the LIAHONA

Miracles by Small Means

the LIAHONA

Miracles by Small Means

ALAN MINER

CFI
An imprint of Cedar Fort, Inc.
Springville, Utah

ISBN 13: 978-1-4621-1137-4

Published by CFI an imprint of Cedar Fort, Inc., 2373 W. 700 S., Springville, UT 84663
Distributed by Cedar Fort, Inc., www.cedarfort.com

LIBRARY OF CONGRESS CATALOGING-IN-PUBLICATION DATA

Miner, Alan C., 1948- author.
The liahona : miracles by small means / Alan C. Miner.
pages cm
Includes bibliographical references.
Summary: Gives details that support the theory that the Liahona was a magnetic compass.
ISBN 978-1-4621-1137-4 (alk. paper)
1. Liahona. 2. Book of Mormon--Antiquities. I. Title.

BX8627.M56 2013
289.3'22--dc23

2012044975

Cover design by Rebecca J. Greenwood
Cover design © 2013 by Lyle Mortimer
Edited and typeset by Whitney A. Lindsley

Printed in the United States of America

10 9 8 7 6 5 4 3 2 1

Printed on acid-free paper

Contents

Introduction 1

Chapter 1: Questions Regarding the Liahona 5

Can the Book of Mormon Narrative and Other Scriptures Support the Idea That the Liahona Contained a Magnetic Spindle?

Chapter 2: More Questions Regarding the Liahona 19

Can the Book of Mormon Narrative and Other Scriptures Support the Idea That the Liahona Contained a Magnetic Spindle?

Chapter 3: Knowledge of Magnetism in Ancient China 39

Was the Magnetic Compass Known in Ancient Times?

Chapter 4: Knowledge of Magnetism and Maritime Navigation in India and Arabia 49

Did Knowledge of Magnetic-related Navigation Reach India and Arabia in Ancient Times?

Chapter 5: Knowledge of Magnetism and Maritime Navigation among the Phoenicians 59

Was There Knowledge of Magnetic-Related Navigation among the Phoenicians?

Chapter 6: Knowledge of Magnetism and Maritime Trade in Ancient Israel. 69

Could Nephi and Lehi Have Been in the Right Place Geographically and at the Right Time Chronologically to Have Become Acquainted with a Magnetic Compass?

Chapter 7: The Native American Documents: Their Origins by Sea and a Special Navigating Instrument 75

Do Native American Documents Support Original Settlers Navigating across the Ocean with a Magnetic "Compass"?

Chapter 8: Knowledge Lost? 79

Could Circumstances Have Combined to Prevent Knowledge of a Magnetic Compass from Flourishing in the West?

Chapter 9: Early Historical Writings Related to American Origins: The Early Chronicles 91

Could Joseph Smith Have Been Influenced to Use the Term Compass *in His Translation by Historical Writings Concerning the American Indians?*

Chapter 10: Early Historical Writings Related to American Origins: Pre-1830 European-American Writers . . . 99

Could Joseph Smith Have Been Influenced to Use the Term Compass *in His Translation by Historical Writings Concerning the American Indians?*

Chapter 11: The World of Joseph Smith: Perceptions and Definitions of the Term *Compass* 107

Could the Term Compass *as Used in the Bible or the Definitions of the Term* Compass *in the Dictionary Have Influenced Joseph Smith's Translation?*

Chapter 12: The World of Joseph Smith: Joseph's Personal Experiences with the Maritime World 115

Did Joseph Smith Have Any Personal Experiences with the Maritime World That Might Have Motivated Him to Include the Term Compass *in His Translation?*

Chapter 13: Personal Testimony from Joseph Smith and the Three Witnesses 121

What Did Joseph Smith and the Three Witnesses Have to Say about the Liahona?

Chapter 14: Some Final Thoughts 125

Notes 129

About the Author 223

INTRODUCTION[1]

Some years ago I came across some information that was completely new to my knowledge of world history. It seems that some eighty years before Columbus sailed across the Atlantic in the Niña, Pinta, and Santa Maria to what would later be termed the West Indies, there was a man in China by the name of Zheng He (pronounced "Cheng Ho")[1] with much superior maritime achievements for the time. Yet these achievements became "lost" to the so-called superior Western civilization and history.

What were those achievements? Well, between AD 1405 and AD 1433, Zheng He led at least seven major maritime expeditions covering at least 50,000 kilometers (31,000 miles) and visiting at least thirty different countries. Zheng He commanded the largest fleet of ships for five centuries to come. His armada included 300 ships and 28,000 sailors. The largest of his ships were over 400 feet long and 160 feet wide with nine masts supporting red silk sails, which makes them the largest wooden ships ever built.[2]

1. Illustration: The ship of Zheng-He compared to Columbus' ship the Santa Maria (**Note*** Possible illustrations that are footnoted at the beginning of each chapter, as well as many other images of people, places, and things within this book, can be obtained in greater numbers and variety on the Internet by use of an "Images" search——for example: "Zheng He ship." For this reason I have not included illustrations with this book and will not repeat the "Images" source in subsequent illustration footnotes.)

One might wonder how Zheng He's ships compare with those of Columbus? Interestingly, the Santa Maria upon which Columbus sailed was only 85 feet long.[3] By comparison, Zheng He's massive Chinese ocean-going fleet had ships that measured almost five times the length of the prize ships of Europe. Even the last and largest of the wooden ships from the United States such as the *USS Constellation* and *USS Constitution* do not compare.[4]

The ships of Zheng He's armada were multifaceted in their design. There were ships with multiple decks and luxury cabins, supply ships to carry horses, troop-transport ships, and tankers to carry fresh water.[5] The full contingent of 28,000 crewmembers included language interpreters, astrologers, astronomers, pharmacologists, ship-construction specialists, doctors, and social protocol officers.

Not only was Zheng He's fleet far ahead of Europe, but the Chinese and Indian empires had been wealthier and more advanced than any place in Europe for thousands of years. At least by the eighth century AD, many people lived their entire lives on large ships; they were born, they married, and they died there. There were multiple dwellings, gardens, and several hundred sailors on board. By Zheng He's time, China and India together accounted for more than half of the world's gross national product. Most current experts readily admit that the ships of Zheng He had the capability to reach Europe by sailing westward across the Indian Ocean and then around Africa, or they could have reached the Pacific Islands or even the American continent by sailing eastward. Whether Zheng He did so, or whether any of his officers did so, is a subject of debate.

So in response to this new knowledge about Zheng He, I asked myself, "In all of my reading about the history of the world over half a century, from elementary school through high school, from college through graduate studies, from beginning readers to books, magazines, and newspaper articles many thousand times over, why had I never heard of this man or the sophistication of China's maritime industry? Had I just missed it or had my pride caused me to ignore it?"[6] Perhaps, I thought, it was more than my selfish pride; perhaps American pride had got in the way. After all, China (to say nothing of Chinese maritime prowess) was never given any in-depth consideration as part of my history classes other than a vague reference to early origins of paper and fireworks. Yet according to what I found in the history of Zheng He, my lack of information regarding this

Chinese admiral might also have been caused by something other than personal ignorance or American/European pride; it might have been the result of a decision by the Chinese themselves to dismantle their maritime armada and isolate their people from the rest of the world.

Toward the end of Zheng He's life, the government of China was overthrown. Confucian scholars, worried about what foreign cultures might do to their morals and values, took control. Not only did they end the voyages of Zheng He's fleet, but they halted construction of any new ships. To prevent any backsliding, they destroyed Zheng He's sailing records and set about dismantling China's navy. By the time of Columbus, the Chinese government had made it a capital offense to build a boat with more than two masts, and twenty-five years later they ordered the destruction of all ocean-going ships. The greatest navy in history, a navy that a century earlier had amassed 3,500 ships, was thus extinguished, and China set a course that would lead to isolationism and decline. And thus the greatest maritime fleet of its time would seemingly disappear from the pages of history.

"This is all well and nice," you might say, "but how does this tidbit of history relate to the Liahona?"[7] My response would be that the story of Zheng He should tell us that sometimes what we have been taught concerning "history" really isn't all there is to history, and that by studying certain events more thoroughly, we might obtain some different perspectives. In other words, by asking questions, by searching, and by touching on various historical perspectives, we might discover a more complete knowledge of history. New light and knowledge might be opened up to us.

My purpose in writing this book has been to seek new light and knowledge on the Liahona, a venerated Nephite instrument mentioned in the Book of Mormon (Alma 37:38). The Liahona was also described as a "compass," a "ball," and a "director."[8] I have approached my examination of the Liahona with five main questions: (1) Can the Book of Mormon narrative and other scriptures support the idea that the Liahona contained a magnetic spindle? (2) If so, was magnetism or the principle of a magnetic compass known in ancient times? (3) Could Nephi and Lehi have been in the right place geographically and at the right time chronologically to have become acquainted with the principle of a magnetic compass? (4) If so, could this knowledge have become "lost"? and (5) If we assume that the term *compass* (which Joseph used in his Book of Mormon translation to describe the Liahona) came from Joseph's own cultural environment, would the meaning of *compass* have implied a magnetic compass?

In attempting to answer these questions I hope that I will provide the reader with some interesting perspectives on the way to possibly restoring "lost" history as it concerns the Liahona.

chapter 1

Questions Regarding the Liahona[2]

Can the Book of Mormon Narrative and Other Scriptures Support the Idea That the Liahona Contained a Magnetic Spindle?

An instrument called a "ball" or "director"[1] is first introduced into the Book of Mormon narrative just prior to Lehi's leaving the Valley of Lemuel (near the Gulf of Aqaba on the Red Sea)[2] and setting off into the wilderness of Arabia toward a promised land. This promised land (the Americas) was seen by Nephi in vision while at the Valley of Lemuel (1 Nephi 12–13). He saw that this New World was separated from the Old World by "many waters" (1 Nephi 13:12). Hence a trip across a great sea or an ocean was inevitable. However, Lehi and Nephi were apparently ignorant of many of the details related to how all this was going to take place. It is reasonable to assume that they entertained myriad questions as they enquired of the Lord regarding their future. One of these concerns apparently had to do with navigation, both across the desert and across the ocean, and was addressed by the Lord just prior to their leaving the Valley of Lemuel. Nephi records the event as follows:

> And it came to pass that as my father arose in the morning, and went forth to the tent door, to his great astonishment he beheld upon the ground a round ball of curious workmanship; and it was of fine brass.

2. Illustration: A representation of the Liahona

> And within the ball were two spindles; and the one pointed the way whither we should go into the wilderness. (1 Nephi 16:10)

Later in the text, we find that this "ball" was specifically termed the "Liahona" (Alma 37:38).[3] The major question I will address here is, "Can the Book of Mormon narrative and other scriptures support the idea that the Liahona contained a magnetic spindle?" I have approached the subject from different points of view to determine whether or not further research is justified.

[**Note*** *For the facility of those readers who initially want to quickly scan my reasoning, I have* italicized *the main question that directed my research, and I have* <u>*underlined*</u> *the words and thoughts that might reflect my summary answer. Where there are options, I have numbered and italicized them.*]

Point #1 *What about those who say I shouldn't speculate on the idea of a magnetic compass when the scriptures are silent on the matter?*

The text of 1 Nephi is silent on many matters. Lehi's group spent at least eight years in the wilderness (1 Nephi 17:4), yet from the time of the appearance of the Liahona in the narrative until the group reached Bountiful,[4] there are only thirty-four verses to describe the experience. In his narrative, Nephi fails to mention other people outside his immediate family group when we know they must have had contact with any number of persons. No mention is made of any animals, yet camels were surely needed to transport tents and supplies (1 Nephi 2:4), and animals were surely needed in order to offer sacrifice and burnt offerings (1 Nephi 2:7, 5:9). Even more telling is the lack of details regarding Nephi's boat. While Nephi tells us that the Lord showed him where to find ore to make some tools (1 Nephi 17:10), Nephi provides no details on the construction of the ship other than saying that they "worked the timbers" (1 Nephi 18:1) and that "I, Nephi, did go into the mount oft, and I did pray oft unto the Lord; wherefore the Lord showed unto me great things" (1 Nephi 18:3). And the record is completely silent regarding how Nephi as well as the others acquired the skills to sail the ship. <u>Given such lack of cultural detail, I have two choices: (1) I can say nothing more than is written in the text, or (2) I can attempt to try to understand the cultural and historical</u>

background in order to gain insight into what is written. John Sorenson notes:

> It continues to strike me how incurious many of our people are, how they want to hear the same thing over and over again. Too much of our scripture "study" is like a bedtime story where, if we get one syllable wrong, the child says, "Oh, that's not the way it goes" . . . The first thing we need is an opening up of curiosity, a willingness to accept that it is okay to be curious, it is okay to try to learn something new.[5]

In my scripture study, I prefer to think that if I don't ask any questions, I can't expect to receive any answers, and if I don't actively seek for knowledge, I shouldn't expect any constructive ideas to come into my mind. "Ask, and it shall be given you; seek, and ye shall find; knock, and it shall be opened unto you" (Matthew 7:7). On that assumption, I will proceed.

Point #2: *Why did Lehi need to receive the Liahona at the time he did?*

I know to some Book of Mormon readers this might seem like a stupid question. Anybody who has read 1 Nephi or who has read most any LDS statement on the Liahona is fully instructed as to how, through "faith and diligence," the instrument helped Lehi and Nephi get through the desert wilderness to the land Bountiful where Nephi would construct a ship (1 Nephi 16:10–17:5; Alma 37:38–42). They would also have read how Nephi used the Liahona in this same manner to navigate that ship to the promised land. Yet while I readily acknowledge that "faith and diligence" were extremely important traits for Nephi to learn and acquire in his journey to the promised land, there might be more to the story than this.

Scholarly investigation over the last half century has revealed details of how Lehi and Nephi must have been following a caravan route called the Frankincense Trail,[6] a route traveled by groups led by experienced caravaneers who knew where they were going and took much less time than eight years to reach their destination. What then would have been the purpose in having Lehi travel separately, with only a Liahona for guidance? And how would this have any bearing on whether the Liahona was in part magnetic?

Scholarship has also revealed that for Lehi and Nephi, the only politically appropriate place where (1) key materials for constructing an ocean-going ship were available; where (2) the basic knowledge and skills of how to build such a ship had been perfected and passed down through generations; and where (3) master sailors experienced in navigating seafaring ships spent the winter months relating their trials at sea, was located on the other side (or southeastern shores) of the Arabian peninsula.[7] There in the land of Bountiful (proposed as being near the port of Khor Rori in the present-day country of Oman on the Dhofar coast of the Indian Ocean[8]) Nephi would be able to obtain the specialized hardwoods for the massive hull and masts, the large amounts of cloth for the many sets of sails, the thousands of feet of rope, and so on. There Nephi would be able to acquire the skills and knowledge of his time so that in overseeing the building of his ship he would know what things to do "after the manner of men" (1 Nephi 18:2). There he also would consult with the Lord on how to construct the tools necessary to make changes such that he could remark: "Now I, Nephi, did not work the timbers after the manner which was learned by men, neither did I build the ship after the manner of men; but I did build it after the manner which the Lord had shown unto me; wherefore, it was not after the manner of men" (1 Nephi 18:2). And there Nephi would be able to sit at the feet of the master ship captains and learn to sail an ocean-going ship not just out of the harbor (a feat in itself) but across the vast Indian Ocean and beyond. Yet if all this learning and preparation (which must have required "faith, heed, and diligence") were to take place in Bountiful, what was it about the Liahona that required Nephi and Lehi to acquire it and learn to use it before they ever got to Bountiful?

I believe one answer to the above question lies in the art of navigation. Navigational training for ocean-going vessels has to do with learning various techniques for ascertaining directions and locations while at sea. The lessons of building a boat, and even sailing a boat, while significant, would not qualify one to navigate that ship on open seas. In Nephi's time, navigational techniques involved measuring the position of the sun, the position of the stars, the directions and intensities of the storms, the flights of birds, and so on (see the section on "Ancient Maritime Navigation" in chapter 4). Suffice it to say, and contrary to what some might believe, these techniques worked quite well most of the time, but not always. There were times when conditions on the sea became sufficiently difficult as to negate the accuracy of every technique. At these perilous times perhaps the usefulness of the Liahona might have made it superior to all the other navigational arts. Local maritime training alone could not cover all difficult navigational situations. And long-term maritime training could not be accomplished by Nephi without significant risk of losing his special ship, his family, and the Liahona itself.[9] Yet by learning to use this "compass" or Liahona to guide his family across the desert under difficult conditions, Nephi would face some similar navigational problems to those encountered while on the ocean, and, furthermore, he would be able to acquire this orienteering training without putting a "one-of-a-kind" ship in jeopardy. Now I know that the above navigational scenario can be seen from the perspective that God provided everything for Nephi, but it can also be seen in light of Nephi learning to navigate by means of a Liahona that was, in part, magnetic.

Point #3: *Who made the "ball" and how did it come to be placed by the tent door?*

The next thing I have probed here (and which is seldom discussed) is the question, "Who made the 'ball' and how did it come to be placed by the tent door?" (1 Nephi 16:10). This sounds like another stupid question; the text is clear that it was "prepared by the hand of the Lord," but some discussion might be insightful.

Unlike Joseph Smith's story about obtaining the plates and interpreters from the angel Moroni, Nephi's narrative record (the Small Plates) is almost void of details concerning the Liahona's origin. He says nothing about the instrument's origin in his retrospective telling of his desert travels (1 Nephi 16:10–30)[10] or his travels at sea (1 Nephi 18:12–22). And the only thing that Nephi does state in his last comment is that "the ball, or compass . . . was prepared for my father by the hand of the Lord, according to that which is written" (2 Nephi 5:12). Yet nothing is written about that preparation! One might suppose that there were details mentioned in the account on the Large Plates of Nephi (which account was translated by Joseph Smith but subsequently lost); however, neither a subsequent author of those Large Plates (Alma) nor the abridger (Mormon) add any details. When given the chance, Mormon only notes that the Liahona "was prepared by the hand of the Lord" (Mosiah 1:16). And Alma writes only that "the Lord prepared it" (Alma 37:38). Thus my focus moves from the lack of details to the question of what the phrase "prepared by the hand of the Lord" implies.

I realize that in helping mankind to move forward in the Lord's work, the Lord has infinite power. I also realize that the Lord usually directs men to help accomplish His work using their own resources and nature as much as they are able. I always refer to this relationship as the Law of Stewardship—that is, the Lord only does for man what man cannot do for himself.[11] Nevertheless, in the scriptural record it seems that whatever might be the proportionate mixture of the Lord's help and man's effort, it is all acknowledged to be "by the hand of the Lord."

For example, Moroni acknowledges that his father Mormon "made this record," and Moroni also acknowledges that "great and marvelous is the destruction of my people, the Nephites." But Moroni then declares, "it is the hand of the Lord which hath done it" (Mormon 8:5–8). Moroni was fully aware that his father, Mormon, gathered ore to molten, and then fashioned the plates, after which he painstakingly inscribed the history of his people on them. Moroni was also aware that Mormon directed his people to prepare for battle against the Lamanites for years and then led his people into the final battles in which carnage the Nephite armies fought to the death against the victorious Lamanite armies. But instead of pointing to any military actions of the people on either side as the cause for the outcome, Moroni simply writes that "it is the hand of the Lord which hath done it."

In the book of Omni, Amaleki records that the people of Zarahemla "journeyed in the wilderness, and *were brought by the hand of the Lord* across the great waters, into the land where Mosiah discovered them . . ." (Omni 1:16, emphasis added). Yet I have never heard anyone interpret this passage to mean that the Lord miraculously transported the Mulekites across the ocean and made them suddenly appear one morning in the Americas without any effort on their part.[12]

In view of the above, the question I have is this: how do we interpret what Nephite record keepers had to say in regards to the Liahona? Alma not only noted, "the Lord prepared it," but added, "there cannot any man work after the manner of so curious a workmanship" (Alma 37:38). But did Alma mean by this phrase that no man had a hand whatsoever in the Liahona's "curious workmanship"? Perhaps not. In a similar situation,

Nephi writes that in building his ship, even his brothers were able to "work timbers of curious workmanship" (1 Nephi 18:1), so it is clear that "curious workmanship" can be worked by ordinary men. What is key to this process of creating "curious workmanship" however, as Nephi acknowledges, is that "the Lord did show [Nephi] from time to time after what manner [he] should work the timbers of the ship." Nephi writes:

> And it came to pass that they [Nephi's brothers] did worship the Lord, and did go forth with me; and we did work timbers of curious workmanship. And the Lord did show me from time to time after what manner I should work the timbers of the ship.
>
> Now I, Nephi, did not work the timbers after the manner which was learned by men, neither did I build the ship after the manner of men; but I did build it after the manner which the Lord had shown unto me; wherefore, it was not after the manner of men. (1 Nephi 18:1–2)

In other words, by following the directions and inspirations of the Lord, these men were able to achieve a result that was something more than if they had done it completely by their own knowledge and power. Although the timbers were physically shaped by men's hands, the result was "curious workmanship" suitable for the Lord's purposes because the Lord was giving inspiration and direction to Nephi. Nephi's statement that he "did not work the timbers after the manner which was learned by men" implies that Nephi had apparently expended the effort to acquire the knowledge of how to build a ship in the normal way "after the manner of men," because he knew the differences. These differences weren't so mysterious as to prevent Nephi's brethren from feeling competent enough to remark that the ship "was good, and that the workmanship thereof was exceedingly fine" (1 Nephi 18:4) especially in view of the fact that they were the ones that had supposedly built the ship and done the workmanship. Once again, while the hand of the Lord is over everything, his purposes are usually accomplished through at least some effort on the part of men. Nephi was required to fulfill his stewardship and do his part. So with these perspectives in mind, I will go back to the original major question in point #3—Who made the ball?—and discuss some possible answers.

(Option #1) The Lord personally made the "ball" and delivered it Himself.

As stated previously, anything is possible with the Lord in dealing with men on earth, and the scriptural references certainly can imply such a scenario. Indeed, the Lord was said to have parted the Red Sea so the children of Israel could cross on dry ground (Exodus 14:8–31), and the Lord was also said to have moved a mountain for the brother of Jared (Ether 12:30). But as I have shown above, the scriptures themselves might also give some subtle hints that men were required to do their part, however small it might seem. In the first instance, Moses was required to "lift thou up thy rod, and stretch out thine hand over the sea, and divide it" (Exodus 14:16). Regarding the brother of Jared, Moroni notes that this man was required to "sa[y] unto the mountain Zerin, Remove—and it was removed. And if he had not had faith it would not have moved" (Ether 12:30).

I will now review another scriptural situation that might provide more insight—the account of the brother of Jared with the stones on mount Shelem.

In the book of Ether, we find an account of a group of inhabitants of the promised land who originally came from the tower (of Babel) and who ultimately had been destroyed. They were led by Jared and his brother. In their migration toward a promised land, they were required to build barges and cross "many waters" before they finally came to "that great sea which divideth the lands" (Ether 2:13). They stayed there four years until one day "the Lord came again unto the brother of Jared, and stood in a cloud and talked with him." (Ether 2:14). The brother of Jared was commanded to build some barges in order to transport them across the great sea. After completing the construction of eight barges "after the manner which they [previously] had built, [and] according to the instructions of the Lord" (Ether 2:16), the brother of Jared found that there was a major problem in these vessels that were supposed to carry them across the waters to the promised land—"in them there is no light; whither shall we steer?" (Ether 2:19). Also when the vessels were sealed up tight, they could not breathe. Upon communicating these problems to the Lord, the Lord is said to have given specific construction solutions for the breathing problem, but interestingly He asked the brother of Jared to come up with his own solution for the light. Here the brother of Jared acts in a peculiar manner. He does not ask the Lord to solve the problem completely for him but comes up with his own plan (apparently with some logical merit, perhaps historical and/or scientific). He moltens out of rock "sixteen small stones" that "were white and clear, even as transparent glass." (Ether 3:1) He carries these stones to the top of the mountain and pleads, "touch these stones O Lord with thy finger, and prepare them that they may shine forth in darkness . . . that we may have light while we shall cross the sea." The Lord then complies by touching the stones "one by one with his finger." (Ether 3:4–6) One can ponder here as to why the brother of Jared bothered to molten the stones at all? Why didn't he just pick up sixteen stones, or ask the Lord to provide him with the stones? The scriptures imply that the brother of Jared had a known objective in mind by the fact that he did molten ore to produce sixteen small stones that were white and clear. Some have speculated that the brother of Jared knew of stones with special luminescent qualities.[13] Whatever the answer, all we know is that the brother of Jared felt obligated to do something on his part, which required his utmost skill and knowledge, yet whose ultimate success depended on the power of "the finger of the Lord."

Returning now to the Liahona, we know that Nephi and Lehi were required to use "faith, diligence, and heed" in working the instrument after they received it. This might have been all the Lord required of them for their part—and yet I still wonder if Nephi was required to do anything regarding how the instrument was made or how it got there in the first place.

(Option #2) The Lord (or an angel) brought the Liahona, which instrument had at an earlier time been in the possession of an inspired man.

An example of this perspective can be found in the interpreters. At the end of a probationary period after the angel Moroni's initial appearance to Joseph Smith, Moroni eventually delivered unto Joseph the abridged plates, the breastplate, and the interpreters (Urim and Thummim). The origin of the abridgment can be traced to Mormon and Moroni (Mormon 6:6; 8:1, 5; Moroni 1:1, 4). The breastplate can be assumed to have originally belonged to either Mormon or Moroni. The interpreters can be traced to the brother of Jared (Ether 3:21–28; Ether 4:4–5, D&C 17:1; see also D&C 10:1), although there might have been an earlier beginning

(Mormon writes: "Now these things were prepared from the beginning, and were handed down from generation to generation, for the purpose of interpreting languages; And they have been kept and preserved by the hand of the Lord" [Mosiah 28:14–15]). There may even have been multiple interpreters in both the Old World and the New World. The interpreters were somehow (perhaps by an angel—Ether?) passed to the Nephite King Benjamin who passed them on to King Mosiah (Mosiah 8:13–18; Ether 4:1)[14] *before* they received the record of Ether (twenty-four gold plates). And in time the interpreters came into the possession of Moroni himself (Ether 3:22–28; 4:1–5)

So if some inspired man (like the brother of Jared and eventually Ether) originally possessed the interpreters, did some inspired man originally possess the Liahona? And did that inspired man (now an angel) bring the Liahona to Lehi? Mormon tells us that the interpreters were "kept and preserved by the hand of the Lord" (Mosiah 28:14), yet they were "handed down from generation to generation" (Mosiah 28:15) Unfortunately, we do not have any previous scriptural account of any man possessing an instrument similar to the Liahona.[15]

(Option #3) The Lord inspired a man (perhaps Nephi) living at the time of Lehi to make or obtain the "ball" according to his given knowledge and abilities and had the man deliver it to Lehi's tent door.

One possible source for the Liahona that might be considered here is Nephi himself.[16] Although it is hard to imagine such a scenario without any direct mention of it by Nephi himself, there are a number of scriptural verses and cultural clues relative to the text that might be interpreted in favor of such a scenario.

To be sure, Nephi seems to have had skill in working metals,[17] and he was familiar with the two metals (brass [an alloy of copper] and iron), which would have been used in constructing a partly magnetic Liahona.[18] Apparently Nephi's metallurgical knowledge and skills were sufficient to give Laman cause to presume that Nephi was using such skills to fashion the Liahona for his own selfish purposes. When they were struggling with the direction that they should take in the desert wilderness, Laman complained to Lemuel and the sons of Ishmael, saying the following:

> Now, he [Nephi] says
>
> [#1] that the Lord has talked with him, and also
>
> [#2] that angels have ministered unto him. But behold, we know that he lies unto us; and he tells us these things, and
>
> [#3] he worketh many things by his cunning arts, that he may deceive our eyes, thinking, perhaps, that he may lead us away into some strange wilderness;
>
> [#4] and after he has led us away, he has thought to make himself a king and a ruler over us, that he may do with us according to his will and pleasure. And after this manner did my brother Laman stir up their hearts to anger. (1 Nephi 16:38)

From the above scripture, I can make a case for Laman's complaint #1 and #2 happening during the time that Lehi's family resided at the Valley of Lemuel.[19] That is, Nephi talked with the Lord and had angels minister to him while his family was there (1 Nephi 2:16; 3:28–29). If this list is chronological in nature, then a case also can be made for the idea that Laman's complaint #3 ("he worketh many things by his cunning arts") happened during the time in the Valley of Lemuel and before they departed into the wilderness. In other words, Nephi possibly made something "by his cunning arts" while at the Valley of Lemuel that seemed to give Nephi some degree of influence in leading his brethren "away into some strange wilderness."

Laman's final complaint (#4) is quite interesting in view of the time it was uttered. Laman claims that Nephi had "thought to make himself a king and a ruler over us." In fact, Nephi himself alluded to this idea at a point much earlier in the text (see 1 Nephi 10:1).[20] In view of the fact that their numbers were apparently limited, what in the world would ever give Nephi the idea that he was a "king and a ruler"? The Book of Mormon tells us that Nephite kings had certain items as proof of kingship: the sword of Laban, the plates of brass, and the Liahona. Historical sources tend to support such regalia as symbols of kingship.[21] Nephi obtained through his own efforts (supported by the Lord) the first two of these items while his family resided at the Valley of Lemuel. That leaves me to wonder whether Nephi also obtained the Liahona in a similar manner during this time at the Valley of Lemuel.

As mentioned above (and which I will discuss in chapter 5), Nephi would have had the materials ("brass" and iron) for constructing the

Liahona (or "ball") at his disposal at this location.

Knowing that his skills were guided by the Lord, and knowing that a complete or total understanding of some of the principles involved (magnetism possibly being one) were beyond his comprehension, Nephi might have chosen to deflect attention from his own skills and efforts in his record by simply attributing the creation of the Liahona to "the hand of the Lord" (2 Nephi 5:12). In a similar manner, Nephi attributed the obtaining of the brass plates and the sword of Laban to the power of the Lord (compare 1 Nephi 3:1–9 with 1 Nephi 5:1–9), even though he knew that he had used his own skills and reasoning in the matter.

There also might be a parallel to the origin of the Liahona in what Nephi later records in chapters 17 and 18 of his narrative in 1 Nephi. Upon arriving at Bountiful, it is Nephi (not Lehi) who receives directions from the Lord on how to build a boat (an instrument to get them across an ocean wilderness). In possibly the same pattern used in constructing the Liahona, the following is said about the ship: (1) Nephi goes to the Lord often in prayer for direction; (2) He asks the Lord for what he did not know (where to obtain ore). Notice that he didn't also ask how to forge the metal or make the bellows; (3) He apparently was able to obtain the other materials needed for constructing the boat by his own means, but (4) He had to go to the Lord to know how to work the materials with "curious workmanship" in order to get the desired result. (5) At the sight of the finished product, his brethren were astonished that the workmanship was "exceedingly fine" even though they did the work; (6) Although the revelation for constructing the ship (the instrument necessary for getting them to the promised land) had come through Nephi (nothing is said of Lehi), the Lord eventually also spoke to Lehi, telling him it was time to leave Bountiful and continue their journey to the promised land; and (7) "On the morrow" they began their trip.

Thus, in view of the pattern listed above regarding the building of Nephi's ship, which tends to correlate with the story of the Liahona, and in view of the complaints of Laman, Nephi might have been more deeply involved in the manufacture of the Liahona than has previously been proposed.

Point #4: *What amount of personal skill was necessary for Lehi or Nephi to determine directions using the Liahona? In other words, was every working part of the Liahona controlled by the Lord exclusively through spirituality?*

From the time the Book of Mormon was first published, it seems that anti-Mormon writers attempted to characterize the Liahona as a magnetic compass, and thus an anachronism. Confronted with those arguments, LDS authors naturally took the opposing view.[22] Interestingly, after the establishment of the Foundation for Ancient Research and Mormon Studies (FARMS), which tended to tie itself to the directionally altered Book of Mormon geography theory of John Sorenson, some writers (but not all) even began extending that opposition to LDS Book of Mormon geography theorists who dared broach the subject of true cardinal directions.[23] Nevertheless, some early LDS writers still commented on the ancientness of knowledge regarding magnetism, and some FARMS writers, along with other LDS writers, flirted with the idea of a magnetic Liahona.[24]

From the beginning, the LDS authors said that the Liahona functioned "*only* according to 'faith, diligence and heed,'" (1 Nephi 16:28, emphasis added; Alma 37:41) emphasizing *only* the spiritual requirements involved in this "miracle."[25] From that perspective, the Lord not only caused the "spindle" to point in the direction that they should travel (1 Nephi 16:10) but also wrote on the Liahona the appropriate complementary spiritual message to go along with that direction (1 Nephi 16:29). Indeed, the words of Nephi seem to back this up. Nephi writes:

> And it came to pass that I, Nephi, beheld the pointers which were in the ball, that they did work according to the faith and diligence and heed which we did give unto them.
>
> And there was also written upon them a new writing, which was plain to be read, which did give us understanding concerning the ways of the Lord; and it was written and changed from time to time, according to the faith and diligence which we gave unto it. And thus we see that by small means the Lord can bring about great things. (1 Nephi 16:28–29)

However, taking another point of view, while all of this spirituality certainly played a significant part, the "all or nothing" / "either/or" argument of spiritual workings as emphasized by some[26] does not necessarily have to be. The dependence on "faith, diligence and heed" does not negate the idea that a mixture of physical and mental efforts might have been required by Nephi or Lehi in order to obtain the desired answer with the Liahona, with or without magnetic spindles. Anciently, while a magnetic compass would have been nice to have on a voyage, most of the time it wasn't necessary to solve the basic questions of ancient navigation. As mentioned previously (and discussed in chapter 4), early mariners were accustomed to take many different signs (sun, moon, stars, waves, winds, birds, and so on) into account before making a navigational correction. But sometimes those systems failed, and in such a stormy, life-threatening, truly electrically charged scenario, all the members of Nephi's party would have been trusting their lives to Nephi's ability to correctly read a volatile (possibly magnetic) spindle.[27] Under such circumstances, Nephi would indeed have needed "faith, diligence and heed."

chapter 2

More Questions Regarding the Liahona[3]

Can the Book of Mormon Narrative and Other Scriptures Support the Idea That the Liahona Contained a Magnetic Spindle?

Point #5: *What about the things that were written on the ball? Doesn't the fact that Nephi relied on these words to help guide him separate the workings of the Liahona from a magnetic compass?*

In chapter 16 of 1 Nephi we find the following:

> And it came to pass that the voice of the Lord said unto him [Lehi]: Look upon the ball, and behold the things which are written.
>
> And it came to pass that when my father beheld the things which were written upon the ball, he did fear and tremble exceedingly . . .
>
> And it came to pass that I, Nephi, beheld the pointers which were in the ball, that they did work according to the faith and diligence and heed which we did give unto them.
>
> And there was also written upon **them** [just the pointers or both the pointers & the ball?] a new writing, which was plain to be read, which did give us understanding concerning the ways of the Lord; and it [the writing] was written and changed from time to time, according to the faith and diligence which we gave unto it. And thus we see that by small means the Lord can bring about great things" (1 Nephi 16:26–29)

3. Illustration: A drawing of the Liahona

In a 1994 FARMS article, Robert L. Bunker writes the following concerning the interpretation in brackets that appears in the verses above:

> Antecedents of pronouns in the Book of Mormon are often ambiguous. Here "them" [verse 29] being plural is assumed to refer to the last plural descriptive noun—"pointers" [verse 28].[1]

But while Bunker focuses on the pointers, it becomes apparent that the antecedent of "them" in verse 29 could possibly refer to both the ball *and* the pointers. After all, how much writing could be written or changed on just the pointers?

In a series of articles, Hugh Nibley linked this writing on the pointers or spindles to the ancient art of belomancy in which, simply said, arrow shafts were labeled, and, depending on how they became arranged after being tossed, they were interpreted to mean basically either "yes" or "no."[2] After a lengthy discussion, Nibley concluded:

> It would be an obtuse reader indeed who needed one to spell out for him the *resemblance* between ancient arrow-divination and the Liahona: two "spindles or pointers" bearing written instructions provide superhuman guidance for travelers in the desert. *What more could you want?* [3]

Yet in response to Nibley's challenge, "What more could you want," I have to declare that my mind begs for more understanding.

In response to Nibley's linkage of the Liahona with the art of belomancy I would pose a few observations and questions of my own. First of all, while I can agree that this divination technique might offer insight into the Book of Mormon story of Lehi in the desert, I would correlate this technique more with Nephi and his brothers "casting lots" on their trip back to Jerusalem rather than with the Liahona. Indeed, I have viewed "casting lots" to be much like our modern practice of "pulling the short straw." In Nibley's article he includes the fact that "Meissner suggests that 'casting lots' in Babylonian (*salu sha puni*) refers to an original shaking or shooting of arrows." (p. 106). In this technique, the arrows ultimately designated either for one to "go" or to "not go." But Nibley seems to stretch this "go" / "don't go" technique too far in order to equate this process with divining directions by a compass.

I might agree with this arrow-tossing divination method (to "go" or "not go") for some aspects of Lehi's trip through the desert because Lehi did have some reference points from time to time such as water wells, caravans, bedouins, tribal sheiks, Frankincense trail halts, mountains, and so on by which to orient himself, and the sun and stars would have usually been visible.[4] The same reasoning becomes somewhat foggy, however, in the midst of an endless ocean on all sides, with stormy overcast skies, and with waves tossing the ship to and fro. For in this watery world, reference points might be absent for long periods of time, and the orientation of the boat could be constantly changing.

Furthermore, as the Book of Mormon narrative implies, Nephi and his brethren were already familiar with the system of "casting lots" (mentioned in conjunction with their trip back to Jerusalem), so why would they need a special instrument to do the same thing? On the other hand, the translation by Joseph Smith of the word Liahona—"being interpreted, a compass"—might indeed imply that the Liahona was at least in part just that, a magnetic compass, with directional words or markings written on the ball and spindles.

But some might counter, "What about the words of the Lord written on the ball that made Lehi 'fear and tremble exceedingly' (1 Nephi 16:27)?" Without negating the direct power of the Lord to miraculously perform this task, I will suggest that Lehi and Nephi had a whole volume of the Lord's words in the form of the brass plates (1 Nephi 5:10–22). Indeed, Nephi wrote (in verse 21):

> And we had obtained the records which the Lord had commanded us, and searched them and found that they were desirable; yea, even of great worth unto us, insomuch that we could preserve the commandments of the Lord unto our children.

In a similar fashion to Nephi's having the words of the Lord written on the brass plates, we today also have whole volumes of the Lord's words collected in what we term the standard works, and quite often when those scriptures are read to us, they specifically reflect on our situation in life and cause us to "fear and tremble exceedingly." Again, without trying to treat lightly the words in the Book of Mormon, I would ask, could the changing of the words on the ball and on the spindles have been accomplished by Nephi with words from the scriptures written on the brass plates? <u>From time to time as Nephi read the brass plates, he could have</u>

inscribed certain important verses on animal skin or metal and attached these words to the ball. Loosely speaking, these words or verses of scripture could then be referred to as words of the Lord written on the ball.

In regards to this process of words being written on the ball, I would like to interject some more thoughts here by Robert Bunker on the passages containing antecedents, which were previously quoted. Bunker writes on the antecedent of the phrase, "and there was also written upon **them**" in verse 29:

> The only other plural [other than "pointers"] in the set of verses quoted is "things which are written" [v. 26] but here too one would find it difficult to say "And there was also written upon them (meaning the 'things which are written') a new writing." People don't tend to write "a new writing" "upon things which are written."

I would like to propose an alternative to Bunker's interpretation. I would suggest that another way of interpreting these verses of scripture previously quoted can be derived from the idea that the Lord teaches us in ways such that our understanding of scripture can be added upon (or 'written upon")—"line upon line, precept upon precept" (2 Nephi 28:30, Isaiah 28:10, D&C 98:12). New scriptural verses from the brass plates could have been inscribed on (or attached to) the outside surface of the "ball," perhaps in the same manner as the names of teams and players are added to a metal sports trophy. These new verses would have enlarged the meaning of the previous verses—in essence they would have been "written [or added] upon them." Some who prefer the miraculous might reply, "How narrow minded and small to think that way." But does not Nephi himself say that the changing of the words on the Liahona was a "small means" to bring about greater things (1 Nephi 16:29)?

Point #6: *Is it significant that in describing their travels through the Arabian desert wilderness, Nephi only refers to the Liahona as a "ball" of "fine brass"?*

An article by John Tvedtnes was published in the online *Meridian Magazine*, titled, "Misunderstanding the Book of Mormon,"[5] in which he begins, "Misconceptions abound concerning the text of the Book of Mormon, among both Latter-day Saints and others. . . . " He then addresses a number of these "misunderstandings," among which appear the comments below on the Liahona:

> One of the well-crafted objects mentioned in the Book of Mormon is the "round ball of curious workmanship" that guided Lehi's party during their travels (1 Nephi 16:10). In Alma 37:38, it is called "a ball, or director . . . Liahona, which is, being interpreted, a compass." Some critics have objected that the "compass" possessed by Lehi's party is an impossibility, since the magnetic compass did not exist until long after that time.
>
> The word "compass" appears many times in the King James version (KJV) of the Bible. The verbal form means "go around"[6] or "surround,"[7] while the noun form means "round" in shape (1 Kings 7:35; 2 Chronicles 4:2)[[8]], which fits the term "ball" by which the Nephites called it. Our magnetic compass takes its name from the fact that it describes the round horizon and the 360 degrees it comprises.
>
> In similar fashion, the compass used to draw circles by draftsmen and carpenters (cfr. Isaiah 44:13)[[9]] is tied to the same principle. So when Nephi calls the Liahona a "compass" (1 Nephi 18:12, 21; 2 Nephi 5:11), he seems to be referring to its round shape, not magnetic qualities.

It is interesting to note here that while writers have continually debated the meaning of the word "compass" as found in the Book of Mormon, they have found little reason to accept or reject the word *Liahona* as part of Nephi's world. That might be because the etymology of the word *Liahona* could not be traced with any surety. However, in 1959 some tablets were discovered in a tiny village called Ras Shamra in Syria (anciently northern Canaan). These tablets were written in a language that scholars have termed Ugaritic. And after compiling and defining a list of all the words in that ancient language (related to Old Hebrew), these scholars found a new word in the Ugaritic tongue, *liahona*, which they interpreted to mean "round."[10] So finally, there is evidence sufficient to at least make the case that *both* the word *Liahona* and the word *compass* are historically adequate for Nephi's narrative and Mormon's (or Alma's) references to that instrument.

Thus some might take the above information as proof that the Liahona was a "round" "ball" (meaning also "compass") and that it did not have any connection to magnetic navigation. Yet from my research on ancient navigation I have found that this proof might not be as absolute as one might assume. To begin with there is a chance that the Ugaritic term *liahona* might possibly be connected to maritime navigation. Historically the northern Canaanite land that produced the Ugaritic language was the land of the Phoenicians, who as we will describe in chapters 4, 5, and 6 were associated with Israel. These Phoenicians were not only sailors and shipbuilders who acquired the skills to traverse the Mediterranean Sea to its westward boundaries and beyond, and had the skills to circumnavigate the continent of Africa, but they had joined forces with the men of King Solomon almost 350 years previous to Nephi's time to build ships on the Red Sea and make three-year voyages to the legendary land of Ophir. The Phoenicians might have assimilated the Ugaritic term *liahona* into their own navigational vocabulary as a name for a "round" instrument that helped them navigate. If the Israelites became acquainted with Phoenician maritime skills, then Nephi was possibly using a known Phoenician term for a navigational instrument, *liahona*, to describe a somewhat similar "ball" or "director" that Nephi himself used in navigating their own journey.

While the above might be speculation, there is a more pertinent point in relation to the term *compass* as it appears in the Book of Mormon text that I would like to address. If Joseph Smith translated the Book of Mormon in his own language, then the question may be asked, how could the term *ball* be sufficient by itself to totally define the Liahona when that instrument was also referred to as a "director" (Mosiah 1:16; Alma 37:38, 45) and had been used to direct the course of Lehi's travels across the wilderness and the ocean? As John Tvedtnes himself pointed out, the words *director* and *compass* seem to be equated in Alma 37:38. According to his own logic the term "compass" was derived from the circular 360-degree horizon. But as can easily be seen, a "ball" (360 degrees) by itself is somewhat useless as a "director" (or for direction-finding) without spindles to point out which degree of direction one should go toward. The term director would lend credence to the idea that the term compass implied more than just a ball (360 degrees), it implied spindles which pointed to specific points on that circular scale. Indeed, Alma declared to his son that, "our fathers called it Liahona, which is, being interpreted, a compass" (Alma 37:38). Thus the concept of a magnetic spindle remains a viable concept.

One other pertinent point that needs to be answered here is that Nephi states in 1 Nephi 16:16 that this "ball" that Lehi found at his tent door "was of *fine brass*." There is no mention of any iron. While this phrase might give support to the opinion that magnetism was not part of the "ball," it does not negate the idea that at least one of the ball's internal parts (a spindle) might have been made of a metal (iron) other than brass. In this respect, in 1 Nephi 16:10, we find that "within *the ball were two spindles; and the one pointed the way whither we should go into the wilderness*" (1 Nephi 16:10). If the outside "ball" was made of brass so that one had to lift the top hemisphere or otherwise peer inside to see the spindles, then the spindles might have been considered apart from the outside sphere. Thus, while the outside "ball" might have been made entirely of "fine brass," perhaps one of the spindles "within" the ball was made of magnetized iron or steel,[11] working at least in part on the principle of magnetism. In fact "brass," being non-magnetic and noncorrosive, would have made an excellent casing for a magnetic pointer.[12]

Point #7: *Why did the Liahona need two spindles to function?*

According to Nephi 16:10, the ball (or Liahona) "was of fine brass. And within the ball were two spindles; and the one pointed the way whither we should go into the wilderness." Strangely the reader is not given the reason at this point for the other spindle. Yet in Alma 37:40 we find "that God could cause that those spindles should point the way they should go." So apparently *both* spindles were involved in ascertaining what direction they should go in. But again, why the need for two spindles?

(Option #1): One spindle pointed miraculously to the direction they should go, and one spindle miraculously had written directions on it.

For those LDS apologists that completely focus on the miraculous nature of the Liahona, both spindles worked on "faith," and according to Alma 37:40 "therefore they had this miracle." From this absolute miraculous perspective, no other explanation need be sought. Indeed, 1 Nephi 16:28 states that Nephi "beheld *the pointers* which were in the ball, that they did work according to the faith and diligence and heed which we did give unto them." John Tvedtnes comments below on the Liahona:

> When Nephi calls the Liahona a "compass" (1 Nephi 18:12, 21; 2 Nephi 5:11), he seems to be referring to its round shape, not magnetic qualities. Neither of the two "spindles" or "pointers" inside the ball pointed north; one pointed the way the group should travel, while the other displayed written directions from the Lord; both worked according to the group's faith (1 Nephi 16:10, 26–30; Alma 37:38–44).[13]

(Option #2): One pointer was magnetic, pointing north, and one pointer was adjusted accordingly to point to the intended direction.

In a 1984 FARMS *Update*, Robert F. Smith writes:

> While the Book of Mormon does not tell us whether the Liahona functioned partly on geomagnetic principles, Nephi did say that it contained two spindles, one of which functioned as a directional pointer, and that the body was made of "fine brass" (1 Nephi 16:10, 28). Brass is an excellent noncorroding and nonmagnetic case for a compass. Those who are familiar with modern compasses might naturally ask whether the Liahona worked on a similar principle, with a magnetic function for one spindle, and a possible azimuth setting [the angle created by plotting from due "north" the point on the eastward horizon where a planet or star arises] for the other.[14]

Thus, one spindle could have been magnetic (pointing north) and by some means the other could have been used, manipulated or interpreted to point the way they should go—both "spindles" being necessary to "point the way they should go." Garth Norman has commented: "My surveyors compass has two pointers, one magnetic, and the other adjustable to the direction I want to walk cross country with a magnetic fix. . . . the Liahona could have functioned in this same way."[15]

When Joseph Smith translated the Book of Mormon plates, he was translating from the reformed Egyptian. The fact of the matter is that nobody knows exactly how and why Joseph chose the English words he did in translating that language. Did those words (like *compass*) incorporate Joseph's understanding at the time of the English vocabulary? Perhaps. The 1828 Webster's dictionary gives one definition of the word *compass* to mean: "An instrument for directing or ascertaining the course of ships at sea." This 1828 dictionary also notes that the word compass can be defined as: "An instrument used in surveying land, constructed in the main like the mariners compass; but with this difference, that the [one] needle is not fitted into the card, moving with it, but plays alone . . . This instrument is used in surveying land, and in directing travelers in a desert or forest, miners, &c."[16]

Option #3: There was only one spindle that pointed. It rotated on the other spindle.

Perhaps the fact that "spindles" (plural) are mentioned here has made the interpretation of the working mechanism of the Liahona oversimplified. Let me explain. Some might wonder just what the word "spindle" implies. According to the *Webster's Dictionary*, a spindle is defined as "any rod, pin, or shaft that revolves or serves as an axis for a revolving part."[17] Thus a spindle might be used to refer to two different working parts, one that revolves and one that serves as an axis. If such was the case, Nephi's description first of "spindles" and then of "the one spindle" might actually refer to the same mechanism; that is, one spindle served as an axis for the second spindle, which revolved around it according to the magnetic alignment. However, before we jump to any conclusions, we need to consider another verse. In 1 Nephi 16:28, Nephi writes that he "beheld *the pointers* which were in the ball, that they did work according to the faith and diligence and heed which we did give unto them" (1 Nephi 16:28). While this might be interpreted nicely by some to mean two or more pointers, it also might describe one magnetic needle which has "pointers" on both ends. The writing on the pointers could have been nothing more than the equivalent of "N" (north) on one point and a "S" (south) on the opposing point so that they could be distinguished from one another and the user would not be confused into a situation where they were orienting themselves from the south magnetic pointer when they assumed they were orienting themselves from the north magnetic pointer. (Intriguingly, while the Western world has always focused on the northern tip of the compass needle to guide us, the Chinese were directed by the southern tip of the needle.) Thus, whether it be the word spindles or pointers in the text, one might still maintain a view that allows for a magnetic needle.

(Option #4): One spindle pointed the direction to travel. The other spindle was a "confirmatory" spindle to either point in the same direction or in an opposite direction (non-confirmatory).

One other variation has been proposed, which applies either to a faith-based interpretation or a magnetic interpretation. In this perspective, BOTH needles worked in the same manner. The second spindle worked as a confirmation of the first. According to Robert L. Bunker:[18]

> This is how it would have worked: if an observer viewed the pointers and saw only a single pointer . . . then they were both aligned in the same direction, one on top of another, and the director was providing correct information. Lehi's party could then follow the indicated direction with confidence that it was the Lord's instruction. If, on the other hand, the two pointers were cross-ways to each other—forming an "x" . . . then the device was not functioning, and the pointing information was not reliable. . . . While this may seem a trivial solution, it nevertheless employs a basic fundamental principle of engineering called "voting of redundant strings," first developed about fifty years ago to make the digital computers of that era more reliable.[19]

While this option might work wonderfully for digital computers, or for some imaginary outside force that attracts the needles, it creates problems for magnetic needles because they would tend to interfere with one another. In other words, great care would have to be taken so that the magnetic activity of the one needle did not influence the magnetic activity of the other (as poles repel and opposite poles attract).

Point #8: *Is it significant that almost immediately after receiving the "ball" from the Lord, Nephi uses a sixteen-point compass term,* south-southeast, *(1 Nephi 16:13) to designate direction?*

In my view, whether the term *south-southeast* came from the mind of Joseph Smith in translating or whether it came from Nephi himself, it is significant because it represents a division of direction into sixteen parts. Perhaps this one-time mention of "south-southeast" might not be considered significant by some, yet when Nephi proceeds to talk about their travels, he continually refers back to this specific directional term (*south-southeast*):

> And it came to pass that we traveled *for the space of four days*, nearly a south-southeast direction . . . (1 Nephi 16:13)
>
> And we did go forth again in the wilderness, following *the same direction* . . . And it came to pass that we did travel *for the space of many days*. (1 Nephi 16:14–15)
>
> And it came to pass that we did again take our journey, traveling *nearly the same course* as in the beginning; and after we had traveled *for the space of many days*. (1 Nephi 16:33)

To me this conveys the meaning that *day-after-day*, in completely different geographical surroundings, with deep wadis meandering wherever the terrain dictated, in different times of the day, in possibly different weather conditions, Lehi and Nephi oriented themselves to a specific *direction* ("south-southeast")—a direction that is found *written* on modern-day compasses (as well as compasses of the past)—a direction to which an orienting needle might be fixed to point the way relative to another magnetic needle continually pointing north.[20] If the workings of the Liahona were completely miraculous, would Nephi have even cared to repeatedly note such a specific direction as south-southeast? And if the aim of Lehi's party was to just follow the direction where the Lord caused the spindle to point, why would there be any need for Nephi to record and repeatedly refer to such a specific direction as south-southeast? Wouldn't it have been more practical under such a situation for Nephi to refer to any direction as either "northward," or "southward," or "eastward," or "westward"? There would be no reason to get any more specific. Despite a spindle miraculously pointing the way to go, Nephi would also have needed to rely on the sun, or the stars, or something else to orient himself as to the directions of north, south, east, or west. It seems to me that without any magnetic spindle pointing north as a reference, and without an adjustable 360-degree set of markings for directions—directions which were also divided into sixteen divisions—it would be very difficult for any person traveling through the desert to claim that they were traveling in a south-southeast direction.

Point #9: *What about when Nephi consulted the Liahona in order to know exactly where to find game for food; doesn't this imply a function of the Liahona completely different from that of a magnetic compass?*

If this is what the scripture really says, then I probably would agree, but let's review the situation. In 1 Nephi 16:30 we read: "And it came to pass that I, Nephi, did go forth up into the top of the mountain, according to the directions which were given upon the ball." In regards to this verse, I first must determine how directions were given on the ball. According to my view, it was the spindles that determined direction of travel and the writing on the ball that more or less reminded one of the spiritual requirements necessary in order to be successful. But a much larger question is whether the Liahona specifically pointed to where game was. I don't think it specifically had to do so. I think there is room for a partially magnetic Liahona functioning as part of an overall orienteering process. Let me explain.

From Nephi's vantage point as he traveled southward on the Frankincense Trail, he probably viewed the mountains on his right (to the west) rising high in the distance many miles away, and he knew that if he traveled there he could probably get game. But as I see it, it wasn't the "getting game" that was the whole problem. It might have been just as difficult or more for Nephi to find his way back to where Lehi had camped. A magnetic compass would allow Nephi to chart a course toward the mountains that could be retraced on the return trip. Although while on top of the mountain Nephi could view everything below in a panoramic perspective, he still had to descend through tortuous paths. In such a descent one can very easily get disoriented and end up coming down the wrong ravine. Through the use of a magnetic compass, Nephi would not only have been able to plot his course back to camp from the top of the mountain but also at various locations in his descent.

To me the words "I, Nephi, did go forth up into the top of the mountain" implies a significant travel distance and an extended hike upward.[21] The words "according to the directions which were given upon the ball" might imply that he carried the Liahona with him. The fact that Nephi "did slay wild beasts" (plural) implies hiking and searching over much terrain to begin with, not to mention how much distance Nephi would have had to travel AFTER hitting his target in order to find the animal.

The word *beast* implies a larger mammal and thus a possibility of a lengthier distance that this animal might travel after suffering the initial arrow penetration and before collapsing and dying. Additionally, for Nephi to focus on finding a wounded animal might have taken him farther away from the memory of the trail he had taken to reach wherever he was, and thus added to the need for the Liahona's directional system (a part of which could have been magnetic) in order to guide him back to camp.

***Point #10**: Why did the "compass" stop working when Nephi was tied up?*

While on the sea journey to the promised land, Nephi reproved his brethren and the sons of Ishmael and their wives for being "lifted up unto exceeding rudeness" insomuch that "they did forget by what power they had been brought thither" (1 Nephi 18:9–10). They became angry with Nephi and bound him with cords (1 Nephi 18:10–12). Nephi then writes:

> And it came to pass that after they had bound me insomuch that I could not move, the compass, which had been prepared of the Lord, did cease to work.
>
> Wherefore, they knew not whither they should steer the ship, insomuch that there arose a great storm, yea, a great and terrible tempest, and we were driven back upon the waters for the space of three days; and they began to be frightened exceedingly lest they should be drowned in the sea . . .
>
> And there was nothing save it were the power of God, which threatened them with destruction, could soften their hearts; wherefore, when they saw that they were about to be swallowed up in the depths of the sea they repented of the thing which they had done, insomuch that they loosed me.
>
> And it came to pass after they had loosed me, behold, I took the compass, and it did work whither I desired it. And it came to pass that I prayed unto the Lord; and after I had prayed the winds did cease, and the storm did cease, and there was a great calm.
>
> And it came to pass that I, Nephi, did guide the ship, that we sailed again towards the promised land. (1 Nephi 18:12–13, 20–22)

The fact that the Liahona stopped working when Nephi was tied up certainly could be connected to a loss of spirituality as the text implies. But it also might imply that Laman and Lemuel had overestimated their own skill in discerning directional orientation (possibly including the use of the Liahona) and that they had underestimated Nephi's navigational skills directing the crew and using the Liahona to keep them away from a storm. In other words, under ideal weather conditions and with Laman and Lemuel and the rest of the crew doing their shipboard duties, it might have seemed to them that one could always rely on the sun or the stars to navigate, and the use of the Liahona seemed incidental. The scriptural story implies that Laman and Lemuel and the crew had become so overconfident that they had neglected their shipboard responsibilities. We read in 1 Nephi 18:9 that "after we had been driven forth before the wind for the space of many days, behold, my brethren and the sons of Ishmael and also their wives began to make themselves merry, insomuch that they began to dance, and to sing, and to speak with much rudeness, yea, even that they did forget by what power [that is, organized and directed effort] they had been brought thither; yea, they were lifted up unto <u>exceeding rudeness</u>." This implies to me that when Nephi saw that their duties were not being strictly executed and commanded them to do their duties, they swore at him and told him that they would do what they pleased when they pleased. Yet Nephi knew he could not keep the boat out of range of the storms or properly prepared for the storms without constant attention to the ship. Perhaps good weather and a wide-open ocean seemed to deceive Laman and Lemuel into thinking they didn't need Nephi's help or the Liahona's help in order to steer a navigable course. But Nephi knew different. He writes, "I, Nephi, began to fear exceedingly lest the Lord should be angry with us, and smite us because of our iniquity, that we should be swallowed up in the depths of the sea; wherefore, I, Nephi, began to speak to them with much soberness; but behold they were angry with me, saying: We will not that our younger brother shall be a ruler over us" (1 Nephi 18:10). Laman and Lemuel soon would have found out that steering the ship in the Indian Ocean was not as simple as they thought, as the following statement on ancient navigation in the Indian Ocean illustrates:

> From an Arab perspective there are three basic monsoon winds. First of all, from April to June, the Kaws wind blows southwest. Later the Dammani SW monsoon blows from August to the middle of October. At this time, the monsoon changes direction, and the Azyab monsoon blows in a NE direction. Ships leaving the Red Sea would start out the

> middle of October, so that they could catch the Azyab monsoon across the Indian Ocean, directly to the Malabar coast, reaching Kulam Mali during December. If they were moving on to China they would have to wait for the cyclones of the Azyab to die down in the Bay of Bengal before journeying on in January, crossing from Mulam Mali round the south of India to Kalah Bar in the Malay Peninsula. . . . you will notice that the south-west monsoon strikes earlier further south, and lasts longer. As it moves northwards its duration shortens. Hence the Malabar coast of India is a dangerous place to be as early as May and remains so through September.[22]

So perhaps Laman and Lemuel didn't know how to navigate sufficiently well so as to keep the ship away from danger, thus (or "insomuch that"), "there arose a great storm" (v. 13). When this stormy weather came up and the stars disappeared, the waves and winds swirled, and the spindles became erratic due to the tossing and turning of the ship and the electrically charged atmosphere, Laman and Lemuel knew they were in trouble. Upon being loosed, Nephi's navigational training (both physical and spiritual) might have allowed him to make use of an erratic but still "workable" (v. 21) magnetic Liahona among other navigational helps in order to exit this stormy situation.

***Point #11:** Why is the term **compass** only used by Nephi in relation to ocean navigation?*

Interestingly, while crossing the Arabian Desert, Nephi only referred to the Liahona as a "ball." It is not until they set forth on the ocean that Nephi refers to the instrument as a "compass" (1 Nephi 18:12). And it is many centuries later that Alma tells us that the real name of this instrument was "Liahona," and that the word *Liahona* is, "being interpreted, a compass" (Alma 37:38).

On the ocean voyage Nephi, refers to troubles with Laman and Lemuel in which the "compass" stopped working. He writes:

> And it came to pass that after they had bound me insomuch that I could not move, the compass, which had been prepared of the Lord, did cease to work.
>
> Wherefore, they knew not whither they should steer the ship, insomuch that there arose a great storm, yea, a great and terrible storm, yea,

> a great and terrible tempest, and we were driven back upon the waters for the space of three days; and they began to be frightened exceedingly lest they should be drowned in the sea; nevertheless they did not loose me.
>
> And on the fourth day, which we had been driven back, the tempest began to be exceedingly sore.
>
> And it came to pass that we were about to be swallowed up in the depths of the sea. And after we had been driven back upon the waters for the space of four days . . . (1 Nephi 18:12–15)

In reporting the effects of the storm at sea when the compass stopped working (but was later restored), Nephi mentions that they were "driven back upon the waters" (1 Nephi 18:13–15). I asked myself, "Just how did he ascertain this knowledge?" One interpretation of this phrase might simply mean that their forward progress had been halted. But how did they determine this? Another interpretation might be as simple as saying that Nephi sensed the storm coming from the direction they were sailing toward and thus deduced that the winds drove them "back." However, a storm can come from many directions, and in the midst of a storm, the waves and winds can swirl. The words of Nephi that they were driven "back" might also imply a knowledge of longitude (east-west position) as well as (or in addition to) latitude (north-south position). While latitude can be measured with a simple instrument while viewing Polaris (the North Star),[23] longitude requires much more sophistication, especially in the middle or after a great storm in which stars are not visible and after which the position of the ship might have been severely altered (thus confusing the calculations of distance from any reference point). This knowledge of position in the aftermath of a storm was unable to be calculated by one single method. It would have required reference points, navigational charts, and directional readings (of which a magnetic "compass" might play an essential part).

On the other hand, traveling in the desert was somewhat different. For the most part, while traveling through the desert, Nephi and Lehi were generally on the Frankincense Trail. This most probably diminished the need for the "compass" function of the Liahona as there were other reference points. Perhaps during those desert times there was more of a need for "faith and diligence" to actually go forward in the direction the spindle pointed, especially when what lay before them seemed forbidding.

Thus, the need for spiritual direction as reflected by the words of the Lord written on the "ball" would have been more important for their ultimate success.

Point #12: *If the Liahona was completely dependent on spirituality, or "faith, diligence and heed," why did it apparently stop working or come into disuse shortly after the Nephite arrival in the promised land?*

After arriving in the promised land, although Nephi took the Liahona with him when he departed from the land of first inheritance to go to the land of Nephi, he does not mention the Liahona's use in guiding him through the wilderness to the land of Nephi (2 Nephi 5:12). Nor does Amaleki specifically mention its use in describing the later Nephite migration from the land of Nephi to the land of Zarahemla (Omni 1:12–14), only that they were led "by preachings and prophesyings." This makes me ask, if they were led by such spiritual manifestations, why didn't these include the Liahona? Later on when Alma speaks of the function of the Liahona, he not only speaks of it in the past tense, he apparently fails to bring up any specific use of it beyond the travels of Lehi. (Alma 37:38–44) Once again I ask myself, why would it not be of use to them in their travels if it was exclusively a spiritual instrument? Had their spiritual abilities diminished?

One partial explanation of the situation might be found in the fact that the Lord saw no need for any continuing use for the Liahona. If such was the case and if Alma specifically tells the readers that "there cannot any man work after the manner of so curious a workmanship" (meaning that the Lord had not given any man since Nephi an understanding of how to interpret the Liahona), then no matter what the natural mechanisms involved, the Liahona would not "work."

On the other hand, while it might be a matter of conjecture, Alma's statement many hundred years after the Lord had first given the Liahona to Lehi that "there cannot any man work after the manner of so curious a workmanship" might also be interpreted to mean that the art of constructing a magnetic compass had been lost. The destructive effects of time and moisture on iron spindles in the Liahona could have complicated matters.[24]

From still another perspective, if "curious workmanship" included the magnetic power to move the spindle, and if no man at that time could give an adequate scientific reason for that magnetic power (much in the same way that the power of electricity or lightning could not be scientifically explained in early times), then the magnetic power would have been attributed to God, and thus the statement, "there cannot any man work after the manner of so curious a workmanship."

Point #13: *What about the use of the term* ***Liahona*** *or* ***compass*** *as a temporal metaphor?*

Many centuries after its actual use, Alma tells us that the real name of this instrument was "Liahona," and that the word *Liahona* is, "being interpreted, a compass" (Alma 37:38).[25] Alma then refers to the Liahona or "compass" metaphorically. Alma writes:

> And now, my son, I would that ye should understand that these things are not without a shadow; for as our fathers were slothful to give heed to this compass (*now these things were* temporal) they did not prosper; even so it is with things which are spiritual.
>
> For behold, it is as easy to give heed to the word of Christ, which will point to you a straight course to eternal bliss, as it was for our fathers to give heed to this compass, which would point unto them a straight course to the promised land.
>
> And now I say, is there not a type in this thing? For just as surely as this director did bring our fathers, by following its course, to the promised land, shall the words of Christ, if we follow their course, carry us beyond this vale of sorrow into a far better land of promise. (Alma 37:43–45)

Here a "temporal" Liahona or "compass" is contrasted with "things spiritual." If by the word *temporal* we are to understand a worldly or earthly mechanism as contrasted to "things which are spiritual" meaning heavenly or eternal in nature, then we might glean some insights. In other words, by following the directions of a "temporal" instrument that functioned, in part, according to the "temporal" principle of magnetism (even though that principle was not fully understood), Nephi was guided to a hoped-for destination (the Americas—a land of promise) without getting lost or dying. In the same manner, by following "spiritual" things or by giving "heed to the word of Christ," even though these principles might not be fully understood, one can be guided to "a far better land of promise" in heaven. This line of metaphorical thinking seems to fit the word *compass* used here for the Liahona. The word *compass* seems to imply the means of heavenly direction (pointers and words) through a life cycle (circle) played out on an earthly globe (ball). This seems to illustrate that the original meaning of the word *compass* is not so simple, even though others have stressed the idea that the word only refers to something round.[26] If a metaphor is only a representation of something that is, or actually was, and if this "compass" functioned according to a magical worldly phenomenon (magnetism), then, paraphrasing the words of Hugh Nibley[27] magic [or the physical movement of a magnetic spindle] becomes religion [or becomes attributed to the spiritual things of God] when the [magnetic] power by which things [or spindles] operate [within the Liahona] is transferred from the things themselves to God. That is, if you can trust God to help you benefit from physical, earthly, "temporal" phenomena that you might not fully understand, you should also trust God to help you benefit from spiritual laws that you might not fully understand. Both require "faith, diligence and heed."

Some Summary Thoughts:

In concluding this point-by-point interrogation on the working principles of the Liahona, I must first note that in my research to come up with perspectives, I have found that the idea of the Liahona having a magnetic spindle has been largely (although not completely) dismissed or ignored by previous LDS writers. However in regards to the points covered here, I believe that I have established that the scriptures do not totally negate the idea that the Liahona may have been, or at least may have been in part, magnetic. I feel that there is enough plausibility for at least a partially magnetic Liahona to warrant further investigation.

chapter 3

Knowledge of Magnetism in Ancient China[4]

Was the Magnetic Compass Known in Ancient Times?

While perusing a small anti-Mormon book printed in 1832, I came across a passage in which the author sarcastically wrote, "The mariners compass was only known in Europe about 300 years ago; but Nephi knew all about . . . the compass 2400 years ago,"[1] meaning that the mention of a "compass" by Nephi was an anachronism, and thus the Book of Mormon was false.

To be sure, the anti-Mormon author misstates the usually accepted time of advent for the magnetic mariners compass in Europe by a few hundred years, but that is not critical to his claim. The grand assumption that he makes is that the Liahona worked on the principle of magnetism. For it is with this assessment that the debate enters murky waters. I could have passed this author's statement off by saying that the Liahona was quite different than the mariner's compass, that according to the narrative itself the Liahona worked on the principles of "faith, heed and diligence" with no mention of magnetism, and that it also had writing that was changed from time to time. But like any self-respecting student of the Book of Mormon these days, I at least wanted to know as much history as possible on the development of the magnetic compass.

4. Illustration: A model of Hoang ti's chariot with the magnetic south-indicating pointer

So going to my computer like any modern-day student and making a search, I was referred to a number of recent articles on the magnetic compass and the following basic information came up on the screen:

> The magnetic compass began to appear in navigation in about [**AD**] **1100**. . . . Early compasses consisted of a piece of naturally occurring *magnetite* [lodestone[2]] attached to one end of a wooden stick, then floated in a pool of water. [[3]] The magnetized stick oriented itself to Earth's magnetic field, rotating until the end supporting the magnetite pointed north. The compass revolutionized navigation.[4]

According to Wikipedia, the free encyclopedia, "The first European mention of the directional compass occurs in Alexander Neckam's *De naturis rerum* (*On the Natures of Things*), probably written in Paris in 1190."[5] This source also noted that the *Dream Pool Essay*, which was written by Chinese Song Dynasty scholar Shen Kua in AD 1086, "contained a detailed description of how geomancers magnetized a needle by rubbing its tip with lodestone, and hung the magnetic needle with one single strain of silk with a bit of wax attached to the center of the needle. Shen Kua pointed out that a needle prepared this way sometimes pointed south, sometimes north."[6] However, "the earliest recorded use of a compass in navigation lies in Zhu Yu's book *Pingzhou Ke Tan* (*Pigzhou Table Talks*) of AD 1117: 'The navigator knows the geography, he watches the stars at night, watches the sun at day; when it is dark and cloudy, he watches the compass.'"[7] "As for the Arab world, Yemeni Sultan al-Ashraf appears to be the earliest confirmed mention of the compass in 1290, though some authors assert an earlier recording, as early as 1242."[8]

I also turned to the *Encyclopaedia Britannica*, which gave me a little bit more information on "magnetite" or "lodestone" and confirmed the above information (although with slightly different chronology) with the following:

> Sometime in the 12th century, mariners in China and Europe made the discovery, apparently independently, that a piece of lodestone, a naturally occurring magnetic ore, when floated on a stick in water, tends to align itself so as to point in the direction of the polestar. This discovery was presumably quickly followed by a second, that an iron or steel needle touched by a lodestone for long enough also tends to align

> itself in a north-south direction. From the knowledge of which way is north, of course, any other direction can be found.[9]

Given such information (although somewhat conflicting), I could have concluded at that point that modern science indeed teaches that the magnetic principle of the mariner's compass was not discovered until almost 1700 years after the time of Nephi and Lehi. But I continued to search, and as I did so I was confronted with some conflicting data. In a 1902 RLDS publication, A. H. Parsons writes: "Donnelly says: 'In **AD 868** it [lodestone] was employed by the Northmen.' (The Landnamabok, vol. 1, chap. 2).[10] According to another source, the Talmud [AD 200–500] speaks of lodestone as "the stone of attraction," and it is alluded to in the early Hebrew prayers as Kalamitah, the same name given it by the Greeks, from the reed upon which the compass floated."[11] This would mean that the principle of magnetism associated with lodestone was known by the Hebrews (and possibly by the Greeks) at least by **AD 500**. Just when the Greeks gave it a name associated with a floating reed is not stated here.

Additionally, in an 1841 book concerning American Indian origins, the author writes the following concerning early navigation and the use of the magnetic compass:

> Mr. Klaproth has traced the communication of the use of the magnetic needle in Europe to the Arabs in the time of the Crusades, and from the Arabs to the Chinese. The latter nation appears to have been acquainted with the attractive power of the loadstone at a remote date; and its property of communicating polarity to iron is noticed in a Chinese work finished **AD 121**,[[12]] and in another work it is stated that ships were steered to the south by the magnet so early as A.D. 429.[13]

So according to the above, by at least AD 500, the power of lodestone (a naturally magnetic rock) was known to the Hebrews and possibly the Greeks, but at an earlier time about AD 429 Chinese ships were said to have been using a magnet to steer ships. And as early as AD 121, the Chinese apparently discovered that this stone could magnetize iron. If these "facts" were correct, I reasoned, then there might be a difference in how people refer to the advent of the compass. Indeed, in order to make some sense out of the arguments on the origins of the compass, I found that I had to first distinguish whether the writer was talking about the origins of just the principle of magnetism (as found in lodestone), or the origins of the navigational use of lodestone. These arguments diverged further when writers talked about the origins of the early primitive navigational "compass" with a floating iron needle versus the much later navigational origins of a more sophisticated instrument called a "compass" with a windrose background and special casing. I further found that I had to distinguish whether the writer was talking about the advent of the compass in China (the East) or the advent of the compass in the European-Mediterranean area (the West). In other words, I realized that in my search for perspectives, instead of limiting my focus to the fact that a refined instrument called the "mariners compass" had finally come into use in the Western world by AD 1100, I might gain some insight into a "magnetic" Liahona by studying the Chinese and other peoples who apparently used the principle of magnetism or a primitive magnetic compass for navigational purposes at a much earlier time. So I continued to search.

My search proved interesting in this regard. I was amazed at the diversity of dates I found for the Chinese knowledge of magnetism and the magnetic compass. I first found an illustration of a Chinese Box Compass. The caption read as follows:

> Most historians agree that the magnetic compass originated in China. A Chinese scholar described a magnetic compass in a text dated about **83 AD** The first magnetic compasses designed for navigation were probably developed in the 11th century by navigators in China and Europe.[14]

So on the one hand this reference was admitting that the magnetic compass was part of the Chinese culture at an early date (here as early as AD 83). Yet at the same time, this same reference was not giving the Chinese credit for using this magnetic principle for navigation any earlier than the eleventh century AD I pondered the question, how could a civilization like the Chinese, bordering on an ocean, have knowledge of magnetism for over a thousand years without adapting it for navigational purposes?

This same question was asked by Josiah Priest just after the publication of the Book of Mormon. In 1831–32 Josiah Priest published a book on American antiquities.[15] It was much like the 600-page series of articles that he had compiled and published in 1825 and then again in 1826.[16] In that earlier book he presented about 140 short accounts or stories concerning people and cultures and lands from various parts of the world. In the 1832 book he focused more on American antiquities. In an article titled, "Voyages and Shipping of the Mongol Tartars, and Settlements on the Western Coast of America" (author not cited), I found the following:

> In AD 1275, the Tartars, under their general, called *Moko*, undertook the invasion of the Japan empire, which lies along adjacent to China, between the western coast of North America and China, with a fleet of 4000 sail, having on board two hundred and forty thousand men. But the expedition proved unsuccessful, as it was destroyed by a storm, driven and scattered about the Pacific ocean. (*Kempfer's History of Japan—Rankin*)
>
> From this we discover the perfect ability of the western nations, that is, west of America, to explore the ocean, as suited their inclinations, in the earliest ages; for we are not to suppose the Tartars had just then, in 1275, come to a knowledge of navigation, but rather, the greatness of this fleet is evidence that the art had arrived to its highest state of perfection.
>
> But did they have a knowledge of the compass? This is an important enquiry. . . .
>
> In the year 2037 BC, or 307 years after the Flood, under the *Hia* dynasty, embassies were sent to China from foreign countries beyond the sea, which came in ships to pay homage to the *Hias* or emperor.
>
> If knowledge of the magnet, and its adaptation to navigation, was known before the Flood, as appears from the remarks of this writer, who derives this discovery from a perusal of the Chinese histories, it was, of necessity, divulged by Noah, to his immediate posterity, who, it is said, went soon after the confusion of the language at Babel, and planted a colony in China, or in that eastern country. As all others of mankind had perished in the Flood, consequently there were none else to promulge it to but this family. . . .
>
> But some may inquire, if the knowledge of the magnet and its application to the great purpose of navigation, and surveying, were understood in any degree, how came one branch of the descendants of the family of Noah, those who went east from Ararat, to have it; and the others, who went in other directions, to be ignorant of it, and had to discover it over again in the course of ages. We can answer this, only by noticing that many arts of the ancients of Europe and of Africa are lost; but how, we cannot tell; but in the same way this art

> was lost. Wars, convulsions, revolutions, sweeping diseases, and so on often change the entire face and state of society, so that if it were even known to all the first generation, immediately succeeding the Flood, a second generation may have lost it, not dwelling in the vicinity of great waters; having no use for such an art, would of necessity lose it, which remained lost until about AD 1300.[17]

In view of the above information, I asked myself, could the principle of magnetism not only have been known in China at a very early date but also used to aid in direction, especially in navigation at the time of Lehi (600 BC)? I searched again and found more of the same diversity of dates. One source speculated "that in **101 BCE** Chinese ships reached the east coast of India for the first time with help from the navigational compass pioneered by the Chinese."[18] One source noted, "the magnetic compass is an old Chinese invention, probably first made in China during the Qin dynasty (**221–206 BC**)[19] Another source stated that Chinese mathematicians invented the magnetic compass in **271 BC**[20]

In accordance with this last dating I came across the following:

> The Chinese may have been aware of magnetism . . . the first mention in writing is from the **fourth century** BC: "When the people of Cheng go out to collect jade, they carry a south-pointer with them so as not to lose their way." [21]

One source stated that at the early date of **1110 BC**, Tcheou Koung is said to have taught the use of the needle and compass to envoys from Youa-tchang. Humboldt writes, "As the ambassadors sent from Cochin China and Tonquin were about to take their departure (which was in the twenty-second cycle, more than 1040 years BC) Tcheou-Koung gave them an instrument which upon one side always turned towards the north and on the opposite side to the south, the better to direct them upon their homeward voyage. This instrument was called tchi-nan (chariot of the south), and it is still the name given to the compass, which leads to the belief that Tcheou-Koung invented the latter" (Humboldt, "Cosmos," vol. 5, p. 51). In his chapter on "the magnetic needle," Humboldt says that the apparatus was called tse-nan (indicator of the south).[22]

This information, if correct, pushed the date for the knowledge of magnetism (not to mention open-sea navigation) back almost 2,000 years from the original stated invention of the mariner's compass. But my research findings were still not complete. In 1832, Josiah Priest wrote the following:

> On this subject [the magnetic compass] we have the following from the pen of the most learned antiquarian of the age, C. S. Rafinesque,[23] whose writings we have several times alluded to in the course of this work. This author says, that in the year of the world 1200, or **2800 BC**, or 450 years before the flood, the magnetic needle was known and in use, and that under the Emperor Hoangti, which was about 130 years nearer the time of the Flood, reckoning from the Creation, ships began to be invented. He even gives the names of two ship builders, *Kong-ku*, and *Ho-ahu*, who by order of the above named emperor, built boats, at first *with hollow trees*, and furnished them with oars, and were sent to explore places where no man had ever been.[24]

In Goodrich's "Life of Columbus," I also found reference to this early time period. He writes: "In the year 2700 BC the Emperor Wang-ti placed a magnetic figure with an extended arm, like the Astarte of the Phoenicians, on the front of carriages, the arm always turning and pointing to the south, which the Chinese regarded as the principal pole."[25] A 1902 RLDS publication by A. H. Parsons adds the following to this event:

> Earliest references to the use of the compass are to be found in Chinese history, from which we learn how, in the sixty-fourth year of the reign of Ho-ang-ti (2634 BC) the Emperor Hiuan-yuan, or Ho-ang-ti, attacked one Tchi-yeou, on the plains of Tchou-lou, and finding his army embarrassed by a thick fog raised by the enemy, constructed a chariot (Tchinan) for indicating the south, so as to distinguish the four cardinal points, and was thus enabled to pursue Tchi-yeou, and take him prisoner. — *Encyclopaedia Britannica*, vol. 6, p. 226.[26]

In an 1895 publication (also on American Indian origins) the author H. B. Root brings up more information to support an ancient knowledge of magnetism. He writes:

> We know that the magnetic qualities of metals were known to the Phoenicians, for Sanchoniathon ascribes to Chronos the invention of "Batulia," or "stones that moved as if they had life." Chronos lived 2,800 years before Christ; the earliest date the compass was known in China was 2,604 BC and was called "Tche chay," or "directing stones."[27]

The above quote was supported by another publication three years later in 1898:

> It is interesting to note that while compasses were not generally known to the world at that early period [Lehi's time], they were not entirely unknown, either. That hundreds of years before the Christian era, the compass was used by the Chinese in making long journeys by land. Article "Compass," in *Chambers' Encyclopedia*, says, "It appears, . . . on very good authority, that it was known in China and throughout the East, generally, at **a very remote period**."[28]

Still another author writes: "The Chinese may have been aware of magnetism since the **second millennium BC**, since houses of the Shang dynasty are aligned with magnetic north."[29]

The next commentary I ran across came from an anonymous blogger adding some insight to an Internet article entitled "Early history of the compass,"[30] posted on November 24, 2005, in which the original author had traced the compass back to the use of lodestones by the Chinese fortune-tellers as early as AD 200. The blogger writes, "Actually the history of the compass is much older and more interesting than the author's version."[31] He then connects the principle of the compass with an ancient Chinese belief system called feng shui. (I will note here that from a search of other sources, I found that feng shui addressed the placement and orientation of buildings to achieve harmony with the environment.) All capital cities of China followed rules of feng shui for their design and layout. "The tombs of Shang kings and their consorts at Xiaotun lie on a north-south axis, ten degrees east of due north. These orientations were first obtained by astronomy, not by the magnetic compass."[32] The oldest known feng shui devices are called Liuren astrolabes.[33] They consist of a two-sided board with astronomical sightlines. These devices are the ancestor of the shi or shipan, which was the first magnetic compass.[34]

The blogger mentioned above continues with the following comments:

> The shipan consisted of a metal plate with a "south-pointing spoon," also cast of metal. The spoon was designed to point south (it requires a long discussion to explain why). The shape of the spoon was designed to reflect the shape of the Ladle constellations (the most recent being

> Beidou, what we call the Big Dipper), because these were astronomical timekeepers for Chinese (and had been for millennia). . . .
>
> The Liuren astrolabe may date back to the Zhou era [278 BCE–209 BCE], but the earliest sightlines seem to date to practices noticed by archaeologists at Banpo (approximately **4000 BCE**, in Yangshao culture), because those practices have a continuity that's displayed to the present.
>
> Liuren from Qin-era [ca. 280 BCE?] tombs display the same markings found thousands of years earlier on jade carvings; the shi and shipan share them as well. In fact, elements of the compass rose design look suspiciously like those carved into a piece of Chinese jade dated c. 3000 BCE.
>
> And all of these devices were the tools not of "Chinese fortune tellers," but of astronomers and other officials in the administrations of rulers.[35]

So once again I assessed my findings. Here was a difference of thousands of years or more between a date acknowledged for the advent of the mariner's compass and the original discovery of the working magnetic principles of lodestone, which were at the heart of the workings of that compass. I asked myself, if the Chinese used a compass to direct them on land "hundreds of years before the Christian era," then why wouldn't a compass also be used in ocean navigation "at a very remote period"? I can only speak for myself, but it didn't take much "horse sense" for me as a young boy to realize that a magnetic compass could help me with directions whether I was on water or on land. So it is hard for me to accept the idea that the Chinese went centuries without adapting a magnetic compass to navigation. But even conceding the idea that the principle of magnetic navigation was known anciently in China, did that knowledge ever reach the Near East by 600 BC?

chapter 4

Knowledge of Magnetism and Maritime Navigation in India and Arabia[5]

Did Knowledge of Magnetic-related Navigation Reach India and Arabia in Ancient Times?

Even conceding the idea that the principle of magnetic navigation was known anciently in China, did that knowledge ever reach the Near East by 600 BC? While the maritime route from China to India had its difficulties, these difficulties were more easily overcome than those encountered in the land routes.[1]

Ancient Maritime Navigation

One of the most informative books on ancient navigation and the magnetic compass was published just recently by Amir D. Aczel,[2] who actually grew up on a ship that his father captained in the Mediterranean. In the first part of his book, Amir Aczel begins his review of ancient navigation with the following comments:

> How did navigators of antiquity find their way at sea in the days before the compass? There is a myth, propagated by people with little understanding of the sea and no faith in human ingenuity, that ancient

5. Illustration: A drawing of an ancient "Iron Fish" compass from India

mariners navigated by hugging the coastline. Nothing is further from the truth. Since time immemorial, mariners have sailed across seas far from the sight of land, and early sailors who inspired the stories of the Bible and Greek mythology were quite adept at navigating in the open seas without the advantages of the compass.[3]

Jim Bailey writes:

> Landsmen often have unrealistic notions of what sea travel is like. Perhaps the most persistent is the idea that it is inherently easier to journey over land than over water. In a country with good roads and efficient vehicles this may be so, but in early times it was far from the truth. Particularly when it came to moving heavy loads the reverse was true. . . .
>
> Another landsman's fallacy is that a sailor looking for safety rather than adventure will hug the shoreline, staying in sight of land. In reality, if you are in a true seagoing boat it is the land that is the danger. In exceptionally heavy weather ships do get overwhelmed by the wind and waves of the deep oceans, but far more are wrecked on coasts. If you are caught off a lee shore in a ship that cannot sail into the wind, it needs only a moderate wind to blow you to inevitable destruction.
>
> The third fallacy is that the world ocean is a fairly homogenous body of water, and sailing across it in one direction is much like sailing in another. It is easy for us to believe this as we speed across it in our power-driven ships, but in the long ages of sails and oars no one could have thought so. Winds and currents make some voyages easy for the most primitive craft and make others nearly or quite impossible for all but ships of advanced design. Our marine knowledge was developed over an immense period of time.[4]

Amir Aczel goes on to explain a number of different ways by which ancient navigators were able to know where they were in open seas as they traveled. He summarizes with the following:

> Ancient mariners were astute observers—their trade was not only a science, it was an art. . . . A captain would use all the tools available to him—astronomical observations, soundings, estimation of the directions of the winds and currents, and even the directions followed by migrating animals—to guide his ship as close as possible to its destination. Once the coastline was sighted, he would use his knowledge of the terrain to correct the vessel's heading accordingly and guide it into port.[5]

Jim Bailey adds to the above comments on the art of ancient navigation with the following:

> Seaweeds, too, vary in different parts of the ocean, and the flights of birds were almost the principal guides. . . . Birds can also be a sure sign of the closeness of land. We know that the Sumerians took their own birds with them to release when they were lost: if they were beyond reach of land the bird would come back to the ship, as in the story of Noah.
>
> The birds were also the first to make use of another navigational aid that may possibly have been used by men in early times. In the heads of some migrating species zoologists have found tiny pieces of magnetic fiber, a naturally magnetized oxide of iron also known as magnetite, which occurs in certain rocks.[6]

So according to Amir Aczel and Jim Bailey, the navigation of the open seas was ancient, using a variety of navigational arts.[7]

India

I figured that if knowledge of magnetism or the compass traveled by sea, then before I searched for clues in Arabia and Palestine, I might find some clues in India, which would have been a natural stopping-off place on any sea journey from China. Before doing so, however, I found it necessary to address Indian beginnings. In an interesting book by Carl Peters dealing with ancient navigation, he goes back to some important beginnings of Indian civilization:

> In the third millennary before the birth of Christ important national movements had taken place along the shores of the Indian Ocean. Aryan tribes had quitted their ancestral homes in Eastern Iran, and had pushed forward, probably through Cabulistan and the western passes of the Hindu Koosh, to India, where they appeared as conquerors in the valley of the Indus, and later also on the Ganges. The particulars of this great migration of nations lie quite beyond our historical tradition.[8]

The location of Iran as the ancestral home of the settlers of India was important because the possible beginnings of seafaring were located in nearby Mesopotamia. So my next step was to get more information. I located a number of evidences for Indian maritime activity in some well-researched articles. Interestingly, one of the articles began with the following comment concerning the historical bias that has ignored such activity:

> Professor A. L. Basham reduced India along with her culture . . . [He] wrote in his book *Wonder That Was India* . . . "certain over-enthusiastic Indian scholars have perhaps made too much of the achievements of ancient Indian seafarers, which cannot compare with those of the Vikings or of some other early maritime peoples."[9]

At the close of the article, after citing much evidence in favor of Indian maritime activity, the above quote is countered with the following:

> Nand Kishore Kumar wonders:
>
> It will be hard to find a secondary source from any part of the world which will endorse Professor Basham's view. Indeed it is difficult to understand, how in view of incontrovertible primary evidence proving Indian maritime activity, extensive respect of space and time-span, intensive in terms of variety, tonnage and value, and altogether of far reaching consequences in material as well as ideational spheres, Professor Basham could have belittled . . . this aspect of Indian civilization. Is it because it is hurtful to the pride of a native of the British Isles which conquered the world through military strength but cannot compare with its erstwhile colony which for over a millennium dominated the world through civilized means?[10]
>
> Dr. Vincent Smith has remarked, "India suffers today, in the estimation of the world, more through the world's ignorance of the achievements of the heroes of Indian history than through the absence or insignificance of such achievement."[11]

So having established this historical background, I found some more pertinent evidence in current articles in favor of Indian maritime activity. Max Duncker, author of *History of Antiquity*, notes that ship-building was known in ancient India by at least **2000 BC**[12] Historian Radha Kumud Mookerji writes that India-built ships were superior in ocean navigation because they were built of teak wood, which resisted the corrosive effects of salt water and weather for a long time. India had an abundant supply of such timber.[13] According to R. C. Majumdar, Chinese texts refer to maritime trade between India and China dating back as far as the seventh century BC Recent excavations in the Philippines, Malay peninsula, and

Indonesia confirm early and extensive trade which continued down to the historical period.[14]

But the Hindus didn't just navigate eastward. Duncker makes it clear that from the earliest times they carried on extensive trade with the west as well.[15] He says, "Trade existed between the Indians and Sabaeans on the coast of South Arabia before the 10th century BC"[16] Archaeological evidence shows that as early as **the eighth century BC**, there was a regular trade relation, both by land and sea, between India on the one hand and Mesopotamia, Arabia, Phoenicia, and Egypt on the other.[17] A. M. T. Jackson writes, "The Buddhist Jatakas and some of the Sanskrit law books tell us that ships from Bhroach and Supara [on the west coast of India] traded with Babylon (Baveru) from the 8th to the 6th century BC"[18] Theophrastos (abt. 300 BC) mentions that Indian teak wood was shipped to the Persian Gulf to be used for shipbuilding there. In fact, there is a town there (Siraf) that was entirely built of this wood. In 1811 teak was found in the walls of a Persian palace near Baghdad (7th century BCE).[19] R. K. Mookerji, author of *Indian Shipping*, sums things up with the following:

> For full thirty centuries India stood out as the very heart of the old world and maintained her position as one of the foremost maritime countries. She had colonies in Pegu, in Cambodia, in Java in Sumatra, in Borneo and even in the countries of the Farther East as far as Japan. She had trading settlements in Southern China, in the Malayan Peninsula, in Arabia and in all the chief cities of Persia and all over the East Coast of Africa.[20]

So if what was stated in these articles was true, I figured that Indian maritime knowledge was perhaps more extensive in ancient times than might be supposed. But I pondered, does the existence of extensive ocean navigation imply the use of the compass? Perhaps not universally, I thought. According to one author, the skies over the Indian Ocean were usually clear, especially during the times that the sailors traveled with the monsoons. Thus the compass might not have been considered important.[21] On the other hand, I found some comments in favor of the early knowledge of magnetism by at least a few Indian sailors. An 1898 *Autumn Leaves* publication reads: "In the ancient language of the Hindoos, (the Sanscrit-which has been a dead language for twenty-two hundred years) the magnet was called 'the precious stone beloved of Iron.'"[22] Thus, according to the above quote, magnetism was apparently known in India by at least 300 BC Another source I came across reads as follows:

> The early Hindu astrologers are said to have used the magnet, in fixing the North and East . . . The Hindu compass was an iron fish that floated in a vessel of oil and pointed to the North. The fact of this older Hindu compass seems placed beyond doubt by the Sanskrit word Maccha Yantra, or fish machine, which Molesworth gives as a name for the mariner's compass.[23]

Thus by combining the Sanskrit dating with the mention of the "iron fish" compass in conjunction with navigation, I had reason to suppose that knowledge of a magnetic compass was known and used for ancient Indian maritime purposes, possibly as early as 300 BC or possibly centuries earlier. Now India is geographically located close to Arabia on the Indian Ocean, and that fact brought me once again to the more pertinent question, did knowledge of the magnetic compass reach Arabia by the time of Lehi?

Arabia

Interestingly, Genesis 10:21–30 says the following about the spread of mankind from Mesopotamia into Arabia:

> Unto Shem also, (the father of all the children of Eber, the brother Japeth the elder), even to him were children born.
>
> The children of Shem; Elam, and Asshur, and Arphaxad, and Lud, and Aram.
>
> And Arphaxad begat Salah; and Salah begat Eber.
>
> And unto Eber were born two sons: the name of one was **Peleg; for in his days was the earth divided**; and his brother's name was Joktan.
>
> And Joktan begat Almodad, and Sheleph, and Hazarmaveth, and **Jerah**,
>
> And Hadoram, and Uzal, and Diklah,
>
> And Obal, and Abimael, and Sheba
>
> And **Ophir,** and Havilah, and Jobab: All these were the sons of Joktan.
>
> And their dwelling was from **Mesha**, as thou goest unto **Sephar a mount of the east**.

In some books by Carl Peters, he elaborates on these verses:[24]

> We have the so-called Table of the Nations of *Genesis* to consider (chap. x). . . .
>
> A. H. Sayce, who is supported in this by Dr. Edward Glaser, explains that this "Table of the Nations" can lay no claim to represent an ethnographical chart. It is purely geographical, i.e., it gives a list of Arabian place-names. . . . The Eber mentioned is perhaps the cradle of the Hebrews, who are thus traced back to South Arabia and the Phoenician country as their place of origin. Ophir here appears between Sheba and Havilah [on the southern coast of the Arabian peninsula]. . . . Mesa or Mesha is, according to Ritter (*Ritters Geography*, vol. xiv, fol. 372), the modern Musa, and Sephar, later known as Dhafar, Dhofar by Mirbat [was] in the incense country [on the southern coast of the Arabian peninsula] . . . "The mountains of the East" is the modern range of incense mountains, called Faguer in the Ekhilil language [which] . . . is a dialect of the remotely ancient Himyaritic tongue.[25]
>
> In the third millennium BC, . . . a movement of Semitic tribes had taken place, starting from the Persian Gulf. . . the "South Phoenicians," founded empires in South Arabia, and pressed as conquerors over East Africa. To this belong the Himyarites, Minaeans, Sabaeans, Kahtanides, Azanians and Abyssinians.[26]

This movement of Semitic peoples into southern Arabia helped give me some background to recent research by LDS authors George Potter and Tim Sedor. They have published some video documentaries in which they outline the reasoning for their theory that the biblical person named Ophir (Genesis 10:29), the brother of Jerah (Jerach,[27] Jare,[28] Jared[29]), came south from the Tower of Babel in the land of Mesopotamia to southern Arabia, and became one of the founders of the empire in Dhofar, establishing a maritime culture, especially at Khor Rori, a spectacular natural port that was supposedly named after the brother of Jerah-Jered (Ophir) and which still remains.[30]

The ideas of Potter and Sedor gave me some background to evaluate the comments I found in another book. In 1995 a revised and expanded edition of Hourani's 1951 *Arab Seafaring* was published. In it I found the following on maritime activity in Arabia:

> Our subject begins when the first Arabs erected a mast and a sail and trusted to the winds on the open sea. . . .

> Arabs were astride two of the world's great trade routes. But the advantages of this geographical position could not be fully exploited until certain difficulties had been overcome. Arabia does not and never did produce wood suitable for building strong seagoing ships. Neither does it contain iron for nailing them, nor is it near to any iron-producing country. It has no navigable rivers and few first-class harbors.
>
> Nothing is known of the seafaring activities of the Arabs before the Hellenic conquest of the Near East [second century BC[31]]. But other nations have left records of their own voyages in Arabian waters long before that time. A brief account of these will show that the coasts of Arabia were in all historical ages in contact by sea with other countries.
>
> Sumerian and Akkadian inscriptions of the **third millennium BC** report maritime relations between Mesopotamia and the countries of Dilmun, Magan and Melukha. Dilmun is probably the island of al-Bahrayn. Magan is now generally agreed to be 'Uman [Oman, the country where Dhofar is located on the southern coast of the Arabian peninsula]. Timber and copper are said to be found there, and there is mention of "the shipwrights of Magan" in the text from Lagash of the time of Shulgi (c. 2050 [BC]).[32]

It is interesting to note here that in the Mesopotamian *Epic of Gilgamesh*, one of the earliest known works of literature dating from the **third millennium BC**,[33] there is a passage in which the sailor Urshanabi says to the king:

> "Gilgamesh, your own hands have prevented you from crossing the ocean; when you destroyed the things of stone, you destroyed the safety of the boat." Gilgamesh protests: "Why are you so angry with me, Urshanabi, for you yourself cross the sea by day and night, at all seasons you cross it." Urshanabi replies: "it was those very stones that brought me safely over." [34]

I asked myself, could pieces of lodestone have been the "things of stone" that were used by Urshanabi and destroyed by Gilgamesh many thousands of years ago? And who were these men? And what was the epic of Gilgamesh?

In attempting to answer these questions, I did more research. I found that various themes, plot elements, and characters in the *Epic of Gilgamesh* can also be found in the Hebrew Bible in the stories of Adam and Eve while in the Garden of Eden, and in the story of Noah and the Flood (with possible implications of Nimrod and the Tower of Babel). More specifically, I found it interesting that in the *Epic of Gilgamesh* a person named Utnapishtim survives the Flood and is made immortal (or gains eternal life). Many have equated Utnapishtim with Noah in the Hebrew flood story. Some have equated Gilgamesh with Nimrod because both rebelled against the things of God (Nimrod = "rebel"), both lived just after the Flood, and both lived in Babylonia.[35]

I found that in the Gilgamesh story, Gilgamesh went to a man named Urshanabi in order to be conveyed across the waters to Utnapishtim (Noah), who had survived the Flood and had become immortal. Gilgamesh (Nimrod) wanted to ask Utnapishtim how he could attain immortality. Urshanabi was Utnapishtim's boatman and the guardian of his special "stones" by which Utnapishtim had navigated across the waters (and by which Urshanabi also crossed the waters). But Gilgamesh destroyed the special "stones," rebelled against what Utnapishtim had to say, and returned to his city which he had built up with his own works (possibly with a tower reaching to heaven).

So once again I asked myself, were these special "stones" mentioned in the *Epic of Gilgamesh* magnetic? I came across the following:

> Scholars have failed to explain what the Stone Things [were] . . . A later fragment of verse suggests that those Stone Things were magical images of some sort, and <u>some scholars have speculated that they were lodestones, a type of mineral that possesses polarity</u>."[36]

So could pieces of lodestone have been the "Stone Things" used by Utnapishtim (Noah) and Urshanabi many thousands of years ago? And were these "Stone Things" actually destroyed by Gilgamesh (Nimrod)? And would correlating Urshanabi with any Bible character provide me with any further understanding of this episode?[37] And if, according to recent research, Dhofar on the southern coast of Oman was involved in seafaring as early as the **third millennium BC**, and if Semitic migration from Sumeria (Mesopotamia) to the southern coast of the Arabian Peninsula would have brought maritime activity and trade down through the Persian Gulf, not only to the southern coast of Arabia but beyond, were the "Stone Things" referred to in the *Epic of Gilgamesh* (which compares to the story of Noah and Nimrod's building of the Tower of Babel) linked in any way to this southern migration (perhaps through "Jered" and Ophir, the brother of Jered)? And even if the original "Stone Things" had been destroyed, did a knowledge of magnetism still exist, at least with some people in Arabia?

As documented above, the people referred to as "South Phoenicians" founded empires in South Arabia, and pressed as conquerors over East Africa. In order to better answer the questions related to Arabia (and India) and the knowledge of magnetism, I found it necessary to understand some other cultures: the Phoenicians and the Israelites.

chapter 5

Knowledge of Magnetism and Maritime Navigation among the Phoenicians[6]

Was There Knowledge of Magnetic-Related Navigation among the Phoenicians?

My search for possible maritime knowledge of a magnetic compass led me to the Phoenicians. The Phoenicians were a group of seafaring people who occupied the Mediterranean coast of the Fertile Crescent and flourished from about 1550 BC to about 300 BC A couple of their major cities were Tyre and Sidon. They distinguished themselves for their remarkable maritime achievements. Interestingly, despite their extensive influence in trade over more than a thousand years, there is a lack of records by the Phoenicians themselves on their own history. Only a single Phoenician work survives. What we know of the Phoenicians comes mainly from their neighbors, the Greeks and Hebrews.

One of those ancient Greek historians was Herodotus, who lived in the fifth century BC He has been called the "Father of History" since he was the first historian known to collect his materials systematically, test their accuracy, and place them in a well-constructed narrative. He wrote a multi-volume series entitled *Histories*. Herodotus's account (written about 440 BC) states,

6. Illustration: A Phoenician ship

> The Phoenicians . . . who had formerly dwelt on the shores of the Erythraean Sea [the sea that borders the southern part of the Arabian peninsula], having migrated to the Mediterranean and settled in the parts which they now inhabit, began at once, they say, to adventure on long voyages, freighting their vessels with the wares of Egypt and Assyria, and touched at other places and at Argos, which at that period in every respect surpassed all those stated which are now comprehended under the general name of Greece." (*Histories,* 1:1)

According to the Hebrews, the Phoenician settlements were part of Canaan:

> And Canaan begat Sidon his firstborn . . . and afterward were the families of the Canaanites spread abroad. And the border of the Canaanites was from Sidon [on the north] . . . unto Gaza [on the south]. (Genesis 10:15–19)

"Sidon" in the native tongue means *fish.* The Phoenicians became famous for the purple dye obtained from the shell*fish,* murex. The word *Phoenician* is derived from the Greek word *phoinios*, meaning purple.

Phoenicia proper, as it was known to the Greeks and Romans from whom the name has come down to us, referred to a maritime people who originally located on the eastern Mediterranean coast to the north of Palestine. The territory in which they were located was not more than 200 miles long, by an average of twenty miles wide. Its coastline was sufficiently irregular to create a number of natural harbors, which provided ports of sufficient dimensions to accommodate fleets of considerable size. The sea that fronted Phoenicia was usually calm and inviting to navigation. On their western horizon, Cyprus was visible, and that led the way to Rhodes, to the coasts of Asia Minor and to Greece.[38]

Yet the navigation of the Mediterranean in general was by no means simple. The eastern end especially was subject to storms that struck terror in the heart of the boldest navigator of those days. These early voyages on the Mediterranean were not conducted by novices, but by seasoned and experienced seamen. The voyages quickly extended beyond coasting (hopping from place to place along the coast). Herodotus, in his account of a memorable voyage to the Argolic coast (Greece), says distinctly that after the completion of their business "they immediately set sail for Egypt." As Egypt lay 800 miles due south of Argos, a coasting voyage was plainly out of the question. Voyages, therefore, covering an even greater distance of 1,500 to 2,000 miles implied an advanced state of naval construction and seamanship.[37]

The Phoenicians became some of the greatest traders of their time. In addition to Tyrian Purple (the special dye used on the clothes of the Greek elite), they traded in wood, Iberian silver, Nubian gold, wine, slaves, and glass. One other trade material worth mentioning is tin from Great Britain.[38] This tin was smelted with copper from Cyprus, creating the durable alloy bronze (brass). By hardening the copper with tin into bronze ("brass"), tools could be produced. The Phoenicians clung to this tin trade with extreme tenacity. Long subsequent to the seventh century they prevented even the Romans from sharing it with them. So skillful did the Phoenicians become in this branch of industry that by a method of treatment known only to them and the Egyptians, and now lost to mankind, they could form bronze into knives and even razors, which carried edges like steel. The manufacture of bronze was peculiarly a Phoenician art. It was a Tyrian artist who fashioned for Solomon (about. 950 BC) the great bronze molten sea or laver, forty-five feet in circumference, supported on the back of twelve oxen, as well as the magnificent bronze pillars, Jachin and Boaz, each forty feet in height, which were accounted among the chief glories of the temple at Jerusalem.[39]

The works of the Phoenicians in metallurgy were not, however, confined to bronze. They were equally skillful in handling the precious metals. Phoenicia was the medium through which silver poured into the East, for all or practically all of the silver mines were either in her possession or under her control as early as 1200 BC And it was Hiram, a Phoenician workman, who fashioned for Solomon's Temple the altars and tables of gold whereon the shewbread was set, as well as the ten candle sticks, the lamps, the flowers, the tongs and snuffers.[40]

During the period from 1300 BC to 1000 BC, Phoenician colonization covered all the islands and shores of the Mediterranean and reached as far as the Atlantic, the coasts of Spain (2,500 miles from Tyre), Britain,[41] and even Norway (2,000 miles beyond Spain). Strabo writes that nearly 300 Phoenician colonies were also planted well down the Atlantic coast of Africa.[42] But the trend of their commerce was also toward the east and south, more especially to the southern coasts of Arabia. From the nature of this trade and the fact that the Phoenicians originally had no ports of their own on the Red Sea, it is apparent that it must have been carried on mainly by caravan, formed by the Nomad tribes of men who from their mode of life were better adapted to this business than the dwellers in the coast towns.[43]

Babylonia was also an important objective. According to Herodotus (*Histories* 1:1 and 3:113), this branch of Phoenician commerce was ancient, tapping as it did the northern road leading to China, through which was obtained the products of the farther Asiatic east and north. All the ancient authorities, including the prophet Ezekiel (27:20), speak of the Babylonian trade.[44]

Yet as significant as the land operations of the Phoenicians were, they were as nothing compared with their sea trade. The carrying trade of the Western world was mainly centered in Phoenicia certainly no later than the twelfth century BC The Phoenicians secured a complete monopoly of the Mediterranean and Atlantic trade and became a merchant of the people for many isles" (Ezekiel 27:3). That an early sea trade existed between Yemen (southern Arabia) and Egypt there can be no question.[45] Yet a question does exist as to what extent Phoenician vessels were involved early on. The Edomites (a people located between Israel and the Red Sea) were in possession of two ports of considerable historic importance on the northern tip of the Gulf of Aqaba—Eloth and Eziongeber. And there is good reason to believe that the Phoenicians might have been permitted to use these ports in connection with the Arabian trade. However, when Edom was conquered by Israel, providing an opening for a more complete control of the Ophir trade (1 Chronicles 18:12, 1 Kings 9:27), the Phoenicians lost no time in making overtures to the Jews and to King Solomon (950 BC) for the transference to their own control of the two ports (Eilat and Eziongeber).

That many of the Phoenician vessels, especially those employed on the Phoenician coasts, were small there can be no question, but many of the Phoenician vessels were of respectable size, and some were huge, even by modern standards. The ship in which St. Paul was wrecked carried 276 persons beside her crew and a cargo of wheat (Acts 27:27). Josephus again tells of his being wrecked in the Adriatic in a vessel that carried 600 passengers. Long-distance vessels referred to as "ships of Tarshish" were employed on voyages to Italy, the Adriatic, the Indian Ocean, and Atlantic ports.[46]

The Phoenicians also acquired advanced navigational knowledge to equal their expanded fleet of ships. That the Phoenicians were accustomed to survey by some means the coasts which they frequented there can be no question, for Herodotus (3:136) makes a positive statement to this effect, supplementing it with the information that when so doing they tabulated their notes for future reference.[47] It should also be apparent from the nature and extent of Phoenician navigation that their voyages were prosecuted by night as well as by day. We also know from Herodotus (3:136) that they made charts of those seas in which they did business, and from the remarks of Strabo (16:757) a later Greek historian (64 BC–ca. AD 24), we learn that they used arithmetical calculation for reckoning the ship's progress at night and the relative position of ports, which leads us to suppose that they were in possession of some instrument like the log for determining the speed of their ships.

From a consideration of these facts there should be no great difficulty in realizing that the Phoenicians had passed far beyond the primitive stages of seamanship and navigation long before the twelfth century BC[48] Yet while those voyages on the eastern seas were by no means impossible during the well determined season of navigation, those to the west would have been extremely hazardous in the high latitudes. Had the Phoenicians depended on astronomical help alone, it is easy to see that a slight change of weather would have left them at night without any accurate means of determining either their position or the direction in which they were sailing. So is it possible that they possessed an instrument that might also be termed a lodestone compass?

Early navigating nations such as China considered the south the important point. Additionally, directions were also oriented according to the sun. To the sun worshipper who faced the sun, the south was the right hand of the world. So what led the Mediterranean nations, and especially the Phoenicians, to orient themselves to the north? The Phoenicians were aware that the pole star was the one constant star in the heavens.[49] But how did the Phoenicians orient themselves to the pole star when the weather was overcast? Was it by means of a magnetic compass?

Intriguingly, a possible reference to magnetism and its peculiar properties is found in *Phoenician History* by Sanchoniathon.[50] *Phoenician History* is the oldest non-coded document of the Western World's historical archives.[51] According to the Christian bishop Eusebius of Caesarea

(AD 260–341), Sanchuniathon was a Phoenician who lived about the twelfth century BC and who authored three works in the Phoenician language. However, only some partial paraphrases and a summary of a Greek translation by Philo of Byblos[52] have survived. A fragment of this history of Sanchoniathon possibly ascribes to the god Ouranos the construction of the first suspended magnet or bactellium. The passage is as follows: "Moreover the god Ouranos devised bactellia-contriving stones that moved as having life."[53] Ouranos was one of the progenitors of the Phoenician race. Some, by comparing Phoenician and Hebrew chronologies, have identified him with Noah (2948–1998 BC). We have, therefore, a traditional account of the discovery and use of possible magnetized stones in the history of one of the most successful maritime nations of ancient times.[54] One can reason that this discovery of "bactellium" would not have been one of the few surviving fragments of Phoenician history unless it had a very definite association with the cultural development of a people whose whole prosperity relied on navigation of the sea. And one can also suppose that since the Phoenicians used the pole star as the principal sign in their navigation, and since they monopolized the sea trade of the Mediterranean for over a millennium, that they certainly would have observed a connection between the directive properties of the bactellium and the direction of the pole star. Otherwise we are left with a unique story in Phoenician history about a magnetic toy for the children of Tyre and Sidon.[55]

If the bactellium was put to use in locating the position of the Phoenician Pole star (north) in stormy and cloudy weather, we are able to establish a most important relationship between the two discoveries. It is difficult to suppose that the Phoenicians actually ventured on long voyages such as those to Ophir (1 Kings 9: 28) and carried valuable cargoes with no better guide than the coastline. The return cargo in gold alone on one voyage amounted to four hundred and twenty talents—an equivalent weight of about 28,000 pounds. To suppose that the Phoenicians left such cargoes to chance is to underestimate the means by which they became the greatest navigating power of the ancient world. It is difficult to conceive of the phenomenal expansion that took place in Phoenician naval construction and navigation unless there was a corresponding advance in the means by which both ships and cargoes were safeguarded.[56]

According to Herodotus, in about 600 BC a Phoenician naval

expedition was commissioned by Pharaoh Necho II of Egypt. In three years these Phoenicians sailed from Ezion-Geber on the Red Sea completely around the continent of Africa.[57] Carl Peters elaborates on this Phoenician expedition and the extent of their seafaring knowledge. He writes:

> Herodotus tells the story, and his account is in every way trustworthy. Now anybody will concede that King Necho, in order to conceive such a plan, must already have had exact information as to the geography of Africa. Such information, however, had been furnished him by the Phoenicians, who again had received it from their cousins in South Arabia and East Africa. We can also infer from this record that the south of the Indian Ocean was already very well known to the Punic nations [from Carthage, on the southwestern coast of the Mediterranean Sea] before 600 BC[58]

It is difficult to know what other seafaring ventures were attempted by the Phoenicians. They guarded their navigational secrets with their lives. However, we find traces of Phoenician presence in localities that they would never have sought and from which it would have been practically impossible to return unless they had been in possession of some instrument that rendered them independent both of a stellar object and weather conditions.[59] Well may the Phoenicians have boasted, as the prophet Ezekiel attributes to them: "Behold thou art wiser than Daniel, there is no secret that they can hide from thee" (Ezekiel 28:3).

Jim Bailey writes concerning the extent of these Phoenician maritime ventures:

> Some people suppose that it must have been far easier for early sailors to get from end to end of the Mediterranean than to cross the Atlantic. The fact is that the Mediterranean is a tricky sea to navigate. By contrast, the Atlantic presents a far more straightforward challenge. Moreover, the shortest distance between Africa and South America is less than the length of the Mediterranean, and the distance from West Africa to the mouth of the Amazon is almost exactly equal to it. But by far the most important factor is the pattern of winds and currents. Two great circular currents swirl endlessly around in the North and South Atlantic, the northern one driving almost straight from the bulge of North Africa to the Caribbean. Above this current the trade

wind blows in the same direction.[60]

Interestingly, Verneil Simmons writes,

> Whatever lingering doubts we might have about the presence of Phoenicians in Mesoamerica disappear when we discover that the ancient art of dyeing cloth with the famous purple dye of the Tyrians was well known in Mesoamerica (Covarrubias, *Mexico South*, pp. 253–256). In the Isthmus of Tehuantepec the Indians know how to extract the dye from the sea snail, in the same process developed in Phoenicia centuries ago, and they obtain the same royal purple color. An excretion is taken from tiny sea snails at just certain times of the year. It is then applied to hanks of yarn, which are next dipped in sea water and then spread out in the sun to wait for the yarn to turn the color of imperial purple. The very complicated process is a most unlikely candidate for independent invention. (The Phoenicians were noted for carefully guarding the destinations of their shipping. They were also secretive about how they produced the famous purple dye.) Examples of such dyed cloth can be viewed today in Mexico City's anthropological Museum. It is said that one can always identify the genuine article by the fishy smell that clings to the cloth for years.
>
> The prophets of old well knew that the sailors of Phoenicia were traveling to far places, and Isaiah clearly states that some of those from Tyre would travel "afar off to sojourn" (Isaiah 23:1, 2, 5–7).[61]

John L. Sorenson provides additional evidence for Phoenician travel to **and from** America. He writes,

> German scientists have examined nine Egyptian mummies by radioimmunoassay and gas chromatography/ mass spectrometry. Cocaine and hashish were found in all nine and nicotine in eight in the hair, soft tissue, and bones. The specimens dated from approximately 1070 BC to AD 395 (see S. Balabanova, F. Parshe, and W. Pirsig, "First Identification of Drugs in Egyptian Mummies," *Natur Wissenshaften* 79/8 (1992): 358). The presence of those substances in the tissues of the mummies can only mean that the Egyptian royalty were active drug-users. Since coca and tobacco plants are American, the question has now become not just of an Egyptian [Phoenician] voyage to America but surely of at least one ship returning, with coca and tobacco seeds aboard, and those plants must have been grown where the pharaohs could utilize them over many centuries. Why those plants have not

> previously been identified by botanists studying Egyptian crops is a good question in itself.[62]

Interestingly, in 350 BC the Phoenician colony of Carthage minted gold coins bearing a pattern which some have interpreted as a map of the Mediterranean with America shown to the west."[63]

Amir Aczel sums up such early navigational exploits as those of the Phoenicians with the following:

> Navigators of antiquity managed well without the advantages afforded by the compass. When the invention was finally made, its effects were more subtle than we might have expected, and yet their consequences changed the world. The compass did not enable navigation—navigation across the seas took place long before the compass was invented—but the compass made navigation much more efficient by opening the seas to winter sailing and by extending a ship's range to regions that were previously unexplored.[64]

So much for the navigational exploits of the Phoenicians and their possible use of a magnetic compass. My investigation now moves to Israel's association with maritime trade and their cultural setting relative to a possible magnetic Liahona.

chapter 6

Knowledge of Magnetism and Maritime Trade in Ancient Israel[7]

Could Nephi and Lehi Have Been in the Right Place Geographically and at the Right Time Chronologically to Have Become Acquainted with a Magnetic Compass?

Some of the earliest evidence of Israel's maritime trade ventures comes from 1 Kings, where it speaks of an alliance by King Solomon with the Phoenicians for a maritime trip to Ophir. Although the scriptural passage in 1 Kings might give the appearance that this was a first foray by the Phoenicians down the Red Sea, they may have been mariners of the Red Sea for many centuries before as "South Phoenicians."[1] In 1 Kings 9, we find the following:

> Now Hiram the king of Tyre [the Phoenician capital city] had furnished Solomon with cedar trees and fir trees, and with gold [for Solomon's temple], according to all his desire, [so] that then king Solomon gave Hiram twenty cities in the land of Galilee.
>
> And king Solomon made a navy of ships in <u>Ezion-geber</u>, which is beside Eloth, on the shore of the Red sea, in the land of Edom.

7. Illustration: The Frankincense Trail linking Israel to southern Arabia and the Indian Ocean

> And Hiram sent in the navy his servants, shipmen that had knowledge of the sea, with the servants of Solomon.
>
> And they came to Ophir, and fetched from thence gold, four hundred and twenty talents, and brought it to king Solomon. (1 Kings 9:11, 26–28)

In his book *Arab Seafaring in the Indian Ocean in Ancient and Early Medieval Times*, George Hourani writes:

> This Ezion-geber [on the northern tip of the Red Sea] can now be identified with confidence as the site at Tall al-Khulayfah, west of al-'Aqabah, which was excavated by an American expedition in 1938–1940. It is quite likely that Solomon himself (c. 974–932 [BC]) built the town and the large copper refinery which has been unearthed there, after the subjection of the Edomites by his father David. But the passage quoted above shows clearly that Solomon's ships were manned by Phoenicians sent by King Hiram of Tyre, and succeeding verses also speak of a separate fleet of Hiram sailing with that of his ally. These ships must have been built at Ezion-geber, and at Tall al-Khulayfah there were actually found large nails of iron and of copper alloyed with iron, fragments of thick ropes, lumps of pitch for caulking, and resin for coating. Wood for planks could be cut from the oak forests then existing in Edom.[2]

Keith Christensen notes that starting about 950 BC,

> King Solomon created at the southern end of the Wadi Araba (near the Red Sea), an industrial establishment to turn his raw materials into manufactured articles . . . the like of which had not been known before his own day, nor was surpassed until comparatively recent times. . . . It is now known that along the entire length of the Wadi Araba (which runs south of the Dead Sea to Ezion-geber) are deposits of copper and iron. . . . Solomon's men employed what is essentially the principle of the Bessemer blast furnace, rediscovered less than a century ago. Ezion-geber was thus not only an important naval base and fortress guarding the crossroads to Arabia and Egypt but also an industrial center. . . . Solomon traded copper and iron to Arabia in return for spices, incense, and other precious objects obtainable there. . . . Solomon and his merchants became rich by shipping out of Ezion-geber copper, iron, olive oil, and possibly many products manufactured in Egypt.[3]

Cleon Skousen gives further perspective on this site. He writes:

> In 1937 Dr. Nelson Glueck of the American School of Oriental Research, took a large expedition into the lower end of the Arabah valley. . . . Eventually Nelson Glueck discovered . . . Tell-el Kheleifeh . . . once Ezion-geber the long sought vanished seaport of King Solomon.

Dr. Glueck said in his official report:

> The whole town of Ezion-geber, taking into consideration place and time, was a phenomenal industrial site, without anything to compare with it in the entire history of the ancient Orient. Ezion-geber was the Pittsburgh of old Palestine and at the same time its most important seaport.[4]

In addition to this trade by sea, an ancient trade route called the Frankincense Trail extended from Israel down to the southern coasts of Arabia. Trade also extended to the East Indies and beyond.[5] The biblical book of 1 Kings records that in addition to the massive amounts of gold brought from Ophir, King Solomon,

> had [the bounty] of the merchantmen, and of the traffick of the spice merchants, and of all the kings of Arabia, and of the governors of the country. . . . For the king [Solomon] had at sea a navy of Tharshish [long-distance vessels][6] with the navy of Hiram [Phoenician vessels]; once in three years came the navy of Tharshish, bringing gold, and silver, ivory, and apes, and peacocks. (1 Kings 10:15, 22)

Recent research indicates,

> Since Solomonic times . . . Israelites were undoubtedly involved in the extensive *incense trade* along the South Arabian caravan routes, as well as in sailing from 'Ezion-Geber [by way of the southern Arabian coastal ports] to India during the summer monsoon, and returning with their spices and other trade goods during the winter monsoon, presumably making stops at ports along the way.[7]

Thus, according to the above accounts, at least by the time of Solomon, Israel obtained maritime knowledge of the Red Sea and the Indian Ocean. But what about the possibility of a "compass" or Liahona?

Revell Phillips notes that about 600 BC there were only two reasonable options for a metal instrument: bronze ("brass") and iron. Iron and simple steel had become commonplace in Jerusalem, yet bronze was retained for special purposes like casting. Bronze was softer and generally inferior to steel for toolmaking, and producing it required a source for its components, copper and tin. This means that iron and "brass" and their properties would have been well known to Lehi and that they would have been available to Nephi at the Valley of Lemuel, located near the shores of the Gulf of Aqaba at the northern end of the Red Sea and close to the Frankincense Trail.[8]

But even if Nephi was supplied with iron and "brass," what could have sparked his imagination relative to the principle of magnetism and a "compass"?

In a book published in 1970, Bill Eyster[9] writes that anciently lodestone or magnetite was found more or less where any good iron ore was found. Then he adds something interesting, especially for Book of Mormon readers. He writes:

> The truth about lodestones is that they found man and not the opposite. Some people believe that the particular man they found was a camel driver. The ugly little brown stones that found him were stuck to the iron nails in his camel's shoe. Nothing can express righteous indignation better than a camel with little stones sticking to his feet and the camel let his driver know it in no uncertain terms![10]

Hugh Nibley, the Hiltons, the Astons, George Potter, and Richard Wellington have all proposed that Lehi and Nephi traveled down through Arabia on the caravan trade route known as the Frankincense trail. This trail had branches that conveyed this precious substance from Oman (on the southern coast of Arabia) northward into Babylonia, Egypt, Israel, Asia Minor, and other parts of the Near East. These routes not only brought trade, but communication to those living vast distances from one another. In those circumstances, stories related by the numerous camel drivers about these lodestones could have reached to all parts of the trail. As noted previously, Solomon had established extensive iron mining operations in the Wadi Araba, which runs south of the Dead Sea to Ezion-geber.

Strangely Eyster discounts the idea that a compass would have any use in caravan trade, noting that the camels "went from one water hole to the next" and that "It is almost impossible to get the lead camel to do anything else."[11] Yet this is an idea that LDS writers from the Hiltons[12] to George Potter and Richard Wellington[13] to Nephi might argue against. Interestingly, Eyster does note that the simplest and most effective way of using lodestone for navigational purposes was "to suspend a piece of lodestone on a string—it will always point north—and at a very early time, the Chinese knew that."[14] This prompted me to wonder whether it would have been too much of a technological leap in 600 BC for an Israelite traveling along the Frankincense Trail to attach lodestone (or some magnetized iron) not just to a string but also to a metal spindle?

While the idea of an Israelite (Nephi) somehow acquiring the knowledge of the properties of lodestone while traveling along the Frankincense Trail might seem much more plausible, another question concerning the Book of Mormon narrative (and the Israelite culture) begs an answer. What about the sixteen-part term *south-southeast* that Nephi used? Could an Israelite living in 600 BC have been exposed to such a system? Amir Aczel notes that the first set of directions are known from the Bible. There were four basic directions and they related to the geographical positioning of those lands and seas surrounding Israel. As maritime activity increased in the Mediterranean with the Phoenicians, these four directions expanded to eight but were tied more to wind direction as the wind not only determined the direction from which power came to push their sails, but also the source and nature of the storms they encountered. Aczel cites the studies of Italian scholar Bachisio Cotzo, who in 1947 connected the sixteen-direction wind rose chronologically and culturally with the Etruscans in the Mediterranean. He notes that the first Etruscan contacts with the Phoenicians and the Greeks were made in the eighth century BC From this culture emerged mystic cults in which priests were believed to hold magical powers and were able to prognosticate events. In determining the origin (and execution) of these events, a sixteen-part directional system was developed in the Mediterranean area that dated to at least the fifth century BC and possibly as early as the eighth century BC[15]

Thus, in summary it might be plausible to say that Nephi was in the right place to be located near the metals iron and "brass" and was in the right place to be located on the Frankincense Trail, where lodestone's magnetic qualities were common. And it might be plausible to say that

Nephi was at the right time to be familiar with the metallurgical techniques necessary to work the iron and brass, at the right time to be aware of the magnetic directional qualities of lodestone, and at the right time to be aware of a sixteen-part directional system. And perhaps all these circumstances came together in order that the Lord could inspire Nephi to either construct a magnetic Liahona or to help Nephi understand its workings.

chapter 7

The Native American Documents: Their Origins by Sea and a Special Navigating Instrument[8]

Do Native American Documents Support Original Settlers Navigating across the Ocean with a Magnetic "Compass"?

Having examined the setting for a magnetic Liahona in the Old World, my attention now turned to the New World to which Nephi and Lehi traveled. The Native American Documents are writings in which the natives of America tried to preserve what traditions and legends of their origins that they could remember before they were destroyed by their conquerors and forgotten. These documents consistently refer to their ancestors crossing a sea and carrying with them a special instrument that helped them in navigation.

The Quiche Indians live in the Country of Guatemala and are a branch of the Maya race. Their native history, the *Popol Vuh*, was apparently written by one or more of the nobles of the Quiches from oral traditions in the 1550s. However, because of the Spanish destruction of Indian manuscripts, it was hidden away. A copy was discovered by Father

8. Illustration: The recording of native Maya codices.

Francisco Ximénez in the Santo Tomas Church at Chichicastenango, Guatemala early in the eighteenth century. Father Ximénez transcribed the record and translated it into Spanish. Ximénez's translation of the *Popol Vuh* from Quiche into Spanish was completed between the years of 1702 and 1725. Concerning that process, Ximénez writes:

> Because I have seen many historians who write about these peoples and their beliefs, say and touch upon some things contained in their histories which were only scattered fragments, [and] since the historians had not seen the actual histories themselves, as they were written, I decided to put here and transcribe all of their histories, according to the way they had written them.

Brasseur de Bourbourg translated the Quiche text into French in 1861. The *Popol Vuh* was first published in English in 1950. Shown below are extracts from the *Preamble* and *First Chapter* of the *Popol Vuh* (after the Brasseur de Bourbourg translation):

> *Preamble*
>
> 1. Here is the origin of the ancient history of the country here called Quiche.
>
> 2. Here we will write and we will commence the history of former times. The beginning and the origin of all that was done in the Quiche nation.
>
> 3. Here then we will introduce the manifestation, the discovery and the shining forth of what was in darkness and the accomplishment of its dawn. By the will of the Creator, and of him who Engenders of him who gives being.
>
> 4. That is what we shall write. Because the National Book, the Popol Vuh is seen no more. <u>The book in which it was clearly seen that we came from the other side of the sea</u>.[179]

The *Popol Vuh* also records that after crossing the sea and just prior to the death of their original leaders, these leaders left their people with a gift from their god—the *Pizom Gagal*. In excerpts from part 4, chapter 5 (Brasseur de Bourbourg translation), we find the following:

> And as they could foresee their death and their soon coming end, they counseled with their children.
>
> They were not ill, they had neither pain nor agony when they gave their (last) advice to their children.

> "Oh my Children! Oh our sons! we are going, we are going away, glorious are the words and wise is the counsel we leave with you.
>
> "And you also, who came from our distant country, oh our wives!" . . . and they bade farewell to each one . . .
>
> These words they said when they bade them farewell. Then Balam-Quitze left the symbol of his being (the Pizom Gagal); "this is a remembrance, I leave it with you. This shall be your power. I take my leave filled with sorrow" he added. Then he left the symbol of his being, the Enveloped Majesty (Pizom Gagal), as it was called. Whose form was not visible because it was wrapped up and could not be unwrapped; the seam did not show because it was not seen when they wrapped it up. [2]

Title of the Lords of Totonicapan is another native Quiche history, written about 1854 by the natives of the town of Totonicapan, Guatemala. It was translated from the Quiche text into Spanish by Dionisio Jose Chonay in 1834. It was translated into English in 1953 by Delia Goetz and published by the University of Oklahoma Press. In this document, there are other references to a journey across the sea and to a sacred "bundle." These Quiche lords declare: "our ancestors . . . had come from the other side of the sea." This native document also reveals that prior to crossing the ocean, the original Quiche ancestors received a gift from their god, which was called the Giron Gagal.

Modern-day LDS author Ammon O'Brien notes that the name Giron Gagal "yields a rather intriguing comparison to the Hebrew words: *gilyown* and *galgal*, which by their English equivalents render a plausible description of the Liahona itself." He then lists the definitions as follows:

Quiche	Hebrew	English definition of Hebrew Word
Giron	*Gilyown*	A tablet for **writing**, a **mirror-like surface**. Also a roll.
Gagal	*Galgal*	"like a rolling thing, or like a **wheel**." Also connotates heaven, or heavenly rolling thing.*

[**Note*** *A "heavenly" thing or a "heavenly rolling thing" might imply heavenly direction being given through a round ball. See my commentary on chapter 2, point #13 for more perspectives.*]

O'Brien further notes that because the Liahona was made of "fine brass" it probably had a mirror-like surface. The Liahona also had spindles that turned on an axis like a wheel. There were also words written on the Liahona from time to time—all of which accords with these definitions.[3]

Now, having noted the above legends of a journey across the sea and of a special gift of god in the Quiche documents, I will next turn to the native history of another Indian nation. *The Annals of the Cakchiquels (Memoirs of Solola)* was written in about 1554 by the Cakchiquel Indians of Solola, Guatemala. Brasseur de Bourbourg translated the Cakchiquel document into French around 1855. American scholar, Dr. Daniel G. Brinton translated the works into English in 1885. It is worth noting that this document also contains details about a precious object—called Chay Abah, which means "Obsidian stone." Much like the Liahona, this object was an oracle or director. In this document we find the following:

> . . . thus the Obsidian Stone was made, for the enclosure (tabernacle) of Tullan. . . .
>
> Then to our mothers and fathers it was commanded . . . So spoke the Obsidian Stone; "There are your hills and plains; there beyond the ocean, are your hills and plains . . . there it is that you shall lift up your faces . . . " thus it was said to the . . . Seven Tribes.[4]

LDS writer Clate Mask notes that the original ancestors of the Cakchiquel had a special instrument to help them in their travels: the *Chay Abah,* or Obsidian Stone, which speaks and tells them to go across the sea where they will find their hills and plains, their riches and their government. The translator says that the real meaning of Obsidian Stone is "Stone that Speaks" or "Oracle Stone." The translator calls the *Chay Abah* "Obsidian Stone" because the Maya-Quiche mistakenly called it that. To avoid further confusion, he also calls it Obsidian Stone (but it really means "Stone that Speaks").[5]

Thus I asked myself, could a lodestone related instrument which "spoke" ("oracle stone") through magnetic movement have been what the Maya-Cakchiquel Indians of Central America referred to in their legends of ancestors coming across the ocean? In other words, could this "oracle stone" or "giron gagal" or "pizom gagal" be compared to the Liahona?

chapter 8

Knowledge Lost?[9]

Could Circumstances Have Combined to Prevent Knowledge of a Magnetic Compass from Flourishing in the West?

In comparing accounts of the ancient use of lodestones for directional purposes with our modern perceptions of when that power actually began to be used for maritime purposes, Bill Eyster makes an intriguing remark. He notes: "There may have been a period of one thousand to five thousand years in which the lodestone was used by the Chinese for nothing except to entertain the kids inside the house on rainy days."[1] Stated another way, how could a period of between one to five thousand years elapse between the discovery of the directive magnetic properties of lodestone in China and the now acceptable date for its use by the Chinese sailors? In other words, how did such knowledge become "lost"?

In this chapter I would like to address some circumstances that I came across in my research that could have combined to prevent knowledge of a magnetic compass from flourishing in the West. These factors are (1) The limitations of writing materials and writers; (2) The purposeful destruction of contemporary records; (3) Secrecy or sacredness; (4) Limited communication between the East and the Western World; (5) Connections between magnetism and divination; and (6) Western bias.

9. Illustration: An artistic rendering of the burning of Mayan religious images and books

Factor #1 The limitations of writing materials and writers

A number of materials were used anciently for writing. Some of these include stone tablets, wooden tablets, clay, pottery sherds, wax cloth, bark, papyrus, parchment, animal bones, knotted ropes, bamboo, bark (Sanskrit), dried palm leaves, and paper. These materials were limited by ease of use, availability of use, cost, ease of storage, preservability, and so on. Papyrus, a paper-like material produced from the papyrus plant, was manufactured in Egypt as far back as the third millennium BC and was stored in rolls. Starting in about the first century BC, parchment (prepared from animal skins) became popular. In about the second century BC, paper was invented in China. In general I can say that non-precious metal records were the most durable, yet their cost was enormous, their manufacture required skill, and inscribing characters on them was time consuming. Other materials like papyrus or parchment were more readily available than precious metals, yet their availability depended on those who could manufacture the product. Moreover, like all plant or animal material, they were subject to deteriorization and decay over time, to say nothing of loss by misplacement or accident. Add to this the fact that the overwhelming population of the ancient world could not read or write and we can see how a vast amount of history could become "lost."

Take the Phoenicians, for example. The Phoenician alphabet was developed around 1200 BC and was used mainly for commercial notes. Ultimately all European alphabets were derived from the Phoenician alphabet. Ironically, the Phoenicians themselves are mostly silent on their own history, one possible reason being that they wrote on perishable materials such as papyrus or skins. Other than some stone inscriptions, Phoenician writing has largely perished. The Phoenicians were described by Sallust and Augustine as having possessed an extensive literature, yet only a single work survives, *Mago's Agriculture* (Latin translation). What is known of the Phoenicians comes mainly from their neighbors, the Greeks and Hebrews.

The Arabs also had problems preserving their records. In 1980, Tim Severin, a geography scholar at Oxford University (as well as other universities) was commissioned by the Sultanate of Oman to build an accurate replica of an ancient Arab sailing ship and make a 6,000-mile journey from the Arabian sea to China. He writes:

> One of the objectives of the project was to find out how the early Arab navigators had succeeded in finding their way to China. It was a stupendous achievement: they had sailed nearly a quarter of the way round the world. . . . The Arabs had steered their routes, not by luck, but by careful calculation. The earliest Arab texts gave few hints as to how they had managed this feat. . . . There were a number of vague references to charts and pilot books which seem to have been carried on board, and which had been compiled from the experience of senior navigators. But no early Arab sea charts have survived, and not until the fifteenth century did a book appear which began to lift the edges of the veil of mystery which surrounded Arab navigation.[2]

Factor #2 The purposeful destruction of contemporary records

Despite the accounts that have been given for the ancient use of magnetism by the Chinese, modern-day scholars tend to verify claims for the advent of the maritime compass based primarily on contemporary records. While the first factor I have discussed (writing materials and writers) that might contribute to "lost" history involves situations that are somewhat involuntary, here I will deal with purposeful destruction. I will cite a few examples to make my point.

The Qin Dynasty of China (221–207 BC) was the first "imperial" dynasty in a long line of dynasties. This dynasty attempted to purge all traces of the old dynasties with the infamous burning of books and burying of scholars incident in 213 BC, which has been criticized greatly by subsequent scholars.[3] Another example of this destruction of records took place in the fifth century when an edict ordered the condensation of all of China's voluminous records and documents concerning the past.[4]

So much for the Chinese. What about the Greeks and Egyptians? The Ptolemy family from Greece ruled Egypt from 305 BC until the Roman conquest of 30 BC Ptolemy had been one of Alexander the Great's generals. After Alexander's death, Ptolemy declared himself king of Egypt. All the male rulers of the dynasty took the name Ptolemy. Ptolemaic queens, some of whom were the sisters of their husbands, were usually called Cleopatra, Arsinoe, or Berenice. During their reign they established a magnificent Royal Quarter in Alexandria with adjacent temples, museums, and the renowned Library of Alexandria.

The destruction of the libraries of Alexandria, Egypt provides another example of lost contemporaneous sources. Because of its location, Alexandria welcomed trade from the east and west on the Mediterranean and soon became an international trade hub. Since Alexandria was the leading producer of papyrus, it became well suited for a repository of papyrus scrolls containing information from many sources. The Royal Library complex was begun under the reign of Ptolemy Soter (ca. 367 BC–ca. 283 BC). Soon it became the largest and most significant library of the ancient world from its construction in the third century BC until at least the first century AD In addition to the library, there were areas of study for anatomy, astronomy, and other subjects. This complex even included a zoo. There were also additional library complexes at the Temple of Serapis and the Caesarian Temple in Alexandria, which helped extend the reputation of Alexandria as the world's center for sciences and literature. This complex of libraries is said to have contained over a half million scrolls of papyrus. While the Royal Library was somewhat private, the last two temples were accessible to the public. This library complex soon became the world's center for research. And as research expanded, new works in mathematics, astronomy, the natural sciences, physics, and other areas of learning were added to its collection. But as vast and important as these libraries were, they didn't survive.

The first assault is said to have come as a result of war, although by accident. In 48 BC Julius Caesar, as part of his military strategy, set fire to some of his own ships in the harbor. Unfortunately the fire spread to the Egyptian fleet and then to part of the city. Some storage areas for papyrus scrolls nearby were burnt and it is estimated that thousands of scrolls were lost.

A second wave of destruction happened because of Christianity. The library collections in Alexandria were located on the precincts of pagan temples. In AD 391 the Emperor Theodosius I issued an edict making paganism illegal. Theophilus, the Bishop of Alexandria, solicited the Emperor to issue an order for the demolition of the heathen temples within the city. The Serapeum was converted into a Christian church and many documents were destroyed.

The last assault on the learning center of Alexandria is said to have come from Moslem Caliph Omar. In AD 640, the Moslems took the city of Alexandria, and after assessing the great collection of scrolls, it is said that the conquering general asked Caliph Omar for instructions on what to do with them. The Caliph has been quoted as replying, "They will either contradict the Koran, in which case they are heresy, or they will agree with it, so they are superfluous." So allegedly, the remaining texts were destroyed.

Although there remains uncertainty in all three of the accounts concerning the amount of destruction, the real certainty is that much of the ancient history and literature of the Mediterranean world was lost forever.[5]

In an intriguing side note here, Ptolemy II Philadelphus was the king of Ptolemaic Egypt from 285 BC to 247 BC Ptolemy II, after banishing his first wife for rumors of treason, married his sister, Arsinoe. Queen Arsinoe II reigned for about seven years with great influence. After her death, the king deified her and dedicated temples in her honor. According to the research of Paul Mottelay:

> Ptolemy ordered Timochares, the architect of the palace, to suspend the iron statue of Arsinoe in the temple of Pharis. The roof of the temple was made all of lodestone so that the statue of the princess seemed to hang in midair without any support.[6]

So with the destruction of the Alexandrian complex, a magnificent demonstration of the power of magnetism was also apparently lost.

My next example focuses on another great maritime nation called Carthage at the western end of the Mediterranean. Sadly, the knowledge of the Carthaginians also suffered destruction. The Carthaginians were termed "Libyphoenicians" [African Phoenicians]. In about 500 BC Hanno of Carthage led an expedition of sixty "fifty-oared ships" and 30,000 men and women to found cities along the western coast of Africa. His feats were inscribed in stone in the temple of Kronos. In a subsequent voyage, Hanno explored all the way around Africa "as far as Arabia." His brother Himilko explored northward to the "outer regions of Europe."[7] When the Romans conquered Carthage in 146 BC, the Roman conqueror, Scipio Africanus, had this inscription translated into Greek, which has been titled "Periplus." Meanwhile, the Romans completely and thoroughly destroyed everything else. Modern scholars have shown that while the record of Hanno is mostly correct as far as navigation, there are certain parts missing so as to preserve those maritime secrets of the Phoenicians that allowed them to maintain control of the worldwide trade of the Mediterranean into the Atlantic for hundreds of years. Sadly, while we do have a record (although edited) of Hanno's voyages, this seems to be the only evidence of the extensive maritime literature of the Carthaginians that has remained.[8]

In America things were not any different. Doris Heyden, translator of Diego Duran's writings on native America, notes the following:

> Mesoamerica, comprised mainly of Mexico and Guatemala and parts of Honduras, Nicaragua, and Salvador, was an area of high culture in prehispanic times and was a land of written books. These ancient codices or painted manuscripts were made of deerskin or bark paper in screenfold form, with pictographic writing painted in mineral colors combined with organic matter. There were also *lienzos*, sheets of cloth (although only colonial examples exist, since no *lienzos* have survived from the prehispanic period) and rolls, which are pictorial manuscripts rolled up rather than folded into screens. Themes included calendars, religious and divinatory material, genealogies, histories, and land claims. Few prehispanic pictorial codices survive since most were destroyed at the time of the conquest. Some were even destroyed or mutilated prior to this, in order to eliminate personages or events that rival factions wished to erase from the historical records. . . .
>
> There are perhaps no more than sixteen extant prehispanic pictorial manuscripts of the type mentioned here.

Factor #3 Secrecy (or Sacredness)

Another contributing factor to lost knowledge in relation to the magnetic compass has to do with secrecy. Amir Aczel writes:

> Although the evidence we have shows that the Chinese used the compass in divination before they used it for navigation, we might not have the full story. It is possible that the compass was used in navigation long before the first records we have found of such use. We know that the Chinese considered their invention of the compass secret.[9]

Aczel notes that in the 1950s, Columbia University scholar Shu-Hua discovered an authentic ancient Chinese text titled *Wu Ching Tsung Yao.* In this text, the author gives complete instructions on how to construct an "iron-fish" compass. The final instruction is that the knowledge of the use and construction of the compass must be kept strictly secret.[10]

Paul Mottelay writes:

> It is related that in AD 235 one Makium, who was ordered by the Chinese emperor to construct "a car which would show the South," succeeded in doing so, and thus recovered the secret of manufacture which had for some time been lost. The "Amer. Journ. of Science and the Arts" (Vol. XL. p. 249) adds that, from this date, the construction of a magnetic car seems to have been a puzzle . . . and the knowledge of the invention appears to have been confined within very narrow limits.[11]

Frank Goodrich writes concerning the secrecy of the Phoenicians:

> A remarkable circumstance connected with the maritime history of the Phoenicians was their jealousy of the influence of foreigners. When a strange ship was observed to keep them company at sea, they would either outsail her, or at night change their course and disappear. On one occasion a Phoenician captain, finding himself pursued by a Roman vessel, ran his ship aground and wrecked her, rather than lose the secret which a capture would have revealed. This act was deemed so patriotic that the government rewarded him, and compensated him for the loss of his vessel.[12]

Factor #4 Limited Communication between the East and the Western World.

A fourth factor influencing lost knowledge relative to the magnetic compass has to do with limited communication between the East and the Western world. From Roman times, caravan traders from Europe began to link up with other traders until they reached Central Asia. Their goods had been brought west from China using a similar multilinked system. These linkages were necessary because of national and tribal forces along the route. Along this route, silk, precious stones and other valuable commodities were transported. Soon after the Roman conquest of Egypt in 30 BC, maritime trade extended from Rome to Arabia, India, Southeast Asia, and China. While oriental goods arrived in the Roman provinces somewhat regularly, Europeans did not have direct knowledge of the mysterious country of China from which they came until the seventh century, when an envoy to Constantinople was sent from a Turkish kingdom in Central Asia. However, within a few years, the conquering Moslems of the Middle East had closed (or tightly controlled) all the land and sea routes east to China. Nevertheless, while Western traders did not venture beyond the Mediterranean, Arab mariners sailed to China, at least until the Chinese ports were closed in the year 878. With the Moslems in control of the Middle East and beyond, the Christian world ceased to have any direct contact with countries east of Constantinople. The Crusades only served to further unite the Moslems against the Christians. In the year 1206, Genghis Khan conquered the northern region of China and within two generations the Mongol domain had spread from China to the outskirts of Western Europe. While the Mongols were not Christian, they weren't Moslems either, and possibilities for trade and missionary work once again opened up to the Western world. It was about this time (AD 1187) that the maritime compass was first mentioned in English writings by an Augustinian monk.[13] Just where he got his information is unknown.

Interestingly, in AD 1204, a Frenchman, Cardinal Jacques de Vitry, after being engaged in the crusades, published a *History of the Crusaders and Their Voyages to the Holy Land.* In this history he describes a primitive compass being in regular use among the saracens on the coast of Syria. A detailed description of this navigational method was later given by an Arabian manuscript.[14]

Factor #5 Connections with Divination

Amir Aczel notes that perhaps one overlooked factor related to the lack of knowledge concerning China's ancient use of the magnetic compass has to do with its connection to divination. In other words, because the compass was used by the Chinese in divination, much of the information about the compass was destroyed. He clarifies:

> Unfortunately, much knowledge about . . . the compass, which could have helped us greatly in understanding Chinese culture, has been lost forever. This happened because of the interference in Chinese affairs by a foreign entity—the [Catholic] Church. The Jesuits, who exerted

control in China in the early seventeenth century, prohibited the reading of books on many subjects, including feng shue [divination arts which included magnetism], and Jesuit missionaries went so far as to order that books on these topics be burned. Thus many immensely valuable Chinese books fell prey to the conflict between Western ignorance and Chinese learning.

Li Ying-shih, who was converted to Christianity in 1602, was a distinguished scholar who had amassed an impressive library with many books on divination and feng shue. He possessed important ancient manuscripts, which he had procured at great expense. These books no doubt had much information on China's civilization and culture and very likely contained details about the invention and use of the magnetic compass in divination. It took three days to burn all of Li Ying-Shih's books. Even the carved plates used in printing such books were burned by the Jesuits—to ensure that the banned books would never be printed again. Thus the European ideal of "holy ignorance" closed forever the doors to knowledge about the origins of the greatest invention China has given the world.[15]

Another example of books being destroyed because of their connection to divination can be taken from the European occupation of Native America. In 1633, Bernardo de Lizana wrote:

[Bishop Diego de Landa] collected the books and the ancient writings and he commanded them burned. . . . They burned many historical books of the ancient Yucatan which told of its beginnings and history, which were of much value if, in our writing, they had been translated because today there would be something original."[16]

Joseph Allen, a writer on Native Mesoamerican origins contributes the following:

Mass destruction of the Maya codices that were extant in the sixteenth century occurred as a result of the Catholic Church's attempts to completely Christianize the Maya natives. In spite of extensive efforts to convert the Maya, the natives commonly reverted to preconquest worshiping activities—much to the dismay of the Catholic friars. Viewing the codices as one avenue of superstitions and lies of the devil, the friars systematically destroyed the books. . . . That destruction "reduced to ashes the scientific backbone of a highly civilized people and sounded

> the deathknell of independent Maya thought" (Blom, *The Conquest of Yucatan*, p. 109).[17]

Thus, many "plain and precious things" written in manuscripts concerning a magnetic "compass" might have been purposely destroyed because of their connection to divination.

Factor #6 Western Bias

A sixth factor contributing to the loss of knowledge regarding the magnetic compass was a Western attitude of superiority. Thus, even if information on the compass did reach "Western civilization," there were still barriers that blocked it. The acclaimed historian Joseph Needham lamented the Western bias against the Chinese. He wrote, "there has also been the usual tendency to presuppose that nothing of real importance could have started outside Europe." He quoted a British source of the 1800s that referred to the ancient Chinese accounts describing a compass as "legends," while calling the late-twelfth-century European reference to the compass "science." Yet Needham notes that all the developmental work on the magnetic compass had been done in China many years before the Europeans. He writes, "people [in China] were worrying about the cause of [magnetic] declination before Europeans even knew the existence of [magnetic] polarity."[18]

This idea is also supported by Cyrus H. Gordon in a book published in 1971. At the time, some considered Gordon to be one of the world's preeminent scholars. Dr. Gordon was head of the Department of Mediterranean Studies at Brandeis University and had published numerous books. In this thoroughly documented book, which represented a lifetime of research, he demonstrated that transoceanic travel across the Atlantic and Pacific to the New World was taking place as long as five thousand years ago. He writes:

> Today it is all too common for the descendants of the most civilized men to lose the great cultures of their ancestors. . . . How abysmal our ignorance is, is described by the term "collective amnesia": when mankind as a whole forgets the experience of the race. This book would never have had to be written were it not that mankind as a whole has forgotten major chapters of its history.[19]

Thus the limitations of writing materials and writers, the purposeful destruction of records, secrecy, limited communication between the East and Europe, religious persecution, and scholarly pride could have combined to prevent knowledge of a magnetic compass from flourishing in the West.

[**Note*** *In regards to knowledge about the use of magnetism that might now be lost, I thought I would add one other amusing little tidbit.*]

An early story known to have been written about 806 BC describes the palace of Ch'in Shi Huang Ti. The palace had what must have been the first metal-detection system in the world. The entire gate of the palace was made of lodestone, and anyone who tried to enter the palace bearing concealed iron weapons would be detected because of the great magnetic pull of the gate and would be immediately arrested.[20]

So we apparently are not the first to employ the walk-through metal-detecting arches for security measures.

chapter 9

Early Historical Writings Related to American Origins: The Early Chronicles[10]

Could Joseph Smith Have Been Influenced to Use the Term Compass *in His Translation by Historical Writings Concerning the American Indians?*

In my studies of how American Indian origins were viewed by Europeans and early American settlers in the years before the coming forth of the Book of Mormon, I came across a multitude of varying opinions related to various peoples, and more important, to the art of ancient navigation. Because I initially found few LDS writers that had addressed the entire scope of thought on American Indian origins,[1] I took it upon myself to collect and study the writings from about 240 of the main historical writers who wrote upon this subject. I believe that my studies are significant in trying to evaluate Joseph Smith's meaning of the word *compass* in relation to the Liahona.

I will now present a few writings from two specific time periods or categories which I will refer to as (A) *The Early Chronicles*, which were written mainly by Catholic fathers or officials of the royal courts of Europe that dealt with the occupation of Mesoamerica and South America; and

10. Illustration: Portrait of Bernardino de Sahagun, a chronicler of American Indian origins

(B) *The Pre-1830 European-American Writings*, which were mainly composed by Europeans with access to early American records, American explorers, early North American religious leaders or missionaries, and a few other secular scholars.

Before I begin with the writings of the early chroniclers, I will give a brief review on European thought regarding the advent of the mariners compass. The compass was first mentioned in **AD 1187**, in the writings of an English Augustinian monk, Alexander Neckam (1157–1217).[2] From St. Albans, Neckam described the workings of the compass but provided no details on where or how he came by this information. The first detailed description of a compass is said to have been made in **AD 1269** by Petrus Peregrinus de Marincourt, a French Crusader. He described a floating compass and a compass with a pivot point.[3] These two accounts were seemingly eclipsed, however, by a false but enduring tradition that the maritime compass was invented in **AD 1302** by an Italian at Amalfi.[4]

Now to some of the more pertinent chroniclers and their writings.

Peter Martyr of Angleria was born in Italy in 1457. He studied medicine and eventually became the doctor to King Louis XI of France. In 1487 he moved to Spain, where in 1492 he was ordained to the priesthood and became the personal chaplain to Queen Isabella. Being close to the Spanish Royal Court, he personally met with Columbus and gathered information from him concerning his voyages to the New World. By **1494** Martyr had written the first two books describing Columbus's voyages. He wrote, "According to Columbus, Hispaniola is the island of Ophir mentioned in the third book of Kings." [5] He elaborates:

> King Solomon built a fleet of ships at Ezion-geber, which is near Eloth on the shore of the Red Sea, in the land of Edom. And Hiram sent with the fleet his servants, seamen who were familiar with the sea, together with the servants of Solomon; and they went to Ophir, and brought from there gold, to the amount of four hundred and twenty talents; and they brought it to King Solomon.
>
> Moreover the fleet of Hiram, which brought gold from Ophir, brought from Ophir a great amount of almug wood and precious stones (I Kings 9:26–28, 10:11).[6]

Most authors that have written on this passage about Columbus by Martyr tend to focus on the gold mines that Columbus found as being the prime motivation for his Ophirian theory, as well as the idea that Ophir was thought to be located somewhere in the East Indies. However, for me, especially in view of the fact that Columbus was one of the premier mariners of his time and that he was acquainted with the most up-to-date navigational knowledge and technology, this Ophirian theory implies much more. It implies that Columbus was comfortable with the idea that it was possible for sailors in the time of Solomon (about 950 BC) to navigate the oceans from the Red Sea to the East Indies (which Hispaniola was compared to) and to return. And in view of Columbus's navigation across the Atlantic, it implies that Columbus thought Ophir (Hispaniola) could also have been reached in Solomon's time either by sailing from Israel to the southern end of the Red Sea and then eastward across the Indian Ocean and beyond, or by sailing westward from the southern end of the Red Sea around the southern tip of Africa and across the Atlantic Ocean.

[**Note*** *An expansion of this Ophir theory appears a number of years later in* ***1572.***[7] *Benito Arias Montano, chaplain to Philip II,*[8] *was an editor for the Polyglot Bible of Antwerp (1569–1572). In his apparatus criticus*[9] *he commented on Genesis 10:25 ("And unto Eber were born two sons; the name of one was Peleg; for in his days was the earth divided; and his brother's name was Joktan."). In this commentary Montano traced the origin of the American Indians to Joktan's son Ophir (Genesis 10:26–29).*

In ***1586*** *Miguel Cabello Valboa (Balboa) details a further expansion on this Ophir theory (although his manuscript was not formally published until 1945). Valboa wrote that after the confusion of tongues at the tower of Babel, Ophir* [*the brother of "Jerah" (or "Jered")*] *traveled to the Far East where he became the ancestor of the seafaring peoples in that location.*[10] *From there the descendants of Ophir apparently sailed to the Americas where they settled in New Spain and Peru.*]

Bernardino de Sahagun was a Franciscan missionary who spent sixty years among the Mexican Indians. Sahagun wrote his voluminous *History of New Spain* in the native Nahuatl language between 1547 and 1569. He translated it into Spanish in the **1570s**, and in that form it was used by such writers as Herrera and Torquemada at the beginning of the seventeenth century. However, it did not appear in published form until 1840. Sahagun's chief purpose in writing was to collect the vast Nahuatl folk literature and legends before they were irreparably lost. According to the *Prologue* to his work, Sahagun writes:

> Concerning the origin of these peoples, the report the old men (of Mexico) give is that they (the ancients) came by sea . . . they came in some wooden boats but it is not known how they were hewn.[11]

Pedro Carrasco, a widely published archaeologist-ethnologist and general expert on Mexican antiquities further adds to this information coming from Sahagun.[12] Carrasco comments thus:

> There is a native tradition however, which reaches farther into the past. It is one recorded by Sahagun (Bk. 10. Chpt. 29 part 12) as part of his account of the Mexica and is here summarized.
>
>> In the distant past the people who first arrived in this land came over the water in boats; they landed in Panotla or Pantla and moved along the coast as far as Quauhtemallan (Guatemala). They were led by their priests, who counselled with their god.
>>
>> Their wise men (tlamatinime) were called amoxoaque (keepers of the books); they soon left and took with them the old books and the art of casting metals. —Carrasco c. 1966 [13]

Here the correlations with Nephi's history are obvious, however there is more. The following comes from Sahagun's writings on the "Mexica" (after Anderson-Dibble's 1950 translation):

> According to tradition, the name of the priest who led the Mexica was Mecitli. . . . wherefore they revered him greatly; and all obeyed the one by whom they were led. And since he led his subjects, therefore they were given the name Mexica.
>
> Behold the story which the old people told. In the distant past, which no one can still reckon, which no one can still remember, . . . those who came to rule in this land, those of the same name, those who seemed to form their (own) little world—came over the water in boats; (and settled in the region of Guatemala) . . .
>
> And these were wise men called Amoxoaque. The wise men remained not long; soon they went. Once again they embarked and carried off the writings, the books, the paintings; they carried away all books, the paintings; they carried away all the crafts, the casting of metals. . . .

> Thereupon departed those who carried the god on their backs; they carried him wrapped—wrapped in a bundle. It is said that their god went advising them. . . . They carried the writings, the books, the paintings. They carried the knowledge.[14]

Jose de Acosta (1540–1600) was a Spanish Jesuit historian who went to Peru in 1571 and spent seventeen years in the New World. He wrote a work titled, "Natural and Moral History of the Indians," which was translated into many languages. The works of Acosta in **1590** and those of Gregorio Garcia in 1607 became the most authoritative works on which later writers relied. Although Acosta did not commit himself on any theory as to Indian origins, he rejected the idea that Indians migrated by sea because knowledge of the compass, he reasoned, was not known anciently in his Mediterranean region of the world. Along these lines Acosta writes[15] (original spelling):

> [p. 47] . . . neither can I perswade my selfe that the first Indians came to this new world of purpose, by a determined voiage; neither will I yeeld, that the Ancients had knowledge in the Art of Navigation, whereby men at this day passe the Ocean, from one part to another, where they please, the which they performe with an incredible swiftnes and resolution; neither do I finde in all Antiquities any markes or testimonies of so notable a thing and of so great importance. Besides, [p. 48] I finde not that in ancient bookes there is any mention made of the use of the Iman or Loadstone, nor of the Compasse to saile by;[16] yea, I beleeve they had no knowledge thereof. And if we take away the knowledge of the compasse to saile by, we shall easily judge how impossible it was for them to passe the great Ocean. . . . it is strange that the Ancients have been so long ignorant of this excellent propertie of the load stone; for Plinie,[17] who was so curious in naturall causes, writing of this load stone, speakes nothing of that vertue and propertie it hath, alwaies to turne the iron which it toucheth towards the North, the which is the most admirable vertue it hath. Aristotle [abt. 340 BC],[18] Theophrastus [abt. 300 BC], Discorides [abt. AD 80], Lucretius [abt. 70 BC],[19] nor any other Writers or naturall Philosophers that I have seene, make any mention thereof, although they treat of the load stone. Saint Augustine [abt. AD 400],[20] writing many and sundry properties and excellencies of the load stone in his bookes of the Citie of God, speakes nothing thereof. . . . There is yet another argument, for Plinie [abt. AD 70],[21] treating of the first inventers of Navigation, and naming all the

> instruments, yet he speakes nothing of the compasse to saile by, nor of the load stone. I say onely, that the art to know the starres was invented by the Phoenicians. . . .
>
> [p. 51] <u>Wee doe not certainely know at what time this Art of sailing was brought to light</u>. But for my part I hold for certaine that it is not verie ancient, . . .
>
> [p. 52] Some <u>approved</u> Authors write in the Historie of the East Indies that the first which began to discover this secret was upon the sea was Vasco da Gama, who, in the heigth of Mosambique,[22] met with certaine Mariners Moores[23] which used this compasse or needle to saile by,[24] and by the meanes thereof he sailed through those seas; <u>yet they write not from whom they learned this Art</u>. And <u>some</u> amongst them are of our opinion, that the Ancients were ignorant of this secret.[25]

[**Note*** *First of all, Acosta does not tell us what qualifies one to be an "approved" author, although I think it has something to do with that author being European. Acosta proudly proclaims that Vasco da Gama was* **<u>the first</u>** *to discover the secret of the compass. Acosta doesn't even feel the need to qualify his statement to read "the first European." That is because Vasco de Gama was the first* **<u>European</u>** *to sail directly from Europe to India. But who should he meet up with in Mozambique (located in southeast Africa opposite the shores of Madagascar) that used the compass? "Moores." That is, he met up with northwest African Muslim sailors! But Africans apparently don't count as intelligent people of merit when it comes to history, according to Acosta. They are not European. Next Acosta includes evidence for his position that "the Ancients were ignorant of this secret* [*the compass*]*." Yet the best he can do is say that only "***<u>some</u>** *amongst them" were of that opinion. Interestingly, he also mentions that others "write not from whom they learned this Art." This seems to imply, at least to me, that the origins of the magnetic compass could have been so far back in time that the details were lost. Furthermore, if the information about the compass didn't come from Europe, where did it come from? Acosta doesn't even bother to speculate beyond the Moors. Apparently Acosta doesn't care to see past Europe.*]

In **1607 Gregorio Garcia** published his *Origen de los indios de el nuevo mundo, e Indias occidentales . . .* at Valencia.[26] In this work, he reviewed all current theories on Indian origins and listed over 1700 authors on the subject of the American Indians. A missionary for twenty years in South

America, Garcia was considered one of the two most significant authorities for decades to come. (The other being Acosta).

One of the most eminent nineteenth-century scholars on American Indian origins, Justin Winsor, wrote the following about Garcia:

> He [Garcia] goes over the supposed navigations of the Phoenicians, the identity of Peru with Solomon's Ophir, and the chances of African, Roman, and Jewish migration—only to reject them all, and to favor a coming of Tartars and Chinese.[27]

In the years that followed Acosta and Garcia, many authors would quote them as authorities on the subject. One of those was Bernabe Cobo. I will comment on Cobo's arguments because they also reflect on previous reasoning, especially that of Acosta.

Bernabe Cobo was a Catholic father whose experiences in Peru led him to write the *History of the New World*.[28] The manuscript was finished in **1653**. He had listened to the legends of the natives regarding their origins, which stated they had come across the sea. He was opposed to such ideas, and in his book he explained his reasoning, although he relied heavily on the reasoning of Jose Acosta (1590). I believe his arguments are worthy of discussion.

One of his arguments was that if the ancients made long voyages across the open sea, they would have kept a record of it. Yet Cobo accepts no sources for this record other than the ancient Greek and Roman historians and philosophers. Cobo disregards the Native American traditions as myth. He makes no mention of Chinese history. Cobo also fails to mention (perhaps he was ignorant of the fact) that the maritime records of the Phoenicians were kept secret, or that the records of the Phoenicians and the Carthaginians were almost completely destroyed by conquering Mediterranean armies. Yet in both instances, the almost infinitesimal fragments that remained speak of lengthy voyages, navigation, and magnetism.

In trying to counter open-sea navigation, Cobo says that while his ancient Greek or Roman historians might speak of stories involving the circumnavigation of Africa, these voyages most certainly would have followed the coastline. However, in another part of his arguments against the early knowledge of a magnetic compass, Cobo says that early mariners feared traveling along the coastline because they could easily be blown out to sea (and become lost). Cobo reasoned that this fear stemmed from the fact that they lacked the means of navigation to return to land—that is, they lacked a magnetic compass. So Cobo seems to contradict himself.

Cobo goes on to question the validity of these stories of circumnavigation around Africa. His reasoning is that although the ancient historian Pliny repeated these stories, he also supported the idea (along with Aristotle and Cicero) that their world was made up of three zones: The Frigid Zone to the north in which mankind could not survive, the middle Temperate Zone in which man existed, and the southern Torrid Zone in which once again, man could not survive. Cobo, speaking from his more advanced seventeenth-century perspectives of travel, notes that Africa extends south of the equator (which would be the Torrid Zone) and thus the ancient Greek and Roman philosophers and historians contradicted themselves. In repeating these stories the ancient historians and philosophers had people voyaging into and beyond the Torrid Zone and yet these same historians and philosophers continued to promote the idea that man could not survive in the Torrid Zone. Cobo considered the ancient Greek and Roman philosophers too intelligent to support this contradiction. He reasons:

> The opinion of all antiquity in feeling that the Torrid Zone was unthinkable [unable to be lived in] was so universally accepted and firmly held in the minds of the wisest men of those times that they would not change their opinion with less certainty and experience to the contrary than we have now, so, although they had some news from men who had sailed those seas, since those voyages were very few in number, not customary and occurring by chance or due to the misfortune of the ones who undertook them, the ancients did not accept the full validity of the authors of the reports, and therefore the evidence was insufficient to make them change their minds.[29]

[**Note*** *And so without admitting the possibility that his ancient Roman and Greek philosophers and historians perhaps weren't as wise as he supposed, or that their knowledge did not represent "all antiquity" (what sacrilege!) or all perspectives,*[30] *Cobo dismisses the evidence and importance of lengthy voyages around Africa.*]

chapter 10

Early Historical Writings Related to American Origins: Pre-1830 European-American Writers[11]

Could Joseph Smith Have Been Influenced to Use the Term Compass *in His Translation by Historical Writings Concerning the American Indians?*

In his book on European thought regarding American Indian origins, Lee Eldridge Huddleston writes:

> Spanish writers dominated the development of ideas concerning the origins of the Indians of America until the beginning of the seventeenth century. After [the year] 1600 the peoples of northern Europe began to take a more active interest—especially the English and the Dutch.[1]

In **1626** an English travel writer named **Samuel Purchas** published his writings on American Indian origins. According to Huddleston, although Purchas might have used some of Acosta's arguments, <u>Purchas conveyed a native belief in a special Oracle or Director which guided the Indian ancestors to their new lands</u>. He writes (original spelling):

11. Illustration: Pierre de Charlevoix, a writer on American Indian origins

> *—The Mexican Exodus and First Founding—*
>
> Having now declared the subversion of this State and Kingdom by the Spaniards, I hold it not amisse to looke backe upon the first people which heere inhabited, with the beginnings and proceedings of the Mexican Empire. . . . The Nauatalcas (an ancient nation of Mexico) paint their beginning and first Territorie in maner of Caves because of their Seven Tribes and men coming out of them. . . . the cause (of their departure they ascribe to their Gods, which spake visibly to them, and bade them seek new Lands . . .
>
> He (their God) promised to make them Lords over all . . . and to give them a land plentiful in riches: whereupon they went forth carrying their Idoll with them in a coffer of Reeds, supported by foure of their principall Priests, with whom he talked, and communicated his Oracles and Directions. . . .
>
> And even as the pillar of Cloud and Fire conducted the Israelites in their passage through the wildernesse, so this apith Divell gave them notice when to advance forwards and when to stay.[2]

In **1761**, a two-volume work was published in London. In this work, a Frenchman by the name of **Pierre de Charlevoix** made an exhaustive review of various ideas and theories concerning Indian origins. In the "Preliminary Discourse on the Origin of the Americans," he writes:

> After reading almost every thing that has been writ on the manner in which America might have been peopled, we seem to be just where we were before this great and interesting question began to be agitated; notwithstanding, it would require a moderate volume to relate only the various opinions of the learned on this subject. For most part of them have given so much into the marvellous, almost all of them have built their conjectures on foundations so ruinous, or have had recourse to certain resemblances of names, manners, customs, religion and languages, so very frivolous, which it would, in my opinion, be as useless to refute, as it is impossible to reconcile with each other.[3]

Charlevoix wrote that after the Flood, people could have sailed across the ocean to America from the tower of Babel since they would have retained the knowledge of shipbuilding:

> Who can seriously believe . . . that Noah . . . the builder and pilot of the greatest ship that ever was . . . should not have communicated to

> those of his descendants who survived him, and by whose means he was to execute the order of the great Creator, to people the universe, I say, who can believe he should not have communicated to them the art of sailing upon the ocean."[4]

Charlevoix concludes with an emphasis on the possibilities of ancient navigation of the seas being the source of the origins of the American Indians, while discounting the possibility of the compass. He writes on the art of navigation:[5]

> Who can ever affirm that it was lost so soon? Strabo [6 BC] says in several places, that the inhabitants of Cadiz, and all the Spaniards, had large vessels, and excelled in the art of navigation. Pliny [AD 70] complains, that in his time, navigation was not so perfect as it had been for several ages before; the Carthaginians and Phoenicians were long possessed of the reputation of being hardy and expert maritimers. Father Acosta [1590] allows, that Vasco de Gama [1500] found, that the use of the compass was known among the inhabitants of Mozambique [on the southeast side of Africa, bordering on the Indian Ocean and opposite the shores of Madagascar] The islanders of Madagascar have a tradition, importing, that the Chinese had sent a colony into their country. And is it not a meer begging of the question, to reject that tradition on account of the impossibility to sail so far without the help of the compass.

In **1773**, **Samuel Mather**, a congregational clergyman from Boston, wrote that America was settled in successive waves not long after the Flood, not by sea, but by land bridges or narrow straights in northern Asia and northern Europe. While he notes that the compass was said not to have been invented until 1302, the Phoenicians were considered "the inventors of the Mariner's Art," and they might have sailed to America and made settlements there. Mather writes[6]:

> But some may ask: Where learned They the Art of navigation? And how came they to understand the Use and Application of the Magnet?—Panormitan [southern Italy] indeed would have it, that Amalphis first discovered the use of the Loadstone to mariners: And there is a Latin Line made to record the Discoverer, Prima dedit Nautis usum Magnetis Amalphis:—By which we are to understand an Italian City, where one John Goa,[7] it is said, found out the Use of the Mariner's Compass,

> about the Year of our Lord 1302—But the Phoenicians [1500 BC–300 BC[8]] were generally thought to be the Inventors of the Mariner's Art; and, from These, the Greeks received it; and, of these, the Cretans first of all, as Pliny acquaints us. But as the Phoenicians first tried the Seas among the Nations at Hand, and then afar off; so Thucydides [abt. 420 BC] tells us, that the Corinthians were the first among the Greeks, who performed Voyages: . . .
>
> The Voyage of Hanno, the Carthaginian, round the Coast of Africa, [425 BC] has already been mention'd: And surely this must discover no small Skill in Navigation. Nor have we any Doubt, that many of the Phoenicians were well skilld in the Mariner's Art: Nor yet is it any unreasonable Supposition, that they might sail to America, and make Settlements here.
>
> Thus it appears with sufficient Probability, that America not very long after the Flood was settled; and that, after the first Settlement of it, there were successive Removals to it, especially from the Northern Parts of Europe and Asia: And then, after some Ages had revolved, the Phoenicians might arrive and trade and settle here. And, by these various Ways, America became very well settled; and vast Numbers of People were found in this Western World, when Columbus, Americus and succeeding Voyagers came to it: And perhaps the Inhabitants here might, for their Numbers, vie with those of the other Continent.

In **1775**, **James Adair**, a man of unknown background but who had spent forty years living among the Indians in what is now the southeast portion of the United States, published what was to become a classic reference work in connecting Indians and their customs and traditions to Hebrew origins. The work was called *The History of the American Indians.*[9] Adair firmly believed that the Indians were descended from the Israelites, either while they were a maritime power in the days of Solomon, or soon after their general captivity (about 600 BC), but no mention is made of the compass. Adair rejected the idea that the Chinese could sail across the ocean to America, being unacquainted with the magnetic properties of loadstone.

In **1778**, **Jonathan Carver** published his studies on America in *Three years Travels through the Interior Parts of North-America.*[10] In reviewing a number of theories on American Indian origins, Carver quoted the comments of Charlevoix in regards to ancient navigation. He also referred to Adair's ideas.

In **1802**, **Jedidiah Morse**, a Congregational pastor in Charlestown, Massachusetts, made a note in his school textbook *Geography Made Easy*[11] that "in Arabia 'the caravans, having no tracks, are guided, as at sea, by a compass.'" This was perhaps the first time in American literature that the compass was associated with caravan travel in Arabia. Nevertheless, Morse says nothing about when the compass first began to be used in caravan travel across Arabia.

In **1816 Elias Boudinot** published *A Star in the West; or, a Humble Attempt to Discover the Long Lost Ten Tribes of Israel.*[12] This book was basically a rehashing of the works of James Adair and Jonathan Edwards, which promoted the lost tribes theory for Indian origins. It became a bestseller because of the fame of its author as the first president of the American Bible Society. According to Boudinot, entry into America was accomplished from Asia over the straits of Kamschatka. No mention is made of the compass or extended travel by sea.

Solomon Spaulding was born in Connecticut, graduated in theology in 1787, and moved to Conneaut, Ohio, in about 1809. During his residence there, he wrote a story in which some Romans sailing to England were blown off course, became lost, and finally landed in America. The manuscript dealt with what they encountered among the Indians. In about 1812, Spaulding moved to Pittsburgh for two years and while there inquired about having his manuscript published. In 1814 he moved again to Amity, Pennsylvania. In **1816** Spaulding died without the manuscript being published.

In the 1830s, an apostate Mormon named D. P. Hurlbut began circulating the idea that the Book of Mormon was plagiarized from Solomon Spaulding's lost manuscript when he had various people relate to him that Solomon Spaulding had been telling a story about an early colony who came to the Americas and lived among the Indians. However, while Hurlbut was gathering material for an 1836 anti-Mormon book, he came across this manuscript, found it did not substantiate his previous claims, and suppressed it. Through various means the whereabouts of this manuscript became known in 1884 to President James H. Fairchild of Oberlin

College, Ohio. A number of years later, a copy of this manuscript was given to the College, and in 1910 a verbatim copy was finally published.

According to Spaulding, this story was translated from papyrus scrolls found buried in a stone box in a cave near the west bank of the Conneaut River, where nearby were found the remains of an ancient fort. According to the story, written in Latin, a Roman named Fabricus, who had been appointed a secretary to Constantine in Rome, was sailing to Britain to carry an important message to the Roman army stationed there. His ship was engulfed in a tremendous storm which drove them out to sea. Spaulding writes concerning navigational circumstances but does not give any hint that they used or knew about the magnetic compass.[13]

In **1823**, Pastor **Ethan Smith** of Poultney, Vermont, published his *View of the Hebrews; or the Tribes of Israel in America*,[14] which became a bestseller. Basically it says the same things that Adair and Boudinot had written, namely that the Indians were of Hebrew origin. The book deals with Jews who were driven out of Jerusalem by the Roman army from AD 67 forward, and also the expulsed Jews of 725 BC, who came to be known as the Lost Ten Tribes. This book is important because anti-Mormon writers have claimed that Joseph Smith borrowed his ideas concerning Indian origins from its pages. In trying to illuminate these charges, B. H. Roberts made a comparison of the Book of Mormon with this book and compiled an impressive list of parallels between them.[15] In Ethan Smith's book, the theory is repeated from various authors he cites that the Lost Ten Tribes traveled northeastward until crossing over into America at the Bering Strait. Nevertheless, Smith writes that technology related to navigation could have been lost by the American Indians:

> Some have felt a difficulty arising against the Indians being the ten tribes, from their ignorances of the mechanic arts, of writing, and of navigation. Ancient Israel knew something of these; and some imagine, that these arts being once known, could never be lost. [Reasons are here given to the contrary] . . . But the savage [American Indian] tribes prevailed; and in process of time their savage jealousies and rage annihilated their more civilized brethren. . . . This accounts for their loss of the knowledge of letters, of the art of navigation, and of the use of iron.[16]

In summary, I have found it intriguing that by the time of Joseph Smith most historical writers (but not all) had the early settlers to the American continent coming by land. The later historical writers seemed to forget (or were ignorant of the fact) that most Native American Indian accounts had their ancestors coming *by sea*. Most historical writers (if not all) discounted the idea that the magnetic compass was used by the early settlers in coming to the American continent. Yet the historical writers tended to forget (or dismiss) the fact that most Native American Indian accounts made mention of <u>a venerated instrument that directed them</u>. Whether Joseph Smith actually read any of the historical writings I have mentioned is a matter of conjecture. What is more important to my discussion of the Liahona is that generally speaking, I can say that just previous to and during Joseph Smith's time, if people entered into oral or written discussions regarding American Indian origins, and if they happened to mention the term *compass*, they would have meant a magnetic compass.

chapter 11

The World of Joseph Smith: Perceptions and Definitions of the Term *Compass*[12]

Could the Term Compass *as Used in the Bible or the Definitions of the Term* Compass *in the Dictionary Have Influenced Joseph Smith's Translation?*

How would Joseph Smith have associated the term *compass* with the Book of Mormon story of the Liahona? In other words, as Joseph Smith translated the Book of Mormon, and especially as he translated the narrative of Nephi and Lehi's travels to the promised land, how did he come up with the word *compass* to describe the Liahona?

Although I do not claim to know all that went into the translation process, I will assume that the descriptive words (although not necessarily the proper names) that were formed in Joseph Smith's mind and that came out of his mouth in translation were in his own language—that is, the language of his times and circumstances. If such was the case, then the meaning of these descriptive words (and more specifically the word *compass*) can be obtained by examining the factors that might have shaped that meaning. And in doing so, I will show that there is a good chance that when Joseph used the word *compass* in his translation, there was an implication that that instrument was, in part, magnetic.

12. Illustration: Webster's 1828 Dictionary

There are four perspectives to Joseph's knowledge that I feel should be examined: (1) The Bible. I will examine the meanings of the term *compass* as found in the King James Bible. The people of Joseph Smith's time gained much of their education from the Bible; (2) The dictionary. I will review the definitions of the term *compass* that were common to the language of the people during Joseph Smith's time; (3) Joseph's personal experiences. I will relate a few circumstances in Joseph's personal life where he might have become personally acquainted with a magnetic compass; and (4) The inclusion of the term *compass* in stories of American Indian origins (which I have already reviewed). I will now address the possible influence on Joseph from the Bible and the dictionary.

The King James Bible, *Webster's 1928 Dictionary*, and Adam Clarke's 1810 *Bible Commentary*

The King James Bible with Apocrypha

Perhaps the most popular version of the Bible during Joseph Smith's time was the King James Version (which also contained at that time the books of the Apocrypha). Within this version the term *compass* is found in a number of different verses with various meanings.

The Adam Clarke Bible Commentary[1]

The most popular and influential Bible commentary of Joseph Smith's time was written by Adam Clarke. In **1810** Adam Clark published the first of his series of commentaries on the Bible. I will quote pertinent commentary for biblical verses that contain the term *compass.*

The 1828 edition of Webster's American Dictionary of the English Language[2]

This dictionary accurately documents the meanings of the term *compass* during Joseph Smith's time and during the period of translation of the Book of Mormon.

Joseph Smith's mother, Lucy Mack Smith, noted in her reminiscences regarding her family and her son Joseph that she was in the habit of gathering the family regularly to read from the Bible. The Bible was a centerpiece of learning during the times of Joseph Smith, so much so that Webster's dictionary refers to various verses in the Bible in its list of definitions for the term *compass*. For these reasons I have chosen to treat the above sources of learning together.

COMPASS, noun.

Definition #1. *Stretch; reach; extent; the limit or boundary of a space, and the space included; applied to time, space, sound, &c.* Our knowledge lies within a very narrow compass. The universe extends beyond the compass of our thoughts. So we say, the *compass* of a year, the *compass* of an empire, the *compass* of reason, the *compass* of the voice. And in that compass all the world contains. [See Proverbs 8:27, 1 Maccabees 14:48.]

Proverbs 8:27
When he prepared the heavens, I was there: when <u>he set a compass upon the face of the depth</u>:

1 Maccabees 14:48
So they commanded that this writing should be put in tables of brass, and that they should be set up <u>within the compass</u> of the sanctuary in a conspicuous place.

Proverbs 8:27
When <u>he set a compass upon the face of the depth.</u>

Adam Clarke notes the following:

Does this not refer to the establishment of the *law of gravitation*? by which all the particles of matter, tending to a common centre, would produce in all bodies the *orbicular* form, which we see them have; so that even the waters are not only retained within their boundaries, but are subjected to the *circular* form, in their great aggregate of seas, as other parts of matter are. This is called here *making a compass, bechukko chug*, <u>sweeping a circle</u>; and even this on the face of the deep, to bring the chaotic mass into form, regularity, and order.

[**Note*** *Would the above definition apply to our modern-day usage of terms like a "moral compass"? When I hear that someone is relying on his or her "moral compass," I envision a situation in which this "moral compass" is*

pointing *him or her away from the temptation or trouble that is in front of him or her. On the other hand, I can envision some improper actions as beyond the limits of what I have committed myself to do. But in that instance, wouldn't I be more inclined to say that the improper actions are* ***beyond*** *my moral compass? The same meaning can be implied in 1 Maccabees 14:48 in which it says that the tables of brass "should be set up* ***within*** *the compass of the sanctuary."*]

Definition #2. *A passing round; a circular course; a circuit.* Time is come round; and where I did begin, there shall I end: My life has run its compass. "They fetched a compass of seven days' journey." 2 Kings 3. 2 Sam. 5. Acts 28. [see also Joshua 15:3] ["round in compass," see 1 Kings 7:35, 2 Chron. 4:2]

2 Kings 3:7–9

And he went and sent to Jehosaphat, the king of Judah, saying, . . . wilt thou go with me against Moab to battle?

And he said, Which way shall we go up? . . .

So the king of Israel went, and the king of Judah, and the king of Edom: and they fetched a compass of seven days' journey . . .

Adam Clarke comments on the above underlined phrase: "By taking a circuitous route, to go round the southern part of the Dead Sea, they probably intended to surprise the Moabites."

2 Samuel 5:22–23

And the Philistines came up yet again, and spread themselves in the valley of Rephaim.

And when David enquired of the Lord, he said, Thou shalt not go up; but fetch a compass behind them, and come upon them over against the mulberry trees.

Acts 28:12–13

And landing at Syracuse, we tarried there three days.

And from thence we fetched a compass, and came to Rhegium; and after one day the south wind blew, and we came the next day to Puteoli.

Adam Clarke notes that the phrase *from thence we fetched a compass* meant "whence we coasted about." He notes, "This will appear evident, when the coast of Sicily is viewed on any correct map."

Joshua 15:3

And it went out to the south side to Maaleh-acrabbim, and passed along to Zin, . . . and went up to Adar, and fetched a compass to Karkaa.

1 Kings 7:34–35

And there were four undersetters to the four corners of one base; and the undersetters were of the very base itself,

And in the top of the base was there a round compass of half a cubit high: and on the top of the base the ledges thereof and the borders thereof were of the same.

2 Chronicles 4:2

And he made a molten sea of ten cubits from brim to brim, round in compass, and five cubits the height thereof; and a line of thirty cubits did compass it round about.

[**Note*** *While this definition ("a passing round" or "circular") might be likened to the term "ball" as it is used in the Book of Mormon (see chapter 2, point 6), it is not totally equivalent to a ball. That is, for one to say that something is round or circular does not necessarily mean that the object is a ball.*]

Definition #3. *Moderate bounds; limits of truth; moderation; due limits.* In two hundred years, (I speak within *compass,*) no such commission had been executed. This sense is the same as the first, and the peculiar force of the phrase lies in the word within.

Definition #4. *The extent or limit of the voice or of sound.*

Definition #5. *An instrument for directing or ascertaining the course of ships at sea, consisting of a circular box, containing a paper card marked with the thirty-two points of direction, fixed on a magnetic needle, that always points to the north, the variation excepted.* The needle with the card turns on a pin in the center of the box. In the center of the needle is fixed a brass conical socket or cap, by which the card hanging on the pin turns freely round the center. The box is covered with glass, to prevent the motion of the card from being disturbed by the wind.

[**Note*** *The Book of Mormon certainly links the term* compass *with directing the course of Nephi's ship. The text does not refer to a "circular box," but to a "ball." The text of the Book of Mormon does not refer to thirty-two points of direction, but to a term "south-southeast," which implies sixteen points of direction. I will also note here that the definition above does NOT appear to allow for an instrument other than a specific magnetic compass. So even if Nephi were to use the term* compass *for an instrument* ***pointing*** *the direction to go, it is a metaphor for a magnetic compass. And so if I suppose the Liahona* ***pointed*** *to the specific direction in which they should go (the traditional interpretation), where was the magnetic "compass" in Nephi's time from which he derived the metaphor?*]

> **Definition #6**. Compass or compasses, [or a pair of compasses, so named from its legs, but pair is superfluous or improper, and the singular number compass is the preferable name,] *an instrument for describing circles, measuring figures, &c., consisting of two pointed legs or branches, made of iron, steel or brass, joined at the top by a rivet, on which they move.* There are also compasses of three legs or triangular compasses, cylindrical and spherical compasses with four branches, and various other kinds. [See Isaiah 44:13]
>
> Isaiah 44:13
>
> The carpenter stretcheth out his rule; he marketh it out with a line; he fitteth it with planes, and he marketh it out with the compass, and maketh it after the figure of a man; according to the beauty of a man; that it may remain in the house.
>
> **Definition #7**. *An instrument used in surveying land, constructed in the main like the mariners compass; but with this difference, that the needle is not fitted into the card,* moving with it, but plays alone; the card being drawn on the bottom of the box, and a circle divided into 360 degrees on the limb. This instrument is used in surveying land, and in directing travelers in a desert or forest, miners, &c.

[**Note*** *This instrument might be likened to the Liahona.*]

[**Note*** *The word* compass *can also be used as a verb. For example, in* Webster's 1828 Dictionary *a few of the meanings given are "to stretch round,"* *"to surround," or "to go or walk round," and so on. Despite this, I will not document anything here because the ONLY verb form for the word "compass" in the Book of Mormon text occurs in the words of Isaiah quoted in 2 Nephi 7:11: "Behold all ye that kindle fire, that compass yourselves about with sparks."*

Another item of note here is that there are NO noun forms of the word compass in the Book of Mormon other than those instances of a direct reference to the Liahona.[3]]

[**Note*** *There is one other verse that is commented on by Clarke that is perhaps more pertinent here in regards to the magnetic compass. It is found in the book of Job (written about 600 BC).*]

> Job 28:18: "No mention shall be made of coral, [or of pearls]: for the price of wisdom is above rubies. The topaz [or lodestone] of Ethiopia shall not equal it . . ." [4]
>
> Adam Clarke makes the following comment on this verse:
>
> That is, it is understood that the wisdom which aided man to make this discovery [of lodestone], and to apply it to the purposes of navigation, on the account of its polarity, is that wisdom which is above the price of rubies. The attractive properties of loadstone must have been observed from its first discovery; and there is every reason to believe that the magnet and its virtues were known in the east long before they were discovered in Europe.

In summary, in examining the Bible, Adam Clarke's *1810 Bible Commentary* and *Webster's 1828 Dictionary*, works that might have influenced the vocabulary of Joseph Smith, the best definition for the term compass as translated and used in the Book of Mormon seems to be a round or, more particularly, a circular instrument that was magnetized.

chapter 12

The World of Joseph Smith: Joseph's Personal Experiences with the Maritime World[13]

Did Joseph Smith Have Any Personal Experiences with the Maritime World That Might Have Motivated Him to Include the Term Compass *in His Translation?*

As Joseph Smith translated the Book of Mormon, and especially as he translated the narrative of Nephi and Lehi's travels to the promised land, did he have any personal experiences, especially with the maritime world, that might have influenced him to use a term like *compass* for a navigational instrument like the Liahona? There are at least three different perspectives that might apply:

(1) Joseph Smith's grandfather Solomon Mack left his family to spend four years sailing the coast of New England and Nova Scotia. He returned to his family in 1788, and from then on he remained relatively close to his daughter Lucy and her family until 1818. He wrote a pamphlet in 1811 in which he detailed his adventures at sea.

(2) Joseph Smith's father had invested in shipping goods to China. In

13. Illustration: Solomon Mack's 1811 pamphlet

doing so, he would supposedly have had some knowledge of the capability of the ship and crew to navigate all the way to China and back.

(3) After his bout with typhus, Joseph Smith accompanied his uncle to Salem, Massachusetts, for rest and relaxation. Salem was a mecca for maritime culture. The East India Marine Society was founded there in 1799.

1. Solomon Mack

About 1799, Solomon Mack followed his daughter Lucy and Joseph Smith Sr. (her husband of 3 years), to Tunbridge, Vermont. While there in Vermont, Solomon wrote his autobiography. As part of his earlier married life, Solomon had gone off to sea with two of his sons for four years (1784–1788), seeking his fortune and leaving his wife and small children at home to fend for themselves. He returned penniless to a penniless family. Tremendously humbled and ashamed, he turned to Christianity. In 1811, in an attempt to earn some money, he compiled a pamphlet from his previous autobiographical writings titled "Narrative." In that pamphlet he describes a few of his sea adventures:

> Soon after I and my two sons went out a privateering. We ship't aboard a privateer of 114 tons, commanded by Captain Havens; there was about eighty men on board. We were chased by five British privateers. . . .
>
> Next we hoisted sail and made for New London. After the war we freighted a vessel and went to Liverpool and sold our loading and ship't aboard Captain Foster's and went [on] a fishing voyage. And so I went two voyage[s], and the third voyage I was in the cabin when I heard a rout on deck. I sprang up as quickly as possible, and there being a terrible hurricane as ever I saw in my life. Both masts was carried overboard, and if they had not we must all have found watery graves—we ought to have been thankful and bless the Lord for it. Our captain and all hands appeared to be greatly surprised, but we was all spared through the tempest. We ought to be thankful to our God for a few moments for repentance, but we thought nothing of these things.
>
> The hands all left her but myself and my son. We stuck fast by the hull, and that night we caught 225 large fish; but by jury masts we worked her into Liverpool. [pp. 12–15][1]

Since Solomon lived close to Lucy and Joseph until about 1818, one might expect that he told and retold his naval exploits to his grandson

Joseph, who he had watched grow from birth to age thirteen. Whether the maritime compass ever entered into any of those stories is a matter of speculation, but there exists the possibility. Moreover, these stories might have inspired Joseph to seek further maritime information on his own.

2. Joseph Smith Sr.

In her reminiscences regarding her family and her heritage, Joseph Smith's mother, Lucy Mack Smith, noted how sometime after 1802, her husband had invested in ginseng:

> Soon after he [Joseph Smith Sr.] commenced business in this place [Randolph, Vermont] he ascertained that crystallized ginseng root sold very high in China, being used as a remedy for the plague which was then raging there. He therefore concluded to embark in a traffic of this article, and consequently made an investment of all the means which he commanded, in that way and manner which was necessary to carry on a business of this kind, viz. crystallizing and exporting the root. . . .
>
> My husband in a short time went to the city of New York with the view of shipping his ginseng and, finding a vessel in port which was soon to set sail, he made arrangements with the captain to this effect—that he was to sell the ginseng in China and return the avails thereof to my husband.[2]

The above might imply that Joseph Smith Sr. became at least somewhat familiar with the abilities of navigation (including instrumentation) as well as the perils of navigation from New York to China and back. As Joseph Smith Sr. ended up losing all he had in this venture (along with Lucy's gift of 1,000 dollars from her brother), this story might have been repeatedly discussed during Joseph Jr.'s boyhood years. But whether Joseph ever heard a word about navigation from his own father, this story about the ginseng trade to China implies that the maritime world (including the magnetic compass) was never far away from New Englanders during Joseph Smith's time.

3. Salem, Massachusetts

In her reminiscences, Lucy Mack Smith recounts Joseph's sufferings with typhus as a young boy. She writes:

> Joseph immediately commenced getting better, and from this onward,

> continued to mend until he became strong and healthy. When he had so far recovered as to be able to travel, he went with his uncle, Jesse Smith, to Salem, for the benefit of his health, hoping the sea-breezes would be of service to him, and in this he was not disappointed.[3]

Lucy does not mention how long Joseph stayed at Salem, nor what he specifically did there. However, I will note that Salem was a seaport city and the collecting-point for maritime art and culture. The East India Marine Society had been founded in 1799. This eventually developed into the Peabody Essex Museum. On their website, I found the following:

> The roots of the Peabody Essex Museum date to the 1799 founding of the East India Marine Society, an organization of Salem captains and supercargoes who had sailed beyond either the Cape of Good Hope or Cape Horn. The society's charter included a provision for the establishment of a "cabinet of natural and artificial curiosities," which is what we today would call a museum. Society members brought to Salem a diverse collection of objects from the northwest coast of America, Asia, Africa, Oceania, India and elsewhere.

While I can't say for sure whether the boy Joseph ever was allowed to see any of this collection, or to go on board any of the ships there (and more specifically to view a maritime compass), I can cite a parallel occurrence from later on in Joseph's life. On July 25, 1836, Joseph and a few of the leading brethren of the Church set off on a trip to the New England. They arrived in Salem on about August 4 and stayed there for about three weeks. According to Oliver Cowdery, this visit also had a health motive. He wrote the following to his brother Warren, who was back in Kirtland:

> It would be altogether uninteresting to lead you all the round of scouting to, and bathing in the sea, and how beneficial a change of climate, as well as a recess from business, has so far been to my health. I will therefore pass over these, and leave them till I see you face to face."[4]

Interestingly, Joseph's signature is found on the visitor's album for the Salem East India Marine Society under the date of August 9, 1836. So I wonder to what extent Joseph was repeating the actions of his first trip to Salem as a boy?

In summarizing my brief comments on three of Joseph's own personal experiences that might have familiarized him with maritime practices, I would have to say that he would have become at least somewhat acquainted with the ships and navigation principles of his time. And I do not think that it is too much for me to presume that the term *compass* that came from his mind to his mouth as he translated the Book of Mormon could have carried with it the idea of a round instrument with a magnetic spindle.

chapter 13

Personal Testimony from Joseph Smith and the Three Witnesses

What Did Joseph Smith and the Three Witnesses Have to Say about the Liahona?[14]

What did Joseph Smith or any of the Three Witnesses have to say regarding the Liahona? As for the testimony of Joseph Smith himself, it is worth noting that in the known recorded teachings of Joseph Smith,[1] in the diaries and journals of Joseph Smith,[2] and in the writings of Joseph Smith,[3] I have found no mention of a "ball," "director," or "Liahona," either in the literal sense or the metaphorical sense. The only thing that I have found is a reference in D&C 17:1 (dated June 1829) in which the Three Witnesses were told that they were to see the "miraculous directors which were given to Lehi while in the wilderness."[4]

Yet according to the testimony of the Three Witnesses in the front of the Book of Mormon, no mention is made of the Liahona. They mention only that

> We have seen the engravings which are upon the plates; and they have been shown unto us by the power of God, and not of man. And we

14. Illustration: The Three Witnesses view the Plates and the Liahona

> declare with words of soberness, that an angel of God came down from heaven, and he brought and laid before our eyes, that we beheld and saw the plates, and the engravings thereon.

However David Whitmer, one of the Three Witnesses, later confirmed that they had seen the "Directors."

In a September 7, **1878**, interview of David Whitmer by Joseph F. Smith and Orson Pratt, we find the following:

> Elder O. P. "Do you remember what time you saw the plates?"
>
> D. W. "It was in June, 1829—the latter part of the month, and the eight witnesses saw them, I think, the next day or the day after. (i.e. one or two days after). Joseph showed them the plates himself, but the angel showed us (the three witnesses) the plates, as I suppose to fulfil the words of the book itself. Martin Harris was not with us at this time; he obtained a view of them afterwards, (the same day). Joseph, Oliver, and myself were together when I saw them [the plates]. We not only saw the plates of the Book of Mormon, but also the Brass plates, the plates of the Book of Ether . . . and many other plates. The fact is, it was just as though Joseph, Oliver and I were sitting just here on a log, when we were overshadowed by a light. It was not like the light of the sun nor like that of a fire, but more glorious and beautiful. It extended away round us, I cannot tell how far, but in the midst of this light about as far off as he sits (pointing to John C. Whitmer, sitting a few feet from him), there appeared as it were, a table with many records, or plates, upon it, besides the plates of the Book of Mormon, also the sword of Laban, <u>the directors—i.e., the ball which Lehi had</u>, and the interpreters. I saw them just as plainly as I see this bed (striking the bed beside him with his hand), and I heard the voice of the Lord, as distinctly as I ever heard anything in my life declaring that the records of the plates of the Book of Mormon were translated by the gift and power of God."
>
> Elder O. P. "Did you see the Angel at this time?"
>
> D. W. "Yes, he stood before us. Our testimony as recorded in the Book of Mormon is strictly and absolutely true, just as it is there written." (The Testimony of David Whitmer, as related in an interview with Apostles Orson Pratt and Joseph F. Smith, at Richmond, Missouri, on September 7, 1878. *Millennial Star* 40: 771–74)

In a "Letter From Elder W. H. Kelley" printed in the *Saints' Herald* (March 1, **1882**) we find David Whitmer quoted as saying the following:

> I was plowing in the field one morning and Joseph and Oliver came along with a revelation stating that I was to be one of the witnesses to the Book of Mormon. I got over the fence and we went out into the woods, near by, and sat down on a log and talked awhile. We then kneeled down and prayed. Joseph prayed. We then got up and sat on the log and were talking, when all at once a light came down from above us and encircled us for quite a little distance around; and the angel stood before us. He was dressed in white, and spoke and called me by name and said, "Blessed is he that keepeth His commandments." This is all that I heard the angel say. A table was set before us and on it the records were placed. The Records of the Nephites, from which the Book of Mormon was translated, the brass plates, the Ball of Directors, the sword of Laban and other plates. While we were viewing them the voice of God spoke out of heaven saying that the Book was true and the translation correct.

Concerning an 1884 interview of David Whitmer by Edmund C. Briggs and R. Etzenhouser that was published in the *Saints' Herald* (June 21, **1884**), we find the following:

> On April 25th, with Bro. R. Etzenhouser in company, I called upon David Whitmer, which I had longed to do for years. We were very hospitably entertained, and enjoyed the interview much. The following are some of the facts as stated to us:
>
> "In June 1829, I saw the angel by the power of God, Joseph, Oliver and I were alone, and a light from heaven shone round us, and solemnity pervaded our minds. The angel appeared in the light, as near as that young man [within five or six feet]. Between us and the angel there appeared a table, and there lay upon it the sword of Laban, the Ball of Directors, the Record, and interpreters. The angel took the Record, and turned the leaves, and showed it to us by the power of God. They were taken away by the angel to a cave, which we saw by the power of God while we were yet in the Spirit. My testimony in the Book of Mormon is true; I can't deviate from it."

In a letter to Elder Edward Stevenson, dated December 5, **1889**, President Joseph F. Smith, second counselor to President Wilford Woodruff, asked if Elder Stevenson had any knowledge of the cave or room in the Hill Cumorah:

> If you have any knowledge—not supposition—in regard to "the room in the Hill Cumorah" containing the Records, treasures etc.—or of the same having been shown to the Prophet and Oliver, I would be greatly obliged to you to inform me on the subject.

Then President Smith added the following:

> All I know about the matter is what Pres. B. Young related to me, many years ago when I commenced speaking to the Y.M.M.I. Associations on the early history of the Church. He told me that the Hill [Cumorah] opened, as it were, to Joseph, and Oliver I think, and they saw—as it appeared to them—a chamber containing all the Plates and Records of the Nephites, with the Sword of Laban, the Breast Plate, the Director, the Interpreters etc. etc. But further than this I know nothing but the rumors and stories that are afloat about something of this kind. If you know anything about this matter I would be glad to hear from you on the subject. [5]

[**Note*** *This is the only authoritative mention that I know of where the Director (Liahona) was seen in a cave (**in** the Hill Cumorah).*]

I found no further details on the appearance or function of the Liahona by Joseph or the Three Witnesses.

chapter 14

Some Final Thoughts[15]

Having addressed the issues that I have, I will now present a summary of the perspectives I have presented relative to a partially magnetic Liahona. In the introduction I used the example of the Chinese admiral Zheng He to convey the idea that while the study of "history" is important in gaining new perspectives on the Book of Mormon, in retrospect "history" can be lost, much in the same manner that Zheng He's maritime achievements faded into obscurity when a new Chinese hierarchy changed their priorities (and thus "history").

In the beginning chapters, I was able to view the Liahona from different scriptural perspectives that might relate to it being, in part, a magnetic compass. While my analysis of the wording in the text of the Book of Mormon certainly does not achieve overwhelming proof,[1] I feel that it does provide possible new insights. In summarizing my results, I decided that the text might not completely rule out a magnetic component to the Liahona and that further study might provide some additional insights.

In the next few chapters, I extended my focus beyond what I had previously considered "maritime history" in relation to a magnetic compass and found new perspectives. Where previously I had assumed the maritime compass to be a European invention just previous to Columbus, I now was able to focus on China, the East Indies, Arabia, the Phoenicians, and Israel many centuries earlier with copper metallurgy (bronze

15. Illustration: An artistic rendering of Nephi's ship (and the Liahona) as Lehi's group sails to the promised land

or "brass"), iron metallurgy and lodestone in mind. And where once I thought that men of ages past never ventured far from the shore, I came to view the ability of the ancients to navigate the open seas with more respect. I also examined early Native American writings on Indian origins and found that ancient traditions involved a special instrument that helped direct the original settlers across the sea to this land.

I next evaluated the "legends" against "science." It became apparent that I was faced with the dilemma of trying to decide what was "true." Had authorities missed some "facts" or had "facts" been overlooked in the name of authority? Had precious ancient records of the Far East, the Near East, or the Americas been lost or destroyed? Would those libraries have provided any clues that might be brought to light? While I lacked complete and total answers, I nevertheless presented some examples that might allow one to feel that the Book of Mormon narrative relative to a partially magnetic Liahona was perhaps plausible.

In succeeding chapters I examined early American-European writings on Indian origins and found that the mariner's compass was indeed part of their discussion on ancient navigation to the New World, although ideas were varied as to its use (or non-use) and were limited in scope. In viewing the bias of some of the European writers, I was left with the question, had the "history" of a magnetic compass remained in obscurity in the West (much in the same manner as Zheng He's maritime achievements) in consequence of a European-American mindset that "nothing of real importance could have started outside Europe"?[2] I also examined *Webster's 1828 Dictionary*, the King James Bible, and Adam Clarke's *1810 Bible Commentary* for content that might have influenced the vocabulary of Joseph Smith's time period and found that the only definition for the term *compass* that correlated with the text of the Book of Mormon involved a round or circular instrument that was magnetized. Furthermore, there seemed to be no definition that would allow for a non-magnetic compass.

Finally, I sought for any teachings by Joseph Smith or accounts by Joseph Smith or the Three Witnesses that might add any insight into the idea of a partially magnetic Liahona. My search did not add any pertinent information.

Going back to the introduction of this book, there I mentioned that I had approached the Liahona with five main questions: (1) Can the Book of Mormon narrative and other scriptures support the idea that the Liahona contained a magnetic spindle? (2) If so, was magnetism or the principle of a magnetic compass known in ancient times? (3) Could Nephi and Lehi have been in the right place geographically and at the right time chronologically to have become acquainted with the principle of a magnetic compass? (4) If so, could this knowledge have become "lost"? and (5) If we assume that the term *compass* (which Joseph used in his Book of Mormon translation to describe the Liahona) came from Joseph's own cultural environment, would the meaning of *compass* have implied a magnetic compass?

While I can't claim that I have given definite answers for the original questions proposed in my Introduction, I do believe that I have provided possible answers. At the least I believe that I have broadened perspectives and established a platform for discussion on the possible workings of the Liahona and on early navigation across the sea to the New World. There will always be those "scientific" minds that will dismiss my ideas, claiming that they are based on emotionally-driven legends and myths which have no place in a pure, science-based history. And perhaps there are good reasons for their opinions. I also suppose that there will be some LDS "purists" that will interpret my approach to the Liahona as an attack on the idea that God can work miracles, even though I have made it clear to the reader that I believe God can indeed perform miracles and that a prophet such as Nephi could indeed have received revelation from God through his faith and the medium of the Liahona. And here again, perhaps there are good reasons for their "purist" opinions. But once again, the purpose of my research and writing has been to explore new perspectives, not to determine in one brief foray into the workings of the Liahona what ideas are absolutely right or wrong in every aspect. And in that regard, I hope that what I have written has provoked the reader in a positive way. I have always appreciated the words of Richard L. Bushman, who Terryl Givens, another noted Mormon historian, recently called the "foremost historian of Mormonism":[3]

> A modern believer lives in a kind of postmodern time warp where religious reality is constantly overlaid on conflicting secular reality, making everything seem relative and indeterminate. In the modern world, faith is a choice. One has to choose to believe over against the reigning common sense. This leads to the liberating but disconcerting realization that historical truth is also molded to suit our assumptions

> and desires. Written history rarely survives the threescore and ten years allotted those who write it.[4]
>
> . . . from a religious perspective, at least from a Mormon point of view, there can be no lasting history for mortals. So long as we progress we will enjoy ever broader horizons, and these must inevitably reflect on our understanding of what went before. As our wisdom enlarges, we will see more deeply into all of our experiences. Only when we come to the limits of knowledge and intelligence will we reach the final truth about history. [5]

As I come to the end of my writing, I want to say that it has been a gratifying experience for me to take a good look at "history" and to seek new perspectives not only on the Liahona being, in part, magnetic, but also on the historical background setting that might be implied in the Book of Mormon text.[6]

Notes

Introduction

1. One can find a portrait of Zheng He by making an Internet "Images" search for "Zheng He."

2. There are a number of Internet sites that give information on this subject. Readers can search "Zheng He."

3. A picture by Jan Adkins (1993) illustrating this comparison in size between Zheng He's treasure ship (400 feet) and Columbus's Santa Maria (85 feet) can be found at a number of Internet websites. Readers can find such illustrations by making an Internet "Images" search.

4. A picture of the historic *USS Constellation* can be seen with an "Images" search on the Internet. I have a personal photo of myself standing next to the *USS Constellation*, anchored in Baltimore Harbor, November 2006.

5. For a gallery with illustrations depicting the different types of ships and details of their usage, one can go to http://www.china.org.cn/english/features/zhenghe/131456.htm.

6. In this regard, I searched in a number of old bookstores for encyclopedias from the 1950s to the 1980s. I found a brief two-sentence reference for "Cheng Ho" but only in a 1983 edition. In

addition to my own searches, I asked some friends who had access to some old sets of encyclopedias to search for me. They also failed to come up with anything significant.

7. John A. Tvedtnes explored a related perspective in a short two-page note in *The FARMS Review* ("Can Early Chinese Maritime Expeditions Shed Light on Lehi's Voyage to the New World?" Review of Gavin Menzies, *1421: the Year China Discovered America*, New York: Morrow, 2003. *The FARMS Review* 16, no. 1 [2004], pp. 427–28). After a brief note on Zheng's voyages, he writes:

Zheng's expeditions, it seems, would have taken him over seas earlier crossed by Lehi on his voyage to a promised land. Even if Zheng did not arrive in the New World, his exploration of parts of the Indian and Pacific Oceans may provide useful information for future Book of Mormon research.

8. The scriptures that are listed below directly relate to the Liahona. All of the verses except those in the book of Mosiah have been preserved in the original manuscript. All of the verses have been preserved in the printer's manuscript. I would hope readers will familiarize themselves with the text in preparation for the discussion which follows:

(*Desert Journey and Bountiful*)

1 Nephi 16:10—And it came to pass that as my father arose in the morning, and went forth to the tent door, to his great astonishment he beheld upon the ground a round ball of curious workmanship; and it was of fine brass. And within the ball were two spindles; and the one pointed the way whither we should go into the wilderness.

1 Nephi 16:13—And it came to pass that we traveled for the space of four days, nearly a south-southeast direction, and we did pitch out tents again.

1 Nephi 16:16—And we did follow the directions of the ball, which led us in the more fertile parts of the wilderness.

1 Nephi 16:26—And it came to pass that the voice of the Lord said unto him: Look upon the ball, and behold the things which are written.

1 Nephi 16:27—And it came to pass that when my father beheld the things which were written upon the ball, he did fear and tremble exceedingly, and also my brethren and the sons of Ishmael and our wives.

1 Nephi 16:28—And it came to pass that I, Nephi, beheld the pointers which were in the ball, that they did work according to the faith and diligence and heed which we did give unto them.

1 Nephi 16:29—And there was also written upon them a new writing, which was plain to be read, which did give us understanding concerning the ways of the Lord; and it was written and changed from time to time, according to the faith and diligence which we gave unto it. And thus we see that by small means the Lord can bring about great things.

1 Nephi 16:30—And it came to pass that I, Nephi, did go forth up into the top of the mountain, according to the directions which were given upon the ball.

(Ocean Voyage)

1 Nephi 18:12—And it came to pass that after they had bound me insomuch that I could not move, the compass, which had been prepared of the Lord, did cease to work.

1 Nephi 18:13—Wherefore, they knew not whither they should steer the ship, insomuch that there arose a great storm, yea, a great and terrible storm, yea, a great and terrible tempest, and we were driven back upon the waters for the space of three days; and they began to be frightened exceedingly lest they should be drowned in the sea; nevertheless they did not loose me.

1 Nephi 18:14—And on the fourth day, which we had been driven back, the tempest began to be exceedingly sore.

1 Nephi 18:15—And it came to pass that we were about to be swallowed up in the depths of the sea. And after we had been driven back upon the waters for the space of four days . . .

1 Nephi 18:21—And it came to pass after they had loosed me, behold, I took the compass, and it did work whither I desired it. And it came to

pass that I prayed unto the Lord; and after I had prayed the winds did cease, and the storm did cease, and there was a great calm.

1 Nephi 18:22—And it came to pass that I, Nephi, did guide the ship, that we sailed again towards the promised land.

(Promised Land)

2 Nephi 5:12—And I, Nephi, had also brought the records which were engraven upon the plates of brass; and also the ball, or compass, which was prepared for my father by the hand of the Lord, according to that which is written.

Mosiah 1:16—And moreover, he [Benjamin] also gave him [Mosiah] charge concerning the records which were engraven on the plates of brass; and also . . . the ball or director, which led our fathers through the wilderness, which was prepared by the hand of the Lord that thereby they might be led, every one according to the heed and diligence which they gave unto him.

Mosiah 1:17—Therefore, as they were unfaithful they did not prosper nor progress in their journey, but were driven back, and incurred the displeasure of God upon them; and therefore they were smitten with famine and sore afflictions, to stir them up in remembrance of their duty.

Alma 37:38—And now, my son, I have somewhat to say concerning the thing which our fathers call a ball, or director-or our fathers called it **Liahona**, which is, being interpreted, a compass; and the Lord prepared it.

Alma 37:39—And behold, there cannot any man work after the manner of so curious a workmanship. And behold, it was prepared to show unto our fathers the course which they should travel in the wilderness.

Alma 37:40—And it did work for them according to their faith in God; therefore, if they had faith to believe that God could cause that those spindles should point the way they should go, behold, it was done; therefore they had this miracle, and also many other miracles wrought by the power of God, day by day.

Alma 37:41—Nevertheless, because those miracles were worked by small means [*nevertheless*] it did show unto them marvelous works. They were slothful, and forgot to exercise their faith and diligence and then those marvelous works ceased, and they did not progress in their journey.

Alma 37:42—Therefore, they tarried in the wilderness, or did not travel a direct course, and were afflicted with hunger and thirst, because of their transgressions.

Alma 37:43—And now, my son, I would that ye should understand that these things are not without a shadow; for as our fathers were slothful to give heed to this compass (now these things were temporal) they did not prosper; even so it is with things which are spiritual.

Alma 37:44—For behold, it is as easy to give heed to the work of Christ, which will point to you a straight course to eternal bliss, as it was for our fathers to give heed to this compass, which would point unto them a straight course to the promised land.

Alma 37:45—And now I say, is there not a type in this thing? For just as surely as this director did bring our fathers, by following its course, to the promised land, shall the words of Christ, if we follow their course, carry us beyond this vale of sorrow into a far better land of promise.

[**Note*** *In Alma 37:41 I have inserted the word* nevertheless *into the verse as it appeared in the original manuscript and the first edition of the Book of Mormon. This word was later deleted, but that deletion changes the tone of the verse. For me, a better rendition would be to substitute the word "notwithstanding" for the deleted "nevertheless," thus rendering the verse:*

Nevertheless, because those miracles were worked by small means—notwithstanding it did show unto them marvelous works—they were slothful, and forgot to exercise their faith and diligence and then those marvelous works ceased.]

Chapter 1

1. A number of illustrations depicting the Liahona can be viewed with an Internet "Images" search for "Liahona."

2. For an illustrated map of a proposed location for the Valley of Lemuel near the Gulf of Aqaba, see www.Nephiproject.com/map_room.htm.

3. Jonathan Curci notes that a possibility for the reason that the name *Liahona* does not appear in the Book of Mormon until the book of Alma stems from the fact that the first portion (116 pages) of the translation of the Large Plates was lost. When Joseph resumed translating, he began where he left off—with the first part of the book of Mosiah. After finishing with his translation of the Large Plates, Joseph then translated the small plates (1 Nephi to Mosiah). (See Royal Skousen, "Critical Methodology and the Text of the Book of Mormon," *Review of Books on the Book of Mormon*, 6, no. 1, 1994, pp. 138–139.) (Source: Jonathan Curci, "Liahona: 'The Direction of the Lord': An Etymological Explanation," in *Journal of Book of Mormon Studies*, 16, no. 2 [2007], pp. 60–67, note 5.) If such was the case, then it seems to imply that while it is apparent that the name *Liahona* was not included in the Small Plates, the first portion of the Large Plates (116 lost pages) DID contain the name *Liahona*.

4. For an illustrated map of a proposed location for Bountiful, see www.Nephiproject.com/map_room.htm.

5. "An Interview With John L. Sorenson," *Journal of Book of Mormon Studies* 11, no. 1 (2002): pp. 80–85.

6. For some key pioneering studies, see Hugh Nibley, PhD, *Lehi in the Desert and The World of the Jaredites*, Salt Lake City: Bookcraft, 1952; Lynn and Hope Hilton, *In Search of Lehi's Trail*, Salt Lake City: Deseret Book, 1976; George Potter and Richard Wellington, *Lehi in the Wilderness*, Springville, UT: Cedar Fort, 2003.

7. See the discussion in chapters 4 and 6.

8. See George Potter and Richard Wellington, *Lehi in the Wilderness*, Springville, UT: Cedar Fort, 2003. For an illustrated map depicting Potter and Wellington's proposed location for Bountiful, see www.Nephiproject.com/map_room.htm.

9. It is interesting to note here that Nephi's situation might be compared in some ways to that of the brother of Jared. The brother of Jared planned and implemented his solution on how he was going to get across the sea by first gathering special stones. Only after this did the Lord do His part (Ether 2:22–3:6). In Nephi's situation, he was given a vision of the promised land across the sea. He could have planned a solution. One might ask, did part of that solution involve a magnetic compass? And if it did, what was Nephi's part in regards to this instrument before the Lord did His part?

10. It is worthy of note, however, that in the verse just preceding the discovery of the Liahona, Nephi records, "it came to pass that the voice of the Lord spake unto my father by night, and commanded him that on the morrow he should take his journey into the wilderness" (1 Nephi 16:9). Whether the Lord communicated any details concerning the Liahona is not specified in the record. Nephi also notes that Lehi was "astonished" upon finding the Liahona at his tent door (1 Nephi 16:10). Yet Nephi does not detail the reasons he was astonished.

11. "This is the principle in action. If you want the blessing, don't just kneel down and pray about it. Prepare yourselves in every conceivable way you can in order to make yourselves worthy to receive the blessing you seek. . . . When we are situated that we cannot get anything to help ourselves, then we may call upon the Lord and His servants who can do all. But it is our duty to do what we can within our own power." Harold B. Lee, quoted in *Stand Ye in Holy Places,* pp. 244–45, http://www.gospeldoctrine.com/Ether2.htm.

12. Another example is found in the book of Ether. Moroni comments on Ether's knowledge of Joseph (the birthright son of the house of Israel) who was sold by his brothers and taken into Egypt, only to rise to prominence and save his whole family from starvation and death by bringing them to him. This salvation of the lineage of Joseph (and of Israel) is then compared with Lehi and Nephi's deliverance from the destruction of Jerusalem by journeying to the promised land. He writes:

> For as Joseph brought his father down into the land of Egypt, even so he died there; wherefore, the Lord brought a remnant of the seed of Joseph out of the land of Jerusalem, that he might be merciful unto the seed of Joseph that they should perish not, even as he was merciful unto the father of Joseph that he should perish not. (Ether 13:7)

Here once again, while Lehi and Nephi made great personal efforts to save their family from destruction, it is the Lord who is credited with the overall shaping of these historical matters in the same manner as the Lord is credited with previously shaping history by bringing Joseph and his father to Egypt in order to preserve the lineage.

13. In 1909, B. H. Roberts focused attention on the idea that radioactive materials can produce luminescence, noting that both radium and polonium glow in the dark (see B. H. Roberts, in *New Witness for God*, vol. 3, Salt Lake City: Deseret News, pp. 547–49).

In 1927 Janne M. Sjodahl also drew attention to radioactive experiments that produced light emission. He wrote that it was not "unreasonable to suppose that God could make the stones in the [Jaredite] barges luminous." He also was the first LDS person to discuss the Jewish tradition that Noah's ark was lighted by glowing stones. He writes:

> *Shine Forth in Darkness*
>
> Touch theses stones, O Lord, with thy finger, and prepare them that they may shine forth in darkness—Ether 3:4; 6:3

Noah, it will be remembered, was according to the English Bible translation, commanded to make a "window" to the ark. But it is pretty well agreed that the translation of the word rendered "window" is not good. The word means literally a shining object, and rabbinical tradition has it that the shining object was really a stone which the Patriarch had found in the river Pison and which was made luminous. (Footnote* See Dr. Clark's Commentary) If this tradition is based on fact, the Brother of Jared must have known it, and that would account for his prayer and the miraculous answer that he obtained.

That precious stones can be made to shine seems to have been demonstrated by scientific experiments. In June, 1920, Dr. T. Coke Squance, of Sunderland, England, was reported to have succeeded in changing a sapphire of faint pink hue into a beautiful ruby, by means of the action of radium. "During the process," the report said, "the lustre was increased to such an extent that the stone had almost the brilliance of a diamond." . . . It seems, then, that the Brother of Jared, when praying the Lord to touch the stones and make them luminant, was in possession, by some means, of a knowledge that scientists of today are just beginning to dip into.

A scientific invention was announced in Philadelphia on Oct. 20, 1926, by Dr. W. D. Coolidge before the Franklin institute. It consisted of a new cathode ray tube. According to the accounts, cathode rays in a darkened room became visible as a purple glow, and a crystal of calcite placed in these rays became glowing, as if red hot, although it was perfectly cold, and continued to glow for some time. Granite also became luminous. (Footnote** *Juvenile Instructor*, Dec., 1926, p. 691). (Janne M. Sjodahl, *An Introduction to the Study of the Book of Mormon*, Salt Lake City: Deseret News Press, 1927, pp. 248–49.)

[**Note*** *Sjodahl refers the reader to Dr. Clarke's* Commentary. *In 1810, Adam Clarke published his* Bible Commentary. *In his commentary on Genesis 6:16, "A window shalt thou make," Adam Clarke writes the following:*

What this was cannot be absolutely ascertained. The original word *tsohar* signifies *clear* or *bright*; the Septuagint translate it by ( ), "collecting, thou shalt make the ark," which plainly shows they did not understand the word as signifying any kind of *window* or *light*.

Symmacbus translates it ( ), *a transparency*; and Aquila, ( ), *the noon.* Jonathan ben Uzziel supposes that it was a precious luminous stone which Noah, by Divine command, brought from the river *Pison.* It is probably a word which should be taken in a collective sense, signifying *apertures* for *air* and *light.*]

In the 1956–1957 *Improvement Era* there was a series of articles by Hugh Nibley under the title "There Were Jaredites." One section dealt with "Shining Stones," (pp. 630–32, 672–75). Also in 1957, *An Approach to the Book of Mormon* was published by the Council of the Twelve Apostles for use in Melchizedek Priesthood quorums of the Church. This book also contained a section on "The Luminous Stones" (pp. 295–97). This material was later revised and expanded into another article, "Strange Ships and Shining Stones" and appeared in the 1959 book *A Book of Mormon Treasury.* On page 144 of that book, we find the following:

> But who gave the brother of Jared the idea about the stones in the first place? It was not the Lord, who left him entirely on his own; and yet the man went right to work as if he knew exactly what he was doing. Who put him on to it? The answer is indicated in the fact that he was following the pattern of Noah's ark, for in the oldest records of the human race the ark seems to have been illuminated by just such shining stones. We have said that if the story of the luminous stones was lifted from any ancient source, that source was not the Talmud (with which the Book of Mormon account has only a distant relationship) but a much older and fuller tradition, with which the Ether story displays much closer affinities. The only trouble here is that these older and fuller traditions were entirely unknown to the world in the time of Joseph Smith, having been brought to light only in the last generation.

In a 1963 *Ensign* article, Spencer W. Kimball speculated that perhaps the Jaredite stones were illuminated "with radium or some other substance not yet discovered by our scientists" (*Ensign*, April 1963, pp. 63–64).

In Nibley's 1967 publication, *Since Cumorah* (Salt Lake City: Deseret Book), the shining stones were briefly discussed on page 239.

Nibley's works were edited and reprinted by FARMS during the 1980s.

In a July 1992 FARMS *Insights* article, "New Light on the Shining Stones of the Jaredites," based on research by Nicholas Read, Jae R. Balif, John W. Welch, Bill Evenson, Kathleen Reynolds, and Matt Roper, it was noted that "By touching the stones, the Lord somehow changed them, causing them to emit a light bright enough to illuminate the inside of the barges." Then the author writes:

> Sandia National Laboratories in New Mexico have recently developed radioluminescent lights that invite some interesting comparisons with the Jaredite stones. These lights are intended to "serve needs for lighting where no electricity is readily available" (SNL News Release, p. 1). Their life expectancy is about 20 years and they are described as being "bright" and very "intense." The radioluminescent lights are made from a highly porous silica matrix—"aerogel"—in which a phosphor such as zinc sulfide is dispersed. . . .
>
> Radioluminescent light is consistent with and supplies an intriguing parallel matching the requirements of the Jaredite stones: they are small, long-lasting, and physically harmless. It is possible that the Jaredite stones were <u>created</u> in a similar fashion, <u>according to existing physical laws</u>.

In 1997, an article titled "Glowing Stones in Ancient and Medieval Lore" by John A. Tvedtnes appeared in the *Journal of Book of Mormon Studies* (vol. 6, no. 2, pp. 99–123) in which he reviewed ancient and medieval literature containing reports of glowing stones. According to Tvedtnes, his survey demonstrates "that the marvelous nature of such stones was widespread in earlier times and that traditions about glowing stones are known from Jewish and other Near Eastern sources."

John concludes with the following:

> While some natural explanations might be presented, I can only say that the Book of Mormon account attributes their power to divine influence. This is the same explanation given in many of the early texts we have surveyed. . . .

In 1999 John A. Tvedtnes wrote a follow-up article in FARMS *Insights* in which he reviewed statements concerning the luminescent stones and called attention to stones "composed of phosphorescent minerals . . . also known to glow." He wrote, "Barite will shine for some time in the dark after being exposed to sunlight."

14. For a discussion on this point, I have prepared another paper titled, "The Relationship of the Interpreters to the 24 Plates of Ether and the Book of Ether." But that paper remains unpublished.

15. While there are no other biblical (Jewish) accounts of something similar to the Liahona, there are some interesting comments in the origin stories of other cultures (cultures that might have connections with the Jews) that *do* speak of something similar. I will address this subject later on in my book.

16. In reviewing the literature, I have failed to find anyone previous to this that has proposed this idea. According to the text, Laman proposed that Nephi "worketh many things by his cunning arts" (1 Nephi 16:38) perhaps implying that Nephi made the Liahona, but Laman did not allow Nephi any help from the Lord. In order to give further perspective to this proposal, I will note that there have been a couple of other writers in recent times that have possibly flirted with such an idea before dismissing it in favor of a total divine nature for the Liahona. In a 1984 FARMS paper titled "Was Lehi a Caravaneer?" by John A. Tvedtnes, he argues against the idea that Lehi was a caravaneer. Instead he proposes that Lehi and Nephi were expert metalworkers. On pages 13–14 he writes:

> I believe that there is evidence to show that Lehi and his family were craftsmen and artisans—probably metalworkers. (In the Near East, sons typically enter into the same occupation as their fathers. Hence, the occupation pursued by Nephi can be reasonably expected to be that of his father as well.) For example, we have Nephi's keen interest in the sword of Laban when he encounters him drunk on the streets in 1 Nephi 4:9. Nephi's steel bow (1 Nephi 16:18) might also be an indication of his occupation. (His inability to repair the bow in the desert could be explained by either the lack of iron ore in the region or by the fact that the Lord had forbidden them to make fires.) . . .
>
> When the Lord tells Nephi, in the land of Bountiful, to build a ship, he has to give detailed instructions on how to do it (1 Nephi 17:8;

> 18:1–4). But there is no record that Nephi had to ask how to prepare the metal tools with which he built the ship. Rather, he simply asked the Lord where he could find the "ore to molten, that I may make tools to construct the ship." He then constructed a bellows, lit a fire and fabricated the tools (1 Nephi 17:8–11, 16). . . .
>
> Further evidence for Nephi's metalworking skills came after the group's arrival in the New World. It was he who prepared the plates of ore from which the Book of Mormon ultimately developed (1 Nephi 19:1), smelting the ore and forming the plates themselves. He also manufactured "many swords" based on the pattern of the weapon he had taken from Laban in Jerusalem (2 Nephi 5:14). But the full range of his talents is explained in the verses which follow this entry: "And I did teach my people to build buildings, and to work in all manner of wood, and of iron, and of copper, and of brass, and of steel, and of gold, and of silver, and of precious ores, which were in great abundance" (2 Nephi 5:15–17).

Tvedtnes then writes the following:

> Jack Welch, after reading the first draft of this paper, suggested in private conversations that the skepticism of Laman and Lemuel upon the discovery of the Liahona or compass outside Lehi's tent one morning (1 Nephi 16:10) may be yet another indication of Nephi's metalworking skills. Lehi's elder sons seem not to be impressed by this marvelous instrument. Welch has proposed that this might be because <u>they thought the brass ball-like device had been manufactured by their brother in an attempt to convince them that they were doing the right thing by following their father into the wilderness</u> (Welch notes that 1 Ne 16:38 refers to Nephi's using "cunning crafts").

Thus Welch proposed that Nephi had sufficient metalworking skills that Laman and Lemuel might have attributed the manufacture of the Liahona to him. But rather than even flirting with the idea that Nephi might indeed have been the source of the Liahona in any way, Tvedtnes quickly adds: "If this suggestion is correct, it would explain why Alma was so insistent in his declaration that no human hand could have fabricated the Liahona (Alma 37:38–39)." But contrary to Tvedtnes's assertion, Alma didn't exactly use those words ("no human hand"); he simply said, "there cannot any man work after the manner of so curious a workmanship," which leaves the door open for interpretation. I understand Alma's words to mean that while the Lord's help was necessary in the construction and function of the Liahona, the extent of that help is left undefined.

In a FARMS Update based on research by Robert F. Smith, March 1984, we also find the following ideas that could have linked the manufacture of the Liahona with Nephi, but once again these ideas were quickly dispelled in favor of a lesser assumption that Nephi might have just been familiar with the principle of magnetism rather than capable of constructing a compass. This article was reprinted in *Reexploring the Book of Mormon: The F.A.R.M.S. Updates*, edited by John W. Welch (Salt Lake City: Deseret Book Company and Provo: Foundation for Ancient Research and Mormon Studies, 1992, pp. 44–46). I quote:

> While the Book of Mormon does not tell us whether the Liahona functioned partly on geomagnetic principles, Nephi did say that it contained two spindles, one of which functioned as a directional pointer, and that the body was made of "fine brass" (1 Nephi 16:10, 28). Brass is an excellent noncorroding and nonmagnetic case for a compass. Those who are familiar with modern compasses might naturally ask whether the Liahona worked on a similar principle, with a magnetic function for one spindle, and a possible azimuth setting [the angle created by plotting from due "north" the point on the eastward horizon where a planet or star arises] for the other. Perhaps part of Laman's skepticism was based on some familiarity with just such a technology.

Once again, just as in the Tvedtnes article, the idea is raised that Laman and Lemuel might have had good reasons to suggest that Nephi, by his "cunning artifice," had constructed the Liahona. And once again it is quickly put down. I quote:

> But what sort of "cunning artifice" did Laman imagine Nephi employed in order to transmit divine messages to the surface of the ball-shaped Liahona (1 Nephi 16:26–29)? Moreover, as Laman and Lemuel later learned to their dismay, the Liahona functioned or failed based directly upon the faith, heed, and diligence given to it and to the Lord (1 Nephi 16:28–29); Mosiah 1:16; Alma 37:40–41, 44–45), all of which is very reminiscent of the mode in which the Nephite interpreters-directors,

> Urim and Thummim functioned best (Mosiah 8:13; Alma 37:23; D&C 9:7–9; 10:1–5; Joseph Smith-History 1:35).
>
> Although we do not know specifically what Laman had in mind, it is worth noting that the function of magnetic hematite was well understood in both the Old and New Worlds before Lehi left Jerusalem. Magnetite, or *lodestone*, is, of course, naturally magnetic iron . . .
>
> Whatever the nature of the Liahona, it is intriguing to note that certain properties of compasses might have been familiar to those who were blessed with its guiding functions, and that those who were skeptical of Nephi and the Liahona might have logically turned to those characteristics in seeking to find a plausible rationalization.

In the above quote, Robert F. Smith focuses exclusively on the principle of magnetism as the determining factor in Laman's linking the Liahona with Nephi. By combining Nephi's knowledge of magnetism (as proposed by Smith) with his knowledge of metallurgy (as proposed by Tvedtnes and Welch above) the reasons for Laman's linking the Liahona with Nephi increase significantly.

17. John A. Tvedtnes, "Was Lehi a Caravaneer?" FARMS working paper, 1984.

18. The reader has to go no further than Nephi's mention of two fabricated items: the "plates of brass" (1 Nephi 3:3, 12, 24; 4:16, 24, 38; 5:10, 14, 18, 19; 13:23) and the "rod of iron" (1 Nephi 8:19–20, 24, 30; 11:25; 15:23). In the Bible we find one of the sons of Lamech (fifth in descent from Cain) was "Tubalcain, an instructer of every artificer in brass and iron" (Genesis 4:22).

19. For Nephi talking with the Lord, see 1 Nephi 2:16; see also chapters 11–14. For Nephi being ministered to by an angel, see 1 Nephi 3:29.

20. 1 Nephi 10:1: "And now I, Nephi, proceed to give an account upon these plates of my proceedings, and my reign and ministry; wherefore, to proceed with mine account, I must speak somewhat of the things of my father, and also of my brethren." Note also that at a later time the Lord refers to Nephi's party not as his "family" or "families," but as "thy people" (1 Nephi 17:8).

21. A number of interesting articles have been written on the subject. To begin with, I have presented the following about Nephi's obtaining the plates of brass:

> Nephi says that after he had smitten off Laban's head "with his own sword, [he] took the garments of Laban and put them upon [his] own body; yea, even every whit; and [he] did gird on [Laban's] armor about [his] loins" (1 Nephi 4:19). More than the practical aspect of this narrative, one should appreciate the covenant symbolism here. Raymond Treat notes in his book, *The Miracle of the Scarlet Thread*, that Richard Booker outlined the steps ancient Hebrews typically followed in making a covenant. They exchanged robes and belts, a man's robe was symbolic of all his material possessions. The ancient belts were weapons belts. Therefore, the message of giving one's belt was "all the power I have I now give to you. If necessary, I will defend you to the death." (Raymond C. Treat, "Understanding Our Covenant," in *Recent Book of Mormon Developments*, vol. 2, 34–35)
>
> So the story of what happened to Laban might be representing the symbolic loss of covenant blessings through unrighteousness, and the bestowing of those blessings upon Nephi, who kept the covenant. Laban, as the record attests, was the covenant caretaker of the record of Joseph. Nephi would thus become the new covenant caretaker of the record of Joseph. (Adapted from Alan C. Miner, *Step by Step through the Book of Mormon*, vol. 1, 1 Nephi 5:19)

Concerning the sword of Laban, Brett L. Holbrook has written a revealing article, which he summarizes in an abstract as follows:

> Swords have often been seen as symbols of divine authority and kingship. Numerous examples from the mythology, literature, and history of the world attest to distinct patterns. The sword of Laban from the Book of Mormon fits these patterns and can be compared to the sword of Goliath. The sword of Laban can also be traced as part of the royal regalia that gives authority throughout Nephite history, and later as it appears in the Restoration. ("The Sword of Laban as a Symbol of Divine Authority and Kingship," in *Journal of Book of Mormon Studies* 2, no. 1, 1993, pp. 39–72)

Daniel N. Rolph explains,

> Though the Book of Mormon reveals that the sword of Laban (1 Nephi 4:9) served as an ancestral and hereditary sword of the ancient Nephite prophets, evidence suggests that the weapon may have been the birthright sword of biblical tradition, a sacred heirloom that may have been wielded by the patriarchs up until the time of Joseph of Egypt. Laban, being a descendant of Joseph, inherited the birthright sword and the plates of brass, both treasures eventually coming into the possession of Nephi, who was both a prophet and a descendant of Joseph, ... Was it accidental, or an act of Providence, that Nephi brought the sword as well as the plates out of Jerusalem to the land of promise? It is interesting to learn that, according to Jewish tradition, the antediluvian patriarch Methuselah slew [myriad] demons with a "wonderful sword," a weapon Abraham is also said to have inherited, by which he "conquered the kings . . . Esau thus received it, as heirloom, from Isaac, since he was the first-born. This sword passed to Jacob when he purchased the birth-right. ("Prophets, Kings, and Swords: The Sword of Laban and Its Possible Pre-Laban Origin," in *Journal of Book of Mormon Studies* [Spring 1993]: pp. 73,75–76)

Concerning the Liahona (or "ball"), Gordon Thomasson writes the following:

> The Liahona deserves special attention. The Liahona was a "ball or director, which led our fathers through the wilderness, which was prepared by the hand of the Lord that thereby they might be led, every one according to the heed and diligence which they gave unto him" (Mosiah 1:16). The Liahona was, in fact, a royal treasure, passed from father to son by Nephi's descendants. Few details in the Book of Mormon have been ridiculed more than the Liahona, and yet few more accurately reflect what one might find in an authentic ancient record. . . .
>
> Royal treasure like the Liahona were once well known, such as the one pictured in the Emperor Charles V's left hand. . . . It is an *orbis terrarum, Reichsapfel*, or orb. . . . It is a symbol of earthly rule and heavenly power, and its use in royal and religious iconography is an implicit claim to worldly dominion, symbolizing its possessor's power over this earth. It represents an assertion of "holding the world in the palm of one's hand." (Gordon C. Thomasson, "Mosiah: The Complex Symbolism and Symbolic Complex of Kingship in the Book of Mormon," in *Journal of Book of Mormon Studies* 2, no. 1. [1993]:, p. 28)

22. For example, in 1888 George Reynolds wrote the following:

> Some people have confused this ball, because it is called a compass, with the mariner's compass, that sailors use at sea to direct the course of their ships. But there is a great difference between the two. The Liahona pointed the way that Lehi's company should travel, while the needle in the mariner's compass points to the north. The one showed the way Lehi *should* go, the other informs the traveler which way he is going. The one was specially prepared by the Lord for Lehi and his companions, and was used through faith only; the other can be used by all men, whether believers in the true God, pagans or infidels. At times, also, writing would miraculously appear on the Liahona, giving directions or reproving for sin, as the company most needed. (*The Story of the Book of Mormon* [Salt Lake City: Jos. Hyrum Parry, 1888], p. 35)

In 1909, B. H. Roberts wrote:

> This curious instrument [the Liahona] in an incidental way is called a "compass" in several passages. Whereupon, our opponents seek to bring the Book of Mormon in conflict with supposed historical facts by insisting that the Book of Mormon speaks of the people being in possession of "a mariner's compass, long before the invention of such an instrument!" ("Story of the Mormons," Linn, p. 97)
>
> This writer [Linn] attributes the possession of the "compass" to the Jaredites. Whether it is the slip of a careless writer or an effort on his part to make the matter of the "compass" in the Book of Mormon more ancient, is a question for him or his friends to explain. Many other writers in their anxiety to find anachronisms in the Book of Mormon refer to this "compass." Lamb is positively dishonest in the matter, since he assumes the existence of two instruments. One he calls the "Director," and applies to it the description given above in the text, and the other he calls the "Compass," though clearly this latter word is used in an incidental way in describing the "Director." This is the only way he could create the longed for anachronism and hence he adopted it. This may secure his fame for ingenuity, but what of his honesty? (See "The Golden Bible" Chapter III., Subdivisions "C" and "D")

The director of the Nephites makes no pretensions to being a "mariner's compass" of man's invention, and surely the description given above, supplemented as it is by a fuller description in the Book of Alma, where it is called "Liahona," must dispel all thought of this instrument being considered as an ordinary compass, such as is invented by men for navigating purposes, and which, as everybody knows, has but this one quality, namely, its needle constantly points northward because of the magnetic pole force, and mariners knowing one direction may ascertain others. The silliness of argument, which even supposedly grave and reverend historians and essayists descend to on such a point, is illustrated by an alleged incident with which Linn stoops to render his pages luminous, by pretending to quote the manner in which "Mormons in Utah" are supposed to explain the alleged anachronism of the "compass." He says:

> The ease with which such an error could be explained is shown in an anecdote of a Utah Mormon, who, when told that the compass was not known in Bible times, responded by quoting Acts xxvii: 13, where Paul says: "And from thence we fetched a compass!"
>
> That is, to quote the passage in full—"From thence we fetched a compass, and came to Rhegium."
>
> This is merely the repetition of an old, silly story told against the Mormons long before they arrived in Utah, and was invented by the Rev. Henry Caswell, author of "The Prophet of the Nineteenth Century," published in 1843. It is of that order of stuff as the tales about the Prophet Joseph attempting to walk on the water, and his pretending to raise the simulated dead. (B. H. Roberts, in *New Witness for God*, vol. 3, Salt Lake City: Deseret News, 1909, pp. 550–51, 561)

In 1970, in reviewing a book on Mark Twain for *BYU Studies*, Richard Cracroft writes:

> He [Twain] turns to the passage in 1st Nephi in which Nephi notes that the family of Lehi used an instrument called the "Liahona" in finding their directions while en route from the Old World to the New. Twain seizes on this instrument as an anachronistic "compass," noting smugly that the travelers appear to "have had the advantage of Noah," all the while ignoring the text's explanation that the so-called compass was a miraculously powered ball—not a magnetic compass—which operated commensurate to the faith of the travelers. (Richard H. Cracroft, "The Gentle Blasphemer: Mark Twain, Holy Scripture, and the Book of Mormon," in *BYU Studies* 11, no. 1 [Autumn 1970]: p. 133)

23. In a 1991 article for *FARMS Review of Books*, reviewing LDS author Arthur Kocherhans *Lehi's Isle of Promise*, James Fluegel criticized Kocherhans for even suggesting that the directions pointed out by the Liahona even resembled magnetic compass directions of not only Joseph Smith's day but also modern-day magnetic compass directions. In his book, Kocherhans had written:

> The words "Red Sea" are Old Testament words and, by looking at Map 14, we can see that Lehi's compass or Liahona caused him to travel by what in 1828 still was called nearly "south-southeast" and nearly "east". The compass direction co-ordinates of Joseph Smith's time and of our present day correspond to physical antiquity.
>
> For our purpose in this work, we will rely upon the accuracy of these scriptures and Joseph Smith's translation of the ancient characters. All further direction names such as east and west are consistent within the Book of Mormon and with 1828 compass co-ordinates and direction names.
>
> Nephi had Lehi's compass in crossing the waters to the promised land. It continued to be a recognized instrument of navigation among the Nephites (Alma 37:38, 43) and an instrument called a compass has continued to be used even down to our day for directional purposes. (*Lehi's Isle of Promise*, Placentia, California: Kobo Enterprises, 1989, pp. 97, 99)

James Fluegel wrote the following in his review:

> Here is an example of how he [Kocherhans] insists that the language of the Joseph Smith translation forces Book of Mormon vocabulary to correspond with modern usage. Various references to the 1828 edition of Noah Webster's *Dictionary* are supposed to form a scholarly link between the translation and conditions in the outside world. But in this case, at least, there is no implication in the text of the Book of Mormon itself that the Liahona was a magnetic compass. Rather, it is clearly described as a revelatory device dependent not upon magnetism but upon obedience to the Lord (1 Nephi 18:12). The Book of Mormon makes this explicit, but because the translation also uses "compass" and because Kocherhans interprets that only to be a magnetic compass, he has carefully thought himself into anachronism. (Book Review: Arthur J. Kocherhans, *Lehi's Isle of Promise: A Scriptural Account with Word Definitions and a Commentary*, in *FARMS Review of Books* 3 [1991]: 97–99)

Interestingly, Fluegel didn't bother to explain how coincidental it was that a sixteen-part compass-like direction, *south-southeast*, could appear in the Book of Mormon text and exactly correspond with the direction of the Frankincense Trail, which ran parallel to the south-southeast–oriented coast of the Red Sea. Whatever the original word used by Nephi, it ultimately came through the mind of Joseph Smith and out of his mouth in words of his era when possible. The question once again that Fluegel failed to address was why such a compass-specific term as *south-southeast* was used at all by Nephi and by Joseph Smith in translating. Fluegel simply mandated that "there is no implication in the text of the Book of Mormon itself that the Liahona was a magnetic compass."

24. In reviewing the literature, as far as I have been able to find, the earliest LDS article that speaks positively for the idea that the Liahona was magnetic comes from the 1883 book by George Q. Cannon (*The Life of Nephi, the Son of Lehi*, Salt Lake City, Utah: Juvenile Instructor Office, 1883, p. 39). In this book Elder Cannon made an interesting footnote in reference to the Liahona. Although Elder Cannon first states that the Liahona "differed in several respects from what are known as compasses," he notes the following in connection with the term *compass*:

> In this connection it may be of interest to say a few words about what is known as the mariner's compass. It is claimed that the Chinese used the compass at a very early period; and it is thought probably that Marco Polo, the traveler, introduced it to Europe from China, about 1290 AD, twelve years before Gioja, of Amalfi, its supposed inventor.

Elder Cannon follows this part of his footnote by making some comments on Job 28. But before I get into his commentary, let me lay some groundwork. According to what I read, the authorship and date of the Book of Job is unknown, although from the clues in the text, it is estimated to have been written sometime between the time of Solomon (1000 BC) and 250 BC (with dates around 600 BC being most popular). [*1] *In chapter 28, Job compares the rich metals and gems (stones) of the earth to the value of the wisdom of God. In verses 12–14, 16, 18–20, 23–24 (KJV), Job writes:*

But where shall wisdom be found? and where is the place of understanding?

Man knoweth not the price thereof; neither is it found in the land of the living. . . .

The depth *saith, It is not in me: and* the sea *saith, It is not with me. . . .*

It cannot be valued with the gold of Ophir, . . .

No mention shall be made of ***coral****, or of* ***pearls****: for the price of wisdom is above* ***rubies****.*

The ***topaz*** *of Ethiopia shall not equal it, neither shall it be valued with* pure gold.

Whence then cometh wisdom? and where is the place of understanding? . . .

God understandeth the way thereof, and he knoweth the place thereof.

For he looketh to the ends of the earth, and seeth under the whole heaven.

By consulting various Bible commentaries, I found that whether the word translated here in scripture is "coral" or "pearls" or "rubies" or "topaz," the true meaning is not only a matter of conjecture, but there is a possibility due to the poetic nature of this passage, that they might be connected with different items of value associated with travels across the sea, or "depth" (v. 14). I might note also that the "pure gold" (v. 19), is paralleled (or equated) with the "gold of Ophir" (v. 16), which is the mysterious location that took Solomon's ships three years to visit and return from with their bounty of gold and other gems (2 Chronicles 8:18; 9:21).

Now having said this, let me get back to what George Q. Cannon had to say in his footnote about the "compass" which Lehi and Nephi received at the valley of Lemuel near the Red Sea. He writes:

> Some people contend that the compass is no new invention; but that the ancients were acquainted with it. They say that it was impossible for Solomon to have sent ships to Ophir, Tarshish and Parvaim, without this useful instrument. They insist that it was impossible for the ancients to be acquainted with the attractive virtue of the magnet, and to be ignorant of its polarity; nay, they affirm that this property of the magnet is plainly mentioned in the book of Job, where the loadstone [a naturally magnetic brownish stone discolored by the presence of an iron oxide] is mentioned by the name of *topaz*, or *the stone that turns itself.* (Ency. Brit.)

*Note 1:** "Job, Book of," *in The Illustrated Bible Dictionary,* vol. 2, Wheaton, Ill: Tyndale House Publishers, 1980, p. 791.

Note* *Interestingly, in Adam Clarke's Bible Commentary (1810 -->) for Job 18:18 ("for the price of wisdom is above* ***rubies****.") we find the following:*

> *Some learned men are of the opinion that the magnet or loadstone is meant, and it is thus called because of the remarkable property it has of turning north and south. And this notion is rendered the more likely, because it agrees with another word in this verse, expressive of a different property of the magnet, viz., its attractive influence: for the Hebrew words meshech chochmah mippeninim, which we render, The price of wisdom is above rubies, is literally, The ATTRACTION of wisdom is beyond the peninim, the loadstone; for all the gold, silver, and precious stones, have strong influence on the human heart, attracting all its passions strongly; yet the attraction of wisdom—that which insures a man's happiness in both worlds-is more powerful and influential, when understood, than all of these, and even than the loadstone, for that can only attract iron; but, through desire of the other, a man, having separated himself from all those earthly entanglements, seeketh and intermeddleth with ALL WISDOM.* The attractive property of the loadstone must have been observed from its first discovery; and there is every reason to believe that the magnet and its virtues were known in the East long before they were discovered in Europe. (http://jcsm.org/StudyCenter/Adam_Clarke_Commentary/clarkejob . . .)

Now if wisdom is valued above the price of lodestone, and lodestone is associated with different items of value from travels across the sea, or "depth" (v. 14), then we might take this association one step further and say that lodestone was being used to enable travels across the sea, and thus we might have an allusion here to the existence and use of a primitive compass.

The next LDS comment comes from a 1909 book by B. H. Roberts. He takes a somewhat more cautious position, although still maintaining the possible antiquity of the magnetic compass. One might ask why. It seems that since the time of Cannon's writings, a number of anti-Mormon books had been published, claiming that the Liahona was magnetic (implying a modern-day origin of the Book of Mormon from Joseph Smith's mind). In response, at the end of a whole page of comment by B. H. Roberts directed to prove that the Liahona *was NOT* a magnetic compass as anti-Mormon writers had charged, Roberts ends with the following:

> The antiquity of the compass really, of course, is of no importance in this discussion, since it is not claimed that "Liahona" is a compass, but an entirely different instrument, "and the Lord prepared it"; still, in passing, it may be well to point out that those who have attempted to make capital out of this supposed anachronism have not stated the whole truth concerning the compass.
>
> "The directive power of the magnet," says a respectable authority "seems to have been unknown in Europe till late in the 12th century. It appears, however, on very good authority, that it was known in China, and throughout the east generally, at a very remote period. The Chinese annals indeed assign its discovery to the year 2634 BC, when, they say, an instrument for indicating the sun was constructed by the emperor Hou-angti. At first, they would appear to have used it exclusively for guidance in traveling by land. ("Universal Knowledge," Chambers, p. 203)" ("The marvels of Liahona," in *New Witnesses for God*, vol. 3., Salt Lake City: Deseret News 1909, pp. 550–52)

In March of 1984 the FARMS organization sent out a one-page update titled "Lodestone and the Liahona" (author not named) to those financially contributing members belonging to their Cornerstone Club. Each month the update was sent out to all major contributors and active volunteers. They were "state-of-the-art short studies" reporting the organization's most recent discoveries and works in progress. At the end of 1984 these articles were assembled into one report for distribution. In this article we find the following:

> While the Book of Mormon does not tell us whether the Liahona functioned partly on geomagnetic principles, Nephi did say that it contained two spindles, one of which functioned as a directional pointer, and that the body was made of "fine brass" (1 Nephi 16:10, 28). Brass is an excellent noncorroding and nonmagnetic case for a compass. Those who are familiar with modern compasses might naturally ask whether the Liahona worked on a similar principle, with a magnetic function

for one spindle, and a possible azimuth setting for the other. Perhaps part of Laman's skepticism was based on some familiarity with just such a technology. . . .

Although we do not know specifically what Laman had in mind, it is worth noting that the function of magnetic hematite was well understood in both the Old and New Worlds before Lehi left Jerusalem. Magnetite, or *lodestone*, is, of course, naturally magnetic iron (Fe_3O_4), and the word *magnetite* comes from the name of a place in which it was mined in Asia Minor by at least the seventh century BC, namely Magnesia. (Thales of Miletus is the first known to have mentioned its strange properties, ca. 600 BC). Professor Michael Coe of Yale University, a top authority on ancient Mesoamerica, has suggested that the Olmecs of Veracruz, Mexico, were using magnetite compasses already in the second millennium BC This is based on Coe's discovery during excavations at San Lorenzo-Tenochtitlan of a magnetite "pointer" (M-160) which appeared to have been "machined," and which Coe placed on a cork mat in a bowl of water in a successful test of its function as a true floater-compass. (J. B. Carlson, *Science* 189: 753–60; . . .)

[**Note*** *As noted above, Coe's 1967 discovery was the basis of a 1975 article in the Science journal in which John B. Carlson reported on his analysis of this Olmec artifact (M-160). Carlson writes:*

> *According to Coe's analysis (n3) the fill in which M-160 was unearthed contained no material later than the San Lorenzo A and B Phases, which have been well dated by radiocarbon methods at 1400 to 1000 BC (n4, 5) . . . The analysis of M-160 indicates that the Olmec may have discovered and used the geomagnetic lodestone compass earlier than 1000 BC*

On page 757 of this article, Carlson presents photographs of M-160 along with diagrams representing a floater experiment. After detailing his experiments, Carlson writes the following:

> *Considering the unique morphology (purposefully shaped polished bar with a groove) and composition (magnetic mineral with magnetic moment vector in the floating plane) of M-160, and acknowledging that the Olmec were a sophisticated people who possessed advanced knowledge and skill in working iron ore minerals, I would suggest for consideration that the Early Formative artifact M-160 was probably manufactured and used as what*

> *I have called a zeroth-order compass, if not a first-order compass. . . . That M-160 could be used today as a geomagnetically directed pointer is undeniable. The original whole bar may indeed have pointed close to magnetic north-south. The groove functions well as a sighting mark . . .*

As a matter of reference, the Olmec culture to which this magnetic bar (M-160) belonged had been linked by some Book of Mormon geography theorists with the Jaredite culture (and later the Mulekite culture).]

In 1992 the above update "based on research by Robert F. Smith, March 1984" would be reprinted as "Lodestone and the Liahona," in *Reexploring the Book of Mormon: The F.A.R.M.S. Updates*, edited by John W. Welch (Salt Lake City: Deseret Book Company and Provo: Foundation for Ancient Research and Mormon Studies, 1992, pp. 44–46). Welch also cites the following: See J. B. Carlson, "Lodestone Compass: Chinese or Olmec Primacy?" *Science* 189 (September 5, 1975): 753–60; R. H. Fuson, "The Orientation of Mayan Ceremonial Centers," *Annals of the Association of American Geographers* 59 (September 1969): 508–10; E. C. Baity, *"Archaeoastronomy and Ethnoastronomy So Far,"* Current Anthropology 14 (October 1973): 443.

In 1993 an article written by Deanne Matheny appeared in the publication *New Approaches to the Book of Mormon: Explorations in Critical Methodology* in which she criticized John Sorenson's writings on Book of Mormon culture and geography. One aspect had to do with Sorenson's skewed directional system for Book of Mormon geography. Matheny argued for cardinal directions. Included among her reasonings was the fact that, "Additionally Lehi's party had the Liahona, which is called a "compass" a number of times in the Book of Mormon" (*New Approaches* . . . , SLC: Signature Books, 1993, p. 278). However, In his 1994 rebuttal to Matheny, John Sorenson dismissed the idea of a magnetic compass. (Review of Deanne G. Matheny, "Does the Shoe Fit? a Critique of the Limited Tehuantepec Geography," in *FARMS Review of Books* 6, no. 1 [1994]: p. 310)

In 1993, B. Keith Christensen would circulate his "Appendices to *The Unknown Witness*," a 170-page addition to his 1992 manuscript edition, *The Unknown Witness: Jerusalem, Geology, and the Origin of the Book of Mormon,* which set forth his theory on Book of Mormon geography. On pages 46–53 of this "Appendices," we find some sections on the Liahona (Book of Mormon "Compass"; Obtaining the Compass; Some Mormon Scholars Waffle over the Liahona; Capabilities of Liahona/Compass; The Liahona and the Bible; and The Isthmus of Tehuantepec and the Liahona). These sections argued for the idea that the Liahona was in part a true compass and against the skewed directions used by John Sorenson to support his theoretical narrow neck of land being the Isthmus of Tehuantepec. He proposes that there were two spindles on the Liahona, the one pointing magically to the direction in which Lehi should travel, and the other apparently pointing to magnetic north. In this way they would know in what direction they were going. Christensen does not cite any previously published LDS works in support of a magnetic Liahona and cites only the works of Nibley and Sorenson against such an idea. On pages 46–47, Christensen writes:

> By definition, a compass is a device to tell direction. The Book of Mormon compass (also called the Liahona, ball, or director) had "two spindles," or pointers. Nephi says "one pointed the way whither we should go into the wilderness." The reason for one pointer is explained, but what was the purpose for the other? I have never seen the question discussed.
>
> We will see that the account indicates it was a compass needle, fulfilling the description that the Liahona was a compass in addition to being a "director."
>
> In their journey in the Middle East Nephi describes their direction in precise terms. For example, it was mentioned earlier that part of their journey was in "nearly a south-southeast direction." By observing the sun, moon, and stars, the means typically used anciently for determining direction, they might have been able to locate south-southeast. But does it seem that by these means someone could precisely determine what was "nearly" south-southeast?
>
> On the other hand, if the first pointer in the Liahona pointed out the direction to go as Nephi says it did, and the other pointer or spindle was a compass needle, this second spindle could show what the direction was.

In the Fall 1994 *Journal of Book of Mormon Studies* (vol. 3, no. 2, pp. 1–11) was an excellent article by Robert L. Bunker ("The Design of the Liahona and the Purpose of the Second Spindle"), which has been discussed previously (see note 26). While the article broached the subject of the magnetic compass, no specific proposal was put forth. The focus of the article was on design not function, and the closest the author got to the principle of magnetism was in footnotes #2 and #3. In footnote #2 he writes on the description of a "spindle": "Such a spindle-shaped pointer is often encountered in magnetic compasses (cf n. 3) where some type of marking designates one end as north." But he follows that statement with the following: "The spindle in the Liahona used to designate direction would also have required differentiation between ends, either by color, texture, or shape." In note 3 Bunker comments on an analogous design to a magnetic compass and also hints at function but his ideas are not made clear. He seems to be making contrary statements regarding a magnetic Liahona. He writes: "Since the magnetic compass in Lehi's time was still many centuries from discovery, the use of the word 'compass' by Joseph Smith in translation to refer to the Liahona reinforces not only the analogy of directional function with the modern compass but also of design." It is not clear to me what Bunker had in mind by saying that the word "compass" in the Book of Mormon reinforced "the analogy of directional function with the modern compass."

In a 1996 RLDS book by Glenn A. Scott Jr., he writes:

> Next morning as Lehi left his tent, he saw on the ground a brass ball of "curious [intricate] workmanship" (1 Nephi 5:11 [16:10]. . . . Nephi called it a compass (1 Nephi 5:190 [18:12] for it did serve that purpose. The magnetic compass had been invented in China long before this time. (*Voices from the Dust: New Light on an Ancient American Record,* Independence, Missouri: School of Saints, p. 77)

25. In a February 1961 article by Hugh Nibley ("The Liahona's Cousins," in *The Improvement Era* 64, no. 2, pp. 87–111), after reviewing all the scriptures that treat the Liahona, Nibley lists the salient features that they report. He writes that one of these salient

features of the Liahona was that "It was neither mechanical nor self-operating, but worked solely by the power of God. It functioned only in response to the faith, diligence, and heed of those who followed it" (p. 89). This in spite of the fact that the thrust of the article was to compare the similarity of the workings of the Liahona with the ancient divination technique of Belomancy, "the practice of shooting, tossing, shaking, or otherwise manipulating rods, darts, pointers, or other sticks, all originally derived from arrows." (p. 104). Much of this material would be reprinted in 1967 by Nibley (*Since Cumorah*, Salt Lake City: Deseret Book, pp. 283–96).

In 1976 Daniel H. Ludlow would write: "The word *compass* as used here does not refer to the magnetic instrument of the mariner (the magnetic compass was apparently not known in the western world until about the twelfth century AD)" (*A Companion to Your Study of the Book of Mormon,* Salt Lake City: Deseret Book, 1976, p. 116).

In 1987 Joseph Fielding McConkie and Robert L. Millet would add their commentary: "This seeric device, later identified by Alma as the Liahona (Alma 37:38), was certainly not a compass in the conventional sense. Rather than identify magnetic north, it pointed the direction that they should travel" (*Doctrinal Commentary on the Book of Mormon*, vol. 1, Salt Lake City: Bookcraft, 1987, p. 124).

In 1988 John L. Sorenson would once again affirm the exclusively spiritual function of the Liahona. He writes: "A course was laid by observing one of the spindles inside the Liahona or 'compass,' which 'pointed the way whither we should go' (1 Nephi 16:10; 18:12, 21). I see no reason at all to suppose this device was magnetic, despite the term *compass.* Rather it was faith operated" ("Transoceanic Crossings," in Monte S. Nyman and Charles D. Tate, Jr., eds., *First Nephi: The Doctrinal Foundation*, Provo, UT: Religious Studies Center, Brigham Young University, 1988, p. 263).

In a 2002 Conference of the FAIR organization, John A. Tvedtnes of FARMS delivered an address titled "The Mistakes of Men: Can the Scriptures be Error-Free?" in which he said the following:

> According to the Book of Mormon, Lehi used a "compass" to guide him in his travels to the New World (1 Nephi 18:12–14; Alma 37:38). Critics are wont to point out that the magnetic compass was discovered in the late middle ages in China and was unknown in the ancient Near East. Though the word *compass* in our day usually denotes a device used to determine the direction of magnetic north, it need not have that meaning in the Book of Mormon. The word *compass* may have been the closest equivalent of the original word available to Joseph Smith in the English language. Moreover, *compass* has several other meanings in English and originally meant "circle" (as in the compass used to draw circles). The word *compass* also appears a number of times in the King James Version of the Bible, usually as a verb but sometimes as a noun (Exodus 27:5; 38:4; 1 Kings 7:35; Isaiah 44:13). We should also note that the fact that the Lord had to "prepare" the device for Lehi implies that it was an instrument not known in his day. So we don't have to worry about whether it was a magnetic compass or not, on the grounds that such an instrument didn't exist at that time. The Lord surely knew the principles on which the magnetic compass works, and could have provided one for Lehi. But it's unlikely that this is what the Book of Mormon intended. (http://www.fairlds.org/FAIR_Conferences/2002_Can_the_Scriptures_be_Error-Free.html)

In a 2003 article titled "Liahona," by Neal Elwood Lambert in the *Book of Mormon Reference Companion*, we find the following:

> *Liahona* A device miraculously provided by the Lord to Lehi and his family which gave divine directions and instructions to them for their travels to the land of promise. . . . This "ball, or director" (Alma 37:38) functioned only "according to the faith and diligence and heed" which the people gave to it (1 Nephi 16:28). (*Book of Mormon Reference Companion*, Dennis L. Largey ed., Salt Lake City: Deseret Book Company, 2003, p. 519)

In an August 17, 2004, devotional address given during Campus Education Week at Brigham Young University, Lance B. Wickman, a member of the First Quorum of the Seventy, stated the following:

> He [Lehi] knew something of the lifesaving qualities of a reliable compass. The Liahona guided him—its bearings not coming from a magnetic field but rather through a function of "faith and diligence and

heed" (1 Nephi 16:28). (http://speeches.byu.edu/htmlfiles/Wickman_Lance_08_2004.html)

In a February 27, 2008, article titled, "Misunderstanding the Book of Mormon," on the online *Meridian Magazine*, John A. Tvedtnes writes:

> The word "compass" appears many times in the King James version (KJV) of the Bible. The verbal form means "go around"(n.2) or "surround" (n.3), while the noun form means "round" in shape" (1 Kings 7:35; 2 Chronicles 4:2), which fits the term "ball" by which the Nephites called it. Our magnetic compass takes its name from the fact that it describes the round horizon and the 360 degrees it comprises.
>
> In a similar fashion, the compass used to draw circles by draftsmen and carpenters (cf. Isaiah 44:13) is tied to the same principle. So when Nephi calls the Liahona a "compass" (1 Nephi 18:12, 21; 2 Nephi 5:12), he seems to be referring to its round shape, not magnetic qualities. Neither of the two "spindles" or "pointers" inside the ball pointed north; one pointed the way the group should travel, while the other displayed written directions from the Lord; both worked according to the group's faith (1 Nephi 16:10, 26–30; Alma 37:38–44).
>
> n.2 E.g., Numbers 21:4; 34:5; Joshua 6:3–4,7; 15:3; 2 Samuel 5:23; 1 Kings 7:15,23; 2 Kings 3:9; Psalm 26:6; Jeremiah 31:39; Acts 28:13
>
> n.3 E.g., 2 Kings 11:8; 2 Chronicles 4:2–3; 23:7; Job 16:3; 40:22; Psalms 5:12; 7:7; 17:9; 32:7,10; 49:5; 140:9; 142:7; Jeremiah 52:21; Luke 19:43 (www.ldsmag.com./)

26. In reviewing another author who linked the Liahona with magnetism, John L. Sorenson writes:

> She falls into a nominalist fallacy (p. 278) by letting the translated word 'compass' determine how she thinks about the 'Liahona.' By considering the latter to fit into the same lexical domain as modern English "compass," she supposes that the device must have pointed out (cardinal) directions to Lehi and Nephi. But magnetism could not have been the operative basis, since faith was (see Alma 38:40). If operative on the natural, magnetic principle, why would the Liahona have ceased functioning as soon as Nephi was tied up (1 Ne. 18:12) and start again when he was released? And how would a magnetic compass produce

written messages (see 1 Ne. 16:26–27)? Clearly the Liahona was only vaguely like compasses we know; it was called by the same English word because, indeed, it was a direction pointer, but what it pointed to was the Lord's choice of route, not a fixed direction based on magnetism. (Review of Deanne G. Matheny, "Does the Shoe Fit? a Critique of the Limited Tehuantepec Geography," in *FARMS Review of Books* 6, no. 1 [1994]: p. 310)

27. The following are comments on some of the complications of reading a compass:

"The Compass shows magnetic north, not true north. Keep it away from anything made of iron or steel" [which affect the reading]. ("Bee-hive-Girls, Honor Badge No. 111," in *Improvement Era* 5, May 1935)

"Magnetic storms affect compass needles all over the earth at the same time. A violent magnetic storm in April, 1938, changed compass direction by several degrees within an hour, and in London, England, more than five degrees." (Franklin S. Harris Jr., "Exploring the Universe," *Improvement Era* 3, March 1941)

"At this time, a compass set in Maine will point 18 [degrees] west of the true north, while at the same time one at Fort Yukon in Alaska will point about 36 [degrees] east of north; . . . making a difference in courses, between extreme points east and west, of fifty four degrees." (James H. Martineau, "The Magnetic Needle," in *The Contributor* 5, no. 7, April 1884)

"Another error relative to the magnetic needle is, that it points in the same direction throughout the day. In addition to its yearly or 'secular variation,'" it has also a *daily variation.*" (Ibid.)

"Another very common misunderstanding is the idea that if a compass be set pointing truly north and south, that by turning it to a right angle it will give a true east and west course, running an indefinite distance in either direction. This is not true, from the fact that while a true north and south line is straight, a true east and west line is not straight but *curved.* For a short distance this curvature is not perceptible to the eye, but at the distance of half a mile or more becomes sufficient to lead an inexperienced person into difficulty if not taken into account; the difference between the true and apparent courses increasing rapidly as the length of the course run increases." (Ibid.)

"The question now arises—if the magnetic needle is so unreliable and uncertain, what is it good for? We answer that in the hands of one who understands its deficiencies and errors and knows how to correct them, it becomes of considerable value, giving a close approximation to a true course." (Ibid.)

Chapter 2

1. Robert L. Bunker, "The Design of the Liahona and the Purpose of the Second Spindle," in *Journal of Book of Mormon Studies* 3, no. 2 (Fall 1994): p. 4, notes 4 and 5. Bunker also writes of a differing interpretation. He notes that "the *Book of Mormon Student Manual: Religion 121 & 122* (Salt Lake City: The Church of Jesus Christ of Latter-day Saints, 1989), p. 16, under the heading 'The Liahona,' suggests that the antecedent of all the pronouns in this verse is the 'writing' on the outside of the Liahona." However, it is hard to find substance for this argument that "the writing on the outside of the Liahona" could be the antecedent for the pronoun "them." The only other plural in the set of verses quoted is "things which are written," but here too one would find it difficult to say "And there was also written upon them (meaning the 'things which are written') a new writing." People don't tend to write " a new writing" "upon things which are written."

2. In 1950 in discussing the meanings derived from the word *Liahona*, Hugh Nibley dismissed the idea of finding any definitive parallel. He wrote:

> The name [Liahona] suggests so many possible Hebrew and Egyptian interpretations (it is, "being interpreted, a compass," Alma 37:38) that one man's guess is as good as another's, and it does not concern us here since, as a miraculous thing, it has no parallel in everyday life. (Hugh Nibley, *The Collected Works of Hugh Nibley: Volume 5 The Book of Mormon. Lehi in the Desert*, Salt Lake City: Deseret Book Company and Provo: Foundation for Ancient Research and Mormon Studies, 1988, p. 109)

However, in his third edition of the Melchizedek Priesthood manual, *An Approach to the Book of Mormon* first published in 1957, he modified his opinion. He writes:

> A year after the manual appeared, those Cambridge scholars who first brought "patternism" to light issued an important volume summarizing the work of the past two decades and bringing their conclusions up to date. Suffice it to say that their work confirms all the basic features of "patternism" and fully supports our chapter on the subject-chapter 23 in the manual. In the following year (1959) an Arab scholar published a study on prehistoric Semitic arrow-divination which has allowed us to bestow a certificate of plausibility on the mysterious Liahona. (p. xv)

In February 1961, an article by Hugh Nibley ("The Liahona's Cousins") appeared in *The Improvement Era* (vol 64, no. 2, pp. 87–111). In that article, Nibley compared the working of the spindles in the Liahona to Arab divining sticks and the practice of belomancy. On page 104, he writes:

> Belomancy is the practice of divination by shooting, tossing, shaking, or otherwise manipulating rods, darts, pointers, or other sticks, all originally derived from arrows. Over ten years ago the present writer made a fairly exhaustive study of ancient arrow-divination, and some years later presented in the pages of the *Era* a long discourse on the ritual use of sticks and rods, especially in ancient Israel ("The Stick of Judah and the Stick of Joseph." *Improvement Era* 56 [Jan. to May 1953]). Yet it was not until he saw Fahd's study, the first full-length treatment of old Semitic arrow-divination, that it dawned upon him that these old practices might have some connection with the Liahona.
>
> Fahd begins by pointing out that the "arrows" used in divination, called *qid-h* or *zalam*, were devoid of heads and feathers, being mere shafts or pointers. (T. Fahd, "*Une Prutique cleromantique a la Ka'ba preislamique,*" *Semitica* VIII [1958]: p. 61) Since Lane has given a fuller description of these objects from the sources, we can do no better than quote *his* quotations:
>
> *zalam,* pl. *azlam* [divining-] arrows by means of which the Arabs in Time of Ignorance (i.e. before Islam) sought to know what was allotted to them: they were arrows upon which the Arabs in the Time of Ignorance wrote 'Command' [on one] and 'Prohibition' [on the other];

or upon some of which was written 'My Lord hath commanded me'; and upon some, 'My Lord hath forbidden me': or there were three arrows; upon one of which was written 'My Lord hath commanded me'; etc. . . . and the third was blank; and they put them in a receptacle, and took forth an arrow; and if the arrow upon which was 'Command' came forth, he went to accomplish his purpose; but if that upon which 'Prohibition' was written came forth, he refrained; and if the blank came forth, they shuffled the second time . . . (E. W. Lane, *Arabic-English Lexicon*, I, 1247, s.v. *zalam*.)

3. FARMS seems to concur with Nibley's viewpoint. On their its under the title "Liahona" ("Other Evidence of the Week"), we find a quote from Nibley:

A . . . study by an Arabic scholar has called attention to the long-forgotten custom of the ancient Arabs and Hebrews of consulting two headless arrows whenever they were about to undertake a journey; the usual thing was to consult the things at a special shrine, though it was common also to take such divination arrows along on the trip in a special container. The message of the arrows, which were mere sticks without heads or feathers, was conveyed by their pointing and especially by the inscriptions that were on them, giving detailed directions as to the journey (Nibley, *Prophetic Book of Mormon*, pp. 244–45).

This quote is also part of a book review by Kevin Christensen, in which he says the following:

Vogel also ignores the Old World context of the Book of Mormon completely. For example, consider the context in which Vogel discusses the Liahona. "Debates about such ocean crossings often turned on questions about navigation. Many argued against migration by sea since the ancients had no knowledge of the mariner's compass."(p. 45). For Vogel, the Liahona is best explained as an anachronistic response to local debate.

Although the mariner's compass had not yet been invented, the Lord provided Lehi with a compass-like instrument, described as a "round [brass] ball of curious workmanship." Inside the ball were "two spindles," one of which "pointed the way whither we should go into the wilderness." (p. 51)

> Where Vogel sees a magnetic mariner's compass, Hugh Nibley approaches the text against the purported context and provides an alternate picture.
>
> The Liahona was a hollow bronze sphere in which were mounted two pointers, headless arrows that bore mysterious inscriptions and pointed the way that Lehi's party should travel in the desert. Besides pointing the direction, the arrows and the inscriptions also provided special instructions for the journey. They only worked during the expedition to the New World, after which they ceased to function.
>
> *A recent study by an Arabic scholar has called attention to the long-forgotten custom of the ancient Arabs and Hebrews of consulting two headless arrows whenever they were about to undertake a journey; the usual thing was to consult the things at a special shrine, though it was common also to take such divination arrows along on the trip in a special container. The message of the arrows, which were mere sticks without heads or feathers, was conveyed by their pointing and especially by the inscriptions that were on them, giving detailed directions as to the journey.* (See Hugh W. Nibley, "The Liahona's Cousins," *Improvement Era* 64 (1961, pp. 87–89, 104–6, 108–11; in *CWHN* 7:251–63)
>
> Where Vogel sees a magnetic mariner's compass, Hugh Nibley approaches the text against the purported context and provides an alternative picture. ("Dan Vogel, Indian Origins and the Book of Mormon," *FARMS Review of Books*, vol. 2 (1990), 221)

This idea is also supported in an article by John M. Lundquist, "Biblical Seafaring and the Book of Mormon," which appears in the Appendix (171–75) of Raphael Patai, *The Children of Noah: Jewish Seafaring in Ancient Times,* Princeton, New Jersey: Princeton University Press, 1998.

Another analysis of the Liahona appears in the FARMS *Journal of Book of Mormon Studies*. Under the title "The Design of the Liahona and the Purpose of the Second Spindle," Robert L. Bunker discusses the idea of two pointers being confirmatory of one another. He also comments on the idea that there was writing on the pointers: "The amount of text inscribed on the pointers cannot be ascertained from Nephi's description, but the physical size of the writing must have been small; otherwise, the observation that it "was plain to be read" (1 Nephi 16:29) would have been unnecessary" (*Journal of Book of Mormon Studies* 3, no. 2 (Fall 1994): 5)

4. Although the mention of "famine" in conjunction with the Liahona in Mosiah 1:17 might imply that there were times in the desert that directions might have been uncertain.

5. John A. Tvedtnes, "Misunderstanding the Book of Mormon," *Meridian Magazine*, February 27, 2008 (online, www.lds.mag.com). This article seems to be related to a 2002 address by John Tvedtnes to the conference of the FAIR organization titled, "The Mistakes of Men: Can the Scriptures be Error-Free?" in which he said the following:

> Though the word "compass" in our day usually denotes a device used to determine the direction of magnetic north, it need not have that meaning in the Book of Mormon. The word "compass" may have been the closest equivalent of the original word available to Joseph Smith in the English language. Moreover, "compass" has several other meanings in English and originally meant "circle" (as in the compass used to draw circles). The word "compass" also appears a number of times in the King James Version of the Bible, usually as a verb but sometimes as a noun (Exodus 27:5; 38:4; 1 Kings 7:35; Isaiah 44:13). (http://www.fairlds.org/FAIR_Conferences/2002_Can_the_Scriptures_be_Error-Free.html)

6. For example, Numbers 21:4; 34:5; Joshua 6:3–4, 7; 15:3; 2 Samuel 5:23; 1 Kings 7:15, 23; 2 Kings 3:9; Psalm 26:6; Jeremiah 31:39; Acts 28:13.

7. For example, 2 Kings 11:8; 2 Chronicles 4:2–3; 23:7; Job 16:13; 40:22; Psalms 5:12; 7:7; 17:9; 32:7, 10; 49:5; 140:9; 142:7; Jeremiah 52:21; Luke 19:43.

8. In 1 Kings 7, in describing the ornaments of Solomon's Temple, we find the following:

> (verse 23) And he made a molten sea, ten cubits from the one brim to the other: it was round all about, and his height was five cubits: and a line of thirty cubits did **compass** it about. . . .
>
> (verse 35) And in the top of the base was there **a round compass*** of half a cubit high: and on the top of the base the ledges thereof and the borders thereof were of the same.

2 Chronicles 4:2: "And he made a molten sea of ten cubits from brim to brim, round in compass, and five cubits the height thereof: and a line of thirty cubits did compass it round about."

[**Note*** *Interestingly, in a different Bible translation, 1 Kings 7:35 reads, "On the top of the stand there was a round* <u>*band*</u> *half a cubit high." (http://bible.oremus.org/?passage=1Kings+7)*]

9. Isaiah 44:13: The carpenter stretcheth out his rule; he marketh it out with a line; he fitteth it with planes, and he marketh it out with the **compass**, and maketh it after the figure of a man, according to the beauty of a man; that it may remain in the house.

10. Tony Decker, *Why I Believe the Book of Mormon (And Why Anybody Can)*, Arlington, VA: Stratford Books, 2007, p. 36.

11. Although iron is easily magnetized, it loses its magnetism relatively quickly. Steel, on the other hand, retains its magnetism for an extended period. It will be remembered that Laban's sword was made of "steel" (1 Nephi 4:9) and that Nephi might have been able to copy this metallurgical technique (2 Nephi 5:14). Thus "steel" might have been available at the time.

12. In an article titled "History of Chinese Invention—Invention of the Magnetic Compass" (www.computersmiths.com), there appears an illustration with the following caption: "The figure to the right shows a working model of the first instrument known to be a compass. <u>The spoon is of magnetic lodestone, and the plate is of bronze</u>. See also John W. Welch, "Lodestone and the Liahona," in *Reexploring the Book of Mormon*, SLC: Deseret Book Company and Provo: FARMS, 1992, p. 44.

13. John A. Tvedtnes, "Misunderstanding the Book of Mormon," *Meridian Magazine* (online), www.ldsmag.com, 2/27/2008. This article seems to be related to a 2002 Tvedtnes address to the conference of the FAIR organization titled, "The Mistakes of Men: Can the Scriptures be Error-Free?" in which he said the following:

We should also note that the fact that the Lord had to "prepare" the device for Lehi implies that it was an instrument not known in his day. So we don't have to worry about whether it was a magnetic compass or not, on the grounds that such an instrument didn't exist at that time. The Lord surely knew the principles on which the magnetic compass works, and could have provided one for Lehi. But it's unlikely that this is what the Book of Mormon intended. (http://www.fairlds.org/FAIR_Conferences/ 2002_Can_the_Scriptures_be_Error-Free.html)

14. This material was later reprinted as "Lodestone and the Liahona," in *Reexploring the Book of Mormon*, John W. Welch ed., Salt Lake City: Deseret Book and Provo, UT: FARMS, 1992, p. 44.

15. V. Garth Norman, "Book of Mormon Myths: Rethinking Understanding the Book of Mormon," (www.ancientamerica.org/library/media . . .)

16. http://1828.mshaffer.com/d/word/compass

17. *Websters New World Dictionary of the American Language* (College Edition), New York: The World Publishing Co., 1964, p. 1403.

18. Robert L. Bunker, "The Design of the Liahona," in *Journal of Book of Mormon Studies* 3, no. 2 (Fall 1994): pp. 1–11.

19. Algirdas Avizienis et al., "Fault-Tolerant Computing: An Overview," *IEEE Computer* 4, no. 1 (January–February 1971): 10.

20. See my comments on the chronological evolution from four directions, to eight directions, to sixteen, thirty-two, and so on at the end of chapter 5.

21. The extent of this distance might be affected by a number of factors: (1) whether Nephi was riding on a camel or donkey or traveling on foot; (2) how far away Lehi's base camp was from the top of the mountain. Meat tends to spoil in heat unless proper precautions are taken in dressing the animal and returning to a place where the meat can be smoked. According to David Cope, a friend

and longtime owner of a local meat-processing plant, Nephi would have had only six to eight hours to get the meat back to camp for smoking. (3) A possible third factor could have been associated with Nephi's making a new bow after breaking his steel one. This is not necessarily apparent until a real-world scenario is in place. George Potter and Richard Wellington (*Lehi in the Wilderness*, Springville, UT: Cedar Fort, Inc., 2003), whom I consider to be the most insightful authors on the geographical and cultural aspect of this part of Nephi's narrative, give the following perspectives:

> After Medina the oases were at Turbah, Bishah, Tathlith, Ranyah and Najran, five oases over a distance of more than seven hundred fifty miles. Now, rather than an oasis to rest at every night, they were many days or weeks apart. . . . The trail south from Medina headed inland. In order to skirt the lava fields it stayed in the desert, the entire course being approximately three hundred fifty miles to Bishah. [p. 95]

> The mountains in this part of Arabia are called the Asir, which means "difficult" because of the impact of the terrain on travel. It is the only place in Arabia where the camel is replaced by the donkey as the chief pack animal. The trail headed inland to avoid the mountains and the lava fields. [p. 95]

> Since it is impossible to travel in Arabia during the hot months of May through October, Lehi would have stopped for the summer to rest. . . . Bishah is the closest trail oasis to the mountains, and thus a logical place to leave the trail to find refuge from the heat. From the Frankincense Trail staging center at Bishah, the high wadis of the Asir are no more than sixty-five miles distant, and the summer temperatures are relatively pleasant, for the most part remaining about eighty to ninety degrees Fahrenheit. [p. 98]

> . . . wadi Tabalah and wadi Bishah, pass through or near the town of Bishah. Either of these wadis would have provided a ready-made path into the mountains. Surrounded by mountain peaks, the wadis end at an altitude of approximately 6,000 feet or more. Nephi says that he "did go forth up into the top of <u>the</u> mountain" (1 Ne 16:30) to hunt. This seems to imply that they were already on the slope of a mountain and that he went up to the top to hunt. From this point in the wadi [6,000 ft] Nephi could have continued on foot to the tops of the mountains, which are up to 9,000 feet high. [p. 99]

When Nephi's bow broke, he needed to quickly construct a new one. . . . Could Nephi have found bow wood in the mountains, and if so where? . . . [p. 99]

[Potter & Wellington then note that in researching this question, Neil Holland found out that one of the best woods for constructing a bow was from a tree called the Atim or olive tree.]

[We] learned that [the Atim tree] is found on both the western and eastern slopes of the mountains in the Hijaz, Asir and the Yemen. In the Asir (at 17–18° north longitude) olive is found in association with Juniper trees in "forests" and grows between 2,000 and 2,400 meters (6,500–7,800 feet. Farther south (14–15° north) olive trees range in altitude from 1,600 to 2,700 meters (5,200–8,775 feet). . . [p. 100]

. . . it would seem that if Nephi had made his bow from Atim that it would have been most likely that he would have found the wood in the Asir (southern Saudi Arabia) rather than farther south in the Yemen. [p. 102]

. . . we set out to estimate the northern limits of the Atim trees. We discovered that within fifteen miles south of Al-Baha, the Atim trees disappeared. This would mean that the extent of the Atim tree seemed to range only seventy-two miles north-south in a narrow band of slopes between 6,000 to 7,000 feet in elevation. However, all but the very northernmost trees of the Atim range were too far from the Frankincense Trail for Nephi to have reached them. At Bishah, the Frankincense Trail turned to the east-southeast (rather than south-southeast) for sixty-five miles to reach Tathlith. In other words, once the trail left Bishah it was heading away from the Atim groves. However, the most copious Atim groves we found were due west of Bishah. Add to this the fact that just northwest of Bishah runs a series of long westward valleys, the wadis Tabalah, Huran, Jamah, Runmah, Tarj and Amal, that provide a camel trail through the rocky foothills and into the high wadis between Al-Qadim and jabal Azzh, and it seemed to us most likely that this was the approximate area where Nephi made his bow. [p. 105]

So what bow wood do we think Nephi used? While it is impossible to know with certainty what wood Nephi used to make his bow, we

> may assume that he used a wild tree, since the loss of the bows seemed to lead to hardship and lack of food. . . . If the bow were made below 1,000 meters then tamarisk is a possibility, up to 2,000 meters it was more likely Acacia; above 2,000 meters then olive becomes more probable. [p. 105]

> Since Nephi did not leave the group when he made the bow (1 Ne. 16:23) like he did when he went to hunt (1 Ne. 16:32), the bow appears to have been made from wood near the family's camp. When Nephi went to hunt, he followed the directions he was given on the Liahona. He tells us "I, Nephi did go forth up into the top of the mountain" (1 Ne. 16:30). The Asir is a mountain range with hundreds of peaks, but Nephi seems to mention a specific one and so it may be that he was already on the upper slopes of the mountain . . . If this were the case and the family were already in the mountains, then olive becomes the even more likely possibility. . . . The bow he made seems to have worked well. With one arrow he was able to kill a number of animals, so it must have been accurate enough to kill small game (he couldn't have carried a number of large animals [1 Ne. 16:32]). All of this points towards Atim (olive) as the most likely candidate. [p. 105]

22. "Nabataea: Maritime 2," http://nabataea.net/sailing.html.

23. Jean Michel Kalouguine writes:

> Habit to use stars as celestial landmarks and to take their altitude is old. The most primitive instrument for this purpose is without contest the human body: The arm, extended or folded in front of the eyes, the hand, arm extended fingers closed or apart, . . . the finger thickness became a unit of measure for the Arabic seafarer. (see http://kaloujm.com/page_kamal_uk.php)

This finger measurement technique led to the development of a simple latitude instrument that Arabian navigators at sea and on land (or across the desert) called a "kamal." The Arabian kamal was a rectangular plate about one by two inches with a string inserted in the center. On the string there were approximately nine knots at measured intervals. The rectangle was moved away from one's face until as the person gazed at the plate, the upper edge corresponded to the pole star* and the lower edge corresponded to the horizon. The loose end of the string was then held taut in the teeth. The distance or length of string between the plate and the person's face (the tip of the nose) was then measured by the knots in the string. If the number of knots was less, then the plate was closer to the navigator's face and the plate blocked from view a greater distance between the pole star and the horizon, which meant that the navigator was at a farther north latitude. If the number of knots was more, then the plate was farther away from the navigator's face and blocked out less distance between the pole star and the horizon. Thus the navigator was at a latitude farther south. By keeping track of the relative latitudes of the ports or caravan stops, the Arab navigator could get at least some bearing on where he was. Yet the Kamal was limited. It was only really useful for measuring Polaris in equatorial latitudes, which perhaps explains why it was not common in Europe. (see "Nabataea: Maritime 2" http://nabataea.net/sailing.html)

[**Note*** *While in early times there might not have been a singular north star, navigators would have probably focused on another constellation star that rotated around the north celestial pole.*]

24. Yet Laban's sword of "steel" seemed to be preserved for centuries.

25. As for the meaning of the word "Liahona," there have been a number of attempts to define it. For example, from the Editor's Table of the 1907 *Improvement Era* we find the following:

> The name of the new publication [Liahona] is selected from the Book of Mormon, and means, being interpreted , a compass. . . . The *Deseret News*, in speaking of the probable etymology of the word says: "The word is both Egyptian and Hebrew, and in both languages signifies 'light.' Liahona, or L Jah Ona" - L (to) Jah (Jehovah) On (House of the Sun)-"then, it seems to us, may safely be translated literally: 'To Jehovah is Light.' That is to say, the Lord has indeed light to give to his servants who trust him and obey his word. . . . It would be presumptuous on our part to speak authoritatively on the subject. But it will be admitted that if the conclusions here suggested are correct, the word

Liahona has a very beautiful and significant meaning." ("Liahona," *Improvement Era*, vol. X, April, 1907, No. 6)

Hyrum M. Smith and Janne M. Sjodahl write:

When Lehi perceived the wonderful qualities of this instrument, he exclaimed, in ecstasy *Liahona!* and that became its name (Alma 37:38). Liahona is a Hebrew word with, possibly, a Nephite termination, added later. L means "to"; *Jah* is an abbreviated form of the sacred name, "Jehovah," and *on* means "light." The meaning, then, is, "To Jehovah is light"; that is, "God has light; light comes from God," for He had answered his prayers for light and guidance. Similarly, Hagar, after having seen the Angel of the Lord, said, *Beer-lahai-roi;* that is, "The well of the Living One who seeth me" (Gen. 16:13). (*Doctrine and Covenants Commentary*, First Period, 1823–1830, section 17, p. 78) (See also Hoyt W. Brewster, Jr., *Doctrine and Covenants Encyclopedia*, p. 361; Daniel H. Ludlow, *A Companion to Your Study of the Doctrine and Covenants*, vol. 1, p. 129; Joseph Fielding McConkie and Robert L. Millet, *Doctrinal Commentary on the Book of Mormon*, vol. 3, p. 282.)

Paul R. Cheesman writes:

It is believed by some that the word *Liahona* means "To God Is Light"; that is to say, God gives light as does the sun. ("Lehi's Journeys" in *The Book of Mormon: First Nephi the Doctrinal Foundation*. Monte S. Nyman and Charles D. Tate, Jr. eds, Provo: BYU Religious Studies Center, 1988, p. 244 citing George Reynolds and Janne M. Sjodahl, *The Story of the Book of Mormon*, Salt Lake City: Deseret News Press, 1955, pp. 10–11)

Hugh Nibley writes:

And many people have dealt with the word *Liahona*. We had a teacher from Hebrew University here for a few years; in fact he bought a house in Provo. He was so fond of it he wanted to come and visit often. His name was Shunary. He never joined the church, but the first thing that fascinated him was this name *Liahona*. He traced it back to the queen bee, the leader of bees swarming in the desert. When bees swarm, that's *Liahona*. I took it from a different one. *Yah* is, of course, God Jehovah. *Liyah* means the possessive, "To God is the guidance," *hona* (*Liyahhona*). That's just a guess; don't put it down. But it's a pretty good guess anyway. (Hugh Nibley, *Teachings of the Book of Mormon—Semester 1 . . . Brigham Young University, 1988–1990.* Provo: FARMS, p. 216)

In 2007 Jonathan Curci wrote:

My approach is to transliterate back into the Hebraic idioms of the time of Lehi what I perceive that Joseph Smith saw or heard and dictated. Then I present the grammatical elements used to form the name *Liahona*, which I show to mean quite literally "to Yahweh is the whither" or, by interpretation, "direction of-to the Lord."

Key to my analysis is a methodology based on the premise that *Liahona* was formed according to the traditional Hebrew method of forming names. The Hebrews created new words by combining existing words in accordance with the circumstances in which the need for that new word arose, taking into account the purpose of the object that received the word. . . .

(Liaho "to (of) the Lord") The meaning of the *Liaho* ("to (of) the Lord") part of the word is common to all the above explanations and seems to gather the agreement of most scholars. . .

(The Direction [Director] of YHWH" or literally "To the Lord Is the Whither") How can *Liahona* possibly mean "compass" or "director"? The answer is found in the final part of the word *(liaho)* 'ona: the adverb *'ona* appears several times in the preexilic texts of the Hebrew Bible. It can be translated as "whither." It is often tied to the verb *halakh* "to go." Some instances in which it appears are Genesis 16:8 "whither wilt thou go?" and "whither are you going" (see Genesis 37:30; also 2 Kings 6:6; Genesis 32:17; 37:30). The adverb *'ona* means *direction* or motion to a certain place. . . .

[**Note*** *Perhaps other Bible passages would be more applicable here. In the book of Deuteronomy the word "whither" is used twenty-six times. This is more than in any other book of the Old Testament. (All other books fall way short of that number with the exception of the book of Jeremiah [21 times] and Ezekiel [11 times].) The context is one in which the children of Israel are told by Moses that they should keep the commandments of the Lord, for the land that they are being led to by the Lord is a covenant land. For example, Deuteronomy 4:5 states: "Behold, I have taught you statutes and judgments, even as the LORD my God commanded me, that ye should do so in the land* <u>whither ye</u>

go *to possess it." Previously in Leviticus 20:22 we find, "Ye shall therefore keep all my statutes, and all my judgments, and do them: that the land,* whither I bring you *to dwell therein, spue you not out."*]

> The following passages [in the Book of Mormon] give a contextual meaning of the adverb *'ona* meaning "whither."
>
> And within the ball were two spindles; and the one pointed the way *whither* [*'ona*] we should go into the wilderness. (1 Nephi 16:10)
>
> I, Nephi did make out of wood a bow . . . And I said unto my father: *Whither* [*'ona*] shall I go . . .? (1 Nephi 16:23, 30)
>
> The compass . . . did cease to work. Wherefore, they knew not *whither* [*'ona*] they should steer the ship . . . (1 Nephi 18:12–13, 21)
>
> The adverb *whither* is present with the translations of the word *Liahona.*
>
> The appearance of the terms *compass, ball,* and *director* in the text is usually related to the question, "whither shall we go?" (*'ona nelekh*). This is why they called the compass *Liahona:* it indicated the direction of the Lord. . . .
>
> Thus, when the children of Lehi questioned "Whither shall we go?" the *Liahona* provided the answer in accordance with their faith: it embodied the "direction of the Lord," which is the literal translation of the term *Liahona*. (Jonathan Curci, "Liahona: 'The Direction of the Lord': An Etymological Explanation," in *Journal of Book of Mormon Studies*, Provo, Utah: Maxwell Institute, vol. 16, issue 2, 2007, pp. 60–67)

26. In a February, 1961 article by Hugh Nibley ("The Liahona's Cousins," in *The Improvement Era,* vol 64, num. 2, pp. 87–111), he writes the following:

> Our fathers called it Liahona, which is, being interpreted a compass." Liahona is here clearly designated as an Old World word from the forgotten language of the fathers, which must be interpreted to present readers. But what is a compass? According to the Oxford dictionary, the derivation of the word remains a mystery; it has two basic meanings, but which has priority nobody knows: the one is "to pass or step together," referring always to a *pair* of things in motion; the other refers to the nature of that motion in a circle, "to pass or step completely," to

> complete a "circumference, circle, round," to embrace or enclose completely. Thus whether it refers to the ball or the arrows, "compass" is the best possible word to describe the device, though generations of Book of Mormon critics have laughed their heads off at the occurrence of the modern word in what purports to be an ancient book.

In George Reynolds and Janne M. Sjodahl, *Commentary on the Book of Mormon,* we find the following:

> The "compass" (vv. 12 and 21) is the round ball of curious workmanship described in 1 Ne. 16:10. Some have assumed that the term was meant to convey the idea that Lehi, more than 500 years BC had the mariners' instrument which is supposed to have been unknown in the western world until the 12th century AD, and that "compass" therefore, is an anachronism which furnishes evidence of the very human origin of the Book of Mormon. . . . the word "compass" is a good English word, meaning not only the mariners' instrument but a circle or a globe in general, a round, a circuit. In Num. 34:5 and Joshua 15:13 it refers to the bend in the southern boundary line of the land of Israel, "from Azmon unto the river of Egypt" and from there to the sea. Luke, in Acts 28:13 uses the term for the course steered by the ship from Syracuse to Rhegium. . . . In 2 Sam. 5:23 and 2 Kings 3:9, to "fetch a compass" means to surround a portion of the army of an enemy. In Proverbs. 8:23, "compass" refers to the circular horizon . . . It is clear from these references that the term as applied in the Book of Mormon to the little round ball of Lehi is correct. ("The First Book of Nephi, Chapter 18, verses 12–20," edited and arranged by Philip C. Reynolds, 7 vols., vol 1, p. 188)

27. Hugh Nibley, "The Liahona's Cousins," in *The Improvement Era,* February, 1961, vol 64, num. 2, pp. 87–111. On page 109 he writes: "Religion becomes magic when the power by which things operate is transferred from God to the things themselves. . . . When men lack revelation they commonly come to think of power as residing in things."

Chapter 3

1. Alexander Campbell, *Delusions. An Analysis of the Book of Mormon; With an Examination of Its Internal and External Evidences, and a Refutation of Its Pretences to Divine Authority.* Boston: Benjamin H. Greene, 1832, p. 13.

2. For a picture of magnetite along with some details, see http://en.wikipedia.org/wiki/Lodestone. According to one source "lode" also means "way" in old English ("What Are Natural Magnets" www.ehow.com).

3. For a model of an ancient Chinese water compass using contemporary materials, see http://lambcutlet.org/gallery/Zheng_He_and_Maritime_Asia_Exhibition/A_model_of_an_ancient . . .

4. MSN Encarta—Navigation.

5. "History of the Navigational Compass," *Wikipedia, The Free Encyclopedia*, www.en.wikipedia.org/wiki/Compass

6. Ibid.

7. Ibid.

8. Ibid.

9. "Compass," in *The New Encyclopaedia Britannica*, 15th edition, volume 3, pp. 502–3.

10. A. H. Parsons, *Parson's Text Book*, Lamoni, Iowa: Herald Publishing House, 1902, p. 46. Parsons also writes:

> "Chinese invented the mariners compass eleven centuries before Christ."—See *Light in Darkness*, by J. E. and A. H. Godbey, p. 289.
>
> Chambers' Encyclopedia: "It appears, however, on very good authority, that it [compass] was known in China, and throughout the east generally, at a very remote period."—Vol. 2, p. 546.

11. Ignatius Donnelly, "The Antiquity of Some of Our Great Inventions," in *Atlantis: The Antediluvian World*, 1882, part V: The Colonies of Atlantis.

12. Paul Mottelay writes:

> The most ancient record made of the peculiar property possessed by the loadstone of communicating polarity to iron is explicitly mentioned in the celebrated dictionary "Choue-Wen," which Hin-tchin completed in AD 121, the fifteenth year of the reign of the Emperor Ngan-ti of the Han dynasty.
>
> This dictionary contains a description of the manner in which the property of pointing with one end toward the south may be imparted to an iron rod by a series of methodical blows, and alludes to ("Tseu") the "stone with which a direction can be given to the needle." (Paul Fleury Mottelay, Ph.D, *Bibliographical History of Electricity & Magnetism: Chronologically Arranged*. London: Charles Griffin & Company Limited, 1922, 21)

13. *The Chinese, etc,* by John F. David, vol. ii, 218, as quoted in Alexander W. Bradford's *American Antiquities and Researches into the Origin and History of the Red Race*, New York: Dayton and Saxton, 1841, p. 230.

Paul Mottelay writes:

> AD 265–419.—What is by many believed to be the earliest reliable, distinct mention or actually printed record of the use of the magnet for navigation, appears in the justly prominent Chinese dictionary or rather encyclopaedia, "Poei-wen-yun-fou," wherein it is mentioned that there were during this period (that of the second Tsin dynasty) ships directed to the South by the *ching* or needle. (Paul Fleury Mottelay, PhD, *Bibliographical History of Electricity & Magnetism: Chronologically Arranged*. London: Charles Griffin & Company Limited, 1922, p. 22)

14. The caption to an illustration of a Chinese box compass reads:

> Developed in China around 200 BC, the compass was first used as a fortune telling device. Iron Ore, or Magnetite was used for compass needles. It naturally aligns itself in a North/South position. These

needles were first floated in water on a reed, but later more elaborate compasses were used with markings for the constellations. First believed to be satanic when introduced in Europe, compasses were widely used for navigating in both Europe and China by the 11th century. (http://www.lakesideschool.org/studentweb/worldhistory/GlobalContactsb/Seagoing Inventio . . .)

15. Josiah Priest, *American Antiquities and Discoveries in the West*, Albany: Hoffman & White, 1834. (4th ed.) Copy published by Ancient American Archaeology Foundation, printed by Hayriver Press, Colfax, Wisconsin, 2004.

16. Josiah Priest, *The Wonders of Nature and Providence, Displayed*, Albany: Hoffman & White, 1825.

17. Josiah Priest, *American Antiquities and Discoveries in the West*, Albany: Hoffman & White, 1834. (4th ed.) Copy published by Ancient American Archaeology Foundation (Colfax, WI: Hayriver Press, 2004), pp. 279–81.

18. www.computersmiths.com, "History of Chinese Invention—Invention of the Magnetic Compass."

19. "History of the Magnetic Compass and Navigation Instruments" (http://www.solarnavigator.net/compass.htm).

20. "A Chronology of Significant Events in the History of Science and Technology," History of Science and Technology: Timeline (http://crimsonbird.com/science/timeline.htm).

21. "Maritime Asia," citing *The Book of the Devil Valley Master*, quoted by Robert Temple, *The Genius of China*, p. 151. Interestingly, in another part of the same article it noted that "After collapse of the Shang dynasty [ca. 11th BCE], Chinese general You Houxi led 240,000 troops to the South Pacific and the Americas." (Quanzhou museum caption). "Asian maritime & trade chronology to 1700 CE," http://www.maritimeasia.ws/topic/chronology.html.

According to *Ancient China's Technology and Science:* Compiled by the Institute of the History of Natural Sciences, Chinese Academy of Sciences (Beijing: Foreign Languages Press, 1983, pp. 152–153), a primitive magnetic compass termed *sinan* came into use in the Warring States Period (475–221 BC). A lodestone in the shape of a ladle swinging freely on a very smooth "earth-board," its "handle" naturally points south as the bulk of its body points to the magnetic north. *Sinan* is mentioned in many classics written between the Warring States Period and the Tang Dynasty (i.e., between 475 BC and AD 907). To quote from *Han Fei Zi* (*The Book of Master Han Fei*) written in the third century BC: "The great emperors of the past dynasties created *sinan* to determine the four cardinal directions." An essay in *Gui Gu Zi* (*Book of the Devil Valley Master*) written in the fourth century BC says that when the people of the state of Zheng went far away for quarrying jade they took *sinan* along so as not to lose their bearings. Magnetic ladies in ancient China were carved of lodestone as jade was carved.

In another article, "How Many Times has America been discovered?" in the journal of the Northern Archaeology Group (*Reprint of the Sunday Telegraph*, December 12, 1999 (http://www.n-a-g.freeserve.co.uk/ DOCUMENTS/ISS14_11JAN2000.htm), the following appears:

> In August Xinhua, the Chinese press agency, reported that similarities between almost 300 markings found on pottery, jade and stone at unspecified ancient native sites in central America closely resemble 3,000-year-old Shang dynasty characters for the sun, sky, rain, water, crops, trees and stars. American and Chinese pictographs in 56 matching sets were shown to senior academics at a symposium in Anyang, former capital of the Shang dynasty. . . . Shang legends state that a King led his people on a journey to the east . . .

In another article, "A Link Between Chinese and American Cultures? The Olmec and the Shang," http://www.sinorama.com.tw/en/8605/605006e1.html, we find the following:

> Last year, in a book entitled *Origin of the Olmec Civilization*, Professor Mike Xu, a Chinese who teaches in the foreign languages department at the University of Central Oklahoma, proposed a hypothesis which

> aroused a storm of controversy in archaeological circles. In Xu's view, the first complex culture in Mesoamerica may have come into existence with the help of a group of Chinese who fled across the seas as refugees at the end of the Shang dynasty. The Olmec civilization arose around 1200 BC, which coincides with the time when King Wu of Zhou attacked and defeated King Zhou, the last Shang ruler, bringing his dynasty to a close. . . . Xu had "explosive" evidence in the form of the written word. Over the past three years he has found some 150 glyphs on photographs of and real specimens of Olmec pottery, jade artifacts and sculptures.

In still another article, "The Olmecs and the Shang" (http://members.tripod.com/%7Ekon-artz/cultures/olmshang.htm), the following appears:

> The Shang dynasty began around 1600 BC and ended, when king Zhou was defeated around 1100 BC by the upcoming Zhou people under their leader Wuwang. . . . In order to reach the American shores (assumed they had no powered boats), they needed to pick up an ocean current. Appropriate currents exist at the northern part of the Pacific and they flow from the southern Yellow Sea, past Japan and the Aleutes, right to the coast of western Mexico (and return eventually to the Asian side on a southern route).

22. http://www.ancient-wisdom.co.uk/magnetism.htm. See Peter Lancaster Brown, "Megaliths, Myths and Men," 1977. Book Club Associates. Joseph Ennemoser, *The History of Magic*, London: Henry G. Bohn, p. 1234.

The following added information comes from the most comprehensive and exhaustive compilation of records mentioning lodestone and the magnetic compass: Paul Fleury Mottelay, PhD, *Bibliographical History of Electricity & Magnetism: Chronologically Arranged*, London: Charles Griffin & Company Limited, 1922, p. 3.

> Tcheou-Koung (Ki-tan) was Chinese Minister of State under both Von-Vang (the first emperor of the Tcheou dynasty, who ruled seven years) and Tsching-Vang (second emperor, who ruled thirty-seven years), and lived to be 100 years old. He was one of the most learned and most popular men China has ever known, and is spoken of to this

day by the Chinese "with an admiration bordering upon enthusiasm" (Saillant et Nyon, "Memoires concernant l'Histoire," Paris, 1776, Vol. III. p. 37). . . .

> REFERENCES.—Du Halde, "Description de la Chine . . . ," La Haye, 1736, Vol. I, p.312; Klaproth, "Boussole," p. 81.

23. Constantine Samuel Rafinesque published two works in 1824: *Ancient History, or Annals of Kentucky; with a Survey of the Ancient Monuments of North America*, Frankfort, KY, 1824 and "Ancient History of North America," parts 1–6, in the *Cincinnati Literary Gazette*, Vol. 1, February 21–May 29, Cincinnati, 1824. In these publications Rafinesque maintained that America was populated after the Flood by way of the lost continent of Atlantis.

24. The information on Hoang-ti can be traced to a book by Jean-Baptiste Du Halde, a French Jesuit historian who specialized in China. While he had not personally traveled to China, he collected Jesuit missionary reports and organized the information as to history, culture, and society. The following comes from Paul Fleury Mottelay's *Bibliographical History of Electricity & Magnetism: Chronologically Arranged* (London: Charles Griffin & Company Limited, 1922, p. 1):

> BC 2637 . . . It is related that, during this sixty-first year of the reign of Hoang-ti (Yeou-hioung-che, also named Koung-fun and Hiuen-yuen), the emperor's troops, who were pursuing the rebellious prince Tcheyeou (Tchi-yeou), lost their way, as well as the course of the wind, and likewise the sight of their enemy, during the heavy fogs prevailing in the plains of Tchou-lou. Seeing which, Hoang-ti constructed a chariot upon which stood erect a prominent female figure which indicated the four cardinal points, and which always turned to the south whatever might be the direction taken by the chariot. Thus he succeeded in capturing the rebellious prince, who was put to death.
>
> Some say that upon this chariot stood a needle, to denote the four parts of the world. That, states the French author [Du Halde] writing in 1736, would "indicate the use of the compass, or something very similar to it . . . and it is unfortunate that the device has not been explained more fully."

> REFERENCES.—Du Halde, "Description de la Chine . . . ," La Haye, 1736, Vol. I, pp. 270–271; BC 2634, Klaproth, "Boussole," pp. 33,34,71,74,76,79,82; . . .

> Hoang-ti (Hoang, supreme king), third in the "Period of the Five Emperors" (Claude Auge, "Nouveau Larousse," Vol. 5. p. 134), regarded as the founder of the Chinese Empire, died at the age of 121, after reigning 100 years, BC 2598.

25. See Goodrich's "Columbus," p. 31, etc., as quoted in Ignatius Donnelly, *Atlantis: The Antediluvian World*, 1882, part 5: The Colonies of Atlantis (chapter 9: The Antiquity of Some of Our Great Inventions). This information is also quoted by RLDS author A. H. Parsons, *Parson's Text Book*, Lamoni, IA: Herald Publishing House, 1902, pp. 46–47.

26. A. H. Parsons, *Parson's Text Book*, Lamoni, IA: Herald Publishing House, 1902, pp. 46–47.

27. H. B. Root, "A Review -No. 1- Did the Phoenicians Discover America?" in *Autumn Leaves* 8, no. 5 (May 1895): pp. 197–200. As to where H.B. Root obtained his information he doesn't say; however, I came across similar information from an 1882 book by Ignatius Donnelly. He writes:

> In Goodrich's "Life of Columbus," we find a curious history of the magnetic compass prior to that time, from which we collate the following points: . . . We find in Sanchoniathon's "Legends of the Phoenicians" that Ouranus, . . . devised Baetulia, contriving stones that moved as having life, which were supposed to fall from heaven." These stones were probably magnetic loadstones." [*Atlantis: The Antediluvian World* by Ignatius Donnelly, 1882, part 5: The Colonies of Atlantis. (chapter 9: "The Antiquity of Some of Our Great Inventions")]

28. "Study Course: Landing and First Settlements of the Nephites," in *Autumn Leaves* 11, no. 7 (July): pp. 310–11. This information is also quoted by RLDS author A. H. Parsons, *Parson's Text Book*, Lamoni, IA: Herald Publishing House, 1902, pp. 46–47.

29. "Maritime Asia," citing *The Book of the Devil Valley Master.*

30. "Early history of the compass," www.jestcaching.com/2005/11/early-history-of-compass.html.

31. "Early history of the compass," www.jestcaching.com/2005/11/early-history-of-compass.html.

32. Patti Farley, "Five Elements Feng Shui," www.elements-five.com/HistoryofFengShui.htm.

33. "An astrolabe is a very ancient instrument for calculating the relative position of the sun and stars in relation to time. While the astrolabe became a sophisticated metal instrument in Europe during the Renaissance, the understanding and principles of the astrolabe are said to have been in use in other parts of the world at a much earlier time, even many centuries before Christ. However, the Western world claimed the principles of the astrolabe had their origins with Apollonius in Greece (about 225 BC). The term *astrolabe* is often used in a context that is **not** the same as the classic [more sophisticated] planisipheric astrolabe" ("The Astrolabe: An instrument with a past and a future" at The Astrolabe, www.astrolabes.org/. . .)

34. Patti Farley, "Five Elements Feng Shui," www.elements-five.com/HistoryofFengShui.htm.

35. "Early history of the compass," www.jestcaching.com/2005/11/early-history-of-compass.html.

Chapter 4

1. "Ancient Sailing and navigation," Canbooks, 2002. http://nabataea.net/sailing.html. While some assume that ancient trade between India and China was accomplished entirely by land over what would later be termed the Silk Road, that journey was

anything but safe. Those who attempted the journey had to cross some of the highest mountains in the world in addition to some of the most forbidding deserts. Natural disasters were a way of life. There were multiple kingdoms with their wars, their heavy taxes, their cultural differences, and their robbers. And while people carried provisions for themselves, their pack animals had to be regularly fed and watered along the way.

2. Amir D. Aczel, *The Riddle of the Compass: the Invention That Changed the World.* New York: Harcourt, 2001.

3. Ibid., p. 9–10.

4. Jim Bailey, *Sailing to Paradise: The Discovery of the Americas by 7000 BC* (New York: Simon & Schuster, 1994).

5. Aczel, pp. 27–28.

6. Jim Bailey, *Sailing to Paradise*, p. 46.

7. This idea is also supported by Cyrus H. Gordon *(Before Columbus: Links between the Old World and Ancient America*, New York: Crown Publishers, 1971). At the time, some considered Gordon to be one of the world's most eminent scholars. Dr. Gordon was head of the Department of Mediterranean Studies at Brandeis University and had published numerous books. In this thoroughly documented book, which represented a lifetime of research, he demonstrated that transoceanic travel across the Atlantic and Pacific to the New World was taking place as long as five thousand years ago. He writes:

> Today it is all too common for the descendants of the most civilized men to lose the great cultures of their ancestors. . . . How abysmal our ignorance is, is described by the term "collective amnesia": when mankind as a whole forgets the experience of the race. This book would never have had to be written were it not that mankind as a whole has forgotten major chapters of its history. (pp. 36–37)

8. Carl Peters, *The Eldorado of the Ancients*, London: C.A. Pearson, Ltd., 1902, pp. 308–9.

9. *Bias in Indian Historiography*, edited by Devahuti. D. K. Publishers' Distribution: New Delhi, 1980, pp. 90–100, cited in "A Tribute to Hinduism—Seafaring in Ancient India," http://www.atributetohinduism.com/Seafaring_in_Ancient_India.htm.

10. Ibid.

11. *Eminent Orientalists: Indian European American*—Asian Educational Services, p. 314, cited in "A Tribute to Hinduism—Seafaring in Ancient India," http://www.atributetohinduism.com/Seafaring_in_Ancient_India.htm.

12. Bombay City Gazetteer, Vol. II, chapter IV, p. 3, cited in "A Tribute to Hinduism—Seafaring in Ancient India," http://www.atributetohinduism.com/Seafaring_in_Ancient_India.htm.

13. *Indian Shipping: A History of the Sea-Borne Trade and Maritime Activity of the Indians From the Earliest Times*, 1912, cited in "A Tribute to Hinduism—Seafaring in Ancient India," http://www.atributetohinduism.com/Seafaring_in_Ancient_India.htm.

14. R. C. Majumdar, *Ancient India*, p. 210–16, cited in "A Tribute to Hinduism—Seafaring in Ancient India," http://www.atributetohinduism.com/Seafaring_in_Ancient_India.htm.

15. Bombay City Gazetteer, Vol. II, chapter IV, p. 3, cited in "A Tribute to Hinduism—Seafaring in Ancient India," http://www.atributetohinduism.com/Seafaring_in_Ancient_India.htm.

16. *Encyclopedia Britannica* Vol. XI, p. 459, cited in "A Tribute to Hinduism—Seafaring in Ancient India," http://www.atributetohinduism.com/Seafaring_in_Ancient_India.htm.

17. Cited in "A Tribute to Hinduism—Seafaring in Ancient India," http://www.atributetohinduism.com/Seafaring_in_Ancient_India.htm.

18. Bombay City Gazetteer, Vol. II, chapter IV, p. 3, cited in "A Tribute to Hinduism—Seafaring in Ancient India," http://www.atributetohinduism.com/Seafaring_in_Ancient_India.htm.

19. Prakash Charan Prasad, *Foreign Trade and Commerce in Ancient India*, pp. 203–212, cited in "A Tribute to Hinduism—Seafaring in Ancient India," http://www.atributetohinduism.com/Seafaring_in_Ancient_India.htm.

20. R. K. Mookerjee, *Indian Shipping: A History of the Sea-Borne Trade and Maritime Activity of the Indians From the Earliest Times*, p. 4, and K. L. Jain, *Hindu Raj in the World*, p. 25, cited in "A Tribute to Hinduism—Seafaring in Ancient India," http://www.atributetohinduism.com/Seafaring_in_Ancient_India.htm.

21. "Ancient Sailing and navigation," Canbooks, 2002, http://nabataea.net/sailing.html.

22. "Study Course: Landing and First Settlements of the Nephites," in *Autumn Leaves* 11, no. 7 (July), pp. 310–11. This information is also quoted by RLDS author A. H. Parsons, *Parson's Text Book*, Lamoni, IA: Herald Publishing House, 1902, pp. 46–47. Interestingly there is a Roman story of magnetism in the region of India that dates back to the first century BC in the writings of Lucretius (ca. 99 BC–ca. 55 BC), a Roman philospher (*De rerum natura—On the Nature of Things*), and later Pliny the Elder (AD 23–79), a Roman naturalist (*Naturalis Historia*). Pliny wrote of a hill near the river Indus that was made entirely of a stone that attracted iron. He mentioned the magical powers of magnetite in his writings. ("History of Magnets," howmagnetswork.com/history.html)

23. "Maccha Yantra—The Ancient Indian Mariner's Compass," Navigation—UnitedIndia.co, www.unitedindia.com/navigation_vedic.htm.

24. Carl Peters, *The Eldorado of the Ancients*, London: C.A. Pearson, Ltd., 1902, pp. 308–9. See also Carl Peters, *King Solomon's*

Golden Ophir: A Research into the Most Ancient Gold Production in History. Simpkin, Marshall, Hamilton & Co., Ltd., 1899. Reprinted 1969 by Negro Universities Press, A Division of Greenwood Publishing Corp., New York.

25. Ibid., pp. 292–93.

26. Ibid., pp. 308–9.

27. According to Potter and Sedor, the Greeks called him Jarach. "The Jaredites" 2001, Video documentary by George Potter & Tim Sedor. Available through www.nephiproject.com.

28. The Holy Bible, English, Douai. 1820? (Genesis 10:26) Located at the Harold B. Lee Library (BS 180). See also "The Jaredites," 2001, Video documentary by George Potter and Tim Sedor (Available through www.nephiproject.com), According to Potter and Sedor, St. Jerome called him Jare.

29. According to the *Smith's Bible Dictionary*, London, 1863, he was called Jared. "The Jaredites" 2001, video documentary by George Potter and Tim Sedor. (Available through www.nephiproject.com)

30. For details on this theory the reader is referred to "The Jaredites," 2001 and "Driving the Jaredite Trail," 2003 produced by George Potter and Timothy Sedor. Based on research by George Potter and Richard Wellington. Filmed entirely on location. Available through www.nephiproject.com.

31. "Hellenistic civilization (Greek civilization beyond classical Greeks) represents the zenith of Greek influence in the ancient world from 323 BC to about 146 BC In the second century BC, the Greco-Bactrians seem to have conquered northwest India, forming an Indo-Greek kingdom" ("Hellenistic civilization," Wikipedia).

32. George F. Hourani, *Arab Seafaring in the Indian Ocean in Ancient and Early Medieval Times*, revised and expanded by John

Carswell. Princeton, New Jersey: Princeton University Press, 1995, pp. 4–6.

33. The most complete version existing today is preserved on twelve clay tablets from the library collection of seventh-century BC Assyrian king Ashurbanipal.

The Epic of Gilgamesh was discovered by Hormuzd Rassam in 1853 and is widely known today. The first modern translation of the epic was published in the early 1870s by George Smith (Smith, George, December 3, 1872, "The Chaldean Account of the Deluge," http://www.sacred-texts.com/ane/chad/index.htm).

The most definitive translation is contained in a two-volume critical work by Andrew George. This represents the fullest treatment of the standard edition material. A book review by the Cambridge scholar, Eleanor Robson, claims that George's is the most significant critical work on Gilgamesh in the last seventy years. See: http://bmcr.brynmawr.edu/2004/2004-04-21.html ("Epic of Gilgamesh," http://en.wikipedia.org/wiki/Epic_of_Gilgamesh).

34. Jim Bailey, *Sailing to Paradise: The Discovery of the Americas by 7000 BC*, New York: Simon & Schuster, 1994, pp. 48, 50.

35. Nimrod ultimately built the Tower of Babel in order to reach the heavens by his own design. The failure of the Tower of Babel was during the time of Peleg in which "the earth was divided." This phrase is commonly held to refer to the splitting up of the world's population into various geographical and linguistic groups (Genesis 11:1–9) rather than a division of the continents.

Interestingly, when trying to correlate Utnapishtim, Gilgamesh, and Urshanabi with Noah and his descendants, I found that because of their extended life span, the Patriarchal line from Noah down to Peleg were all contemporary with Nimrod and the Tower of Babel (Gen. 10: 21–30).

	(1)	(2)	(3)	(4)	(5)
Genealogical Line:	Noah -	Ham -	Cush -	**Nimrod**	
Genealogical Line:	Noah -	Shem -	Arphaxad -	Eber -	**Peleg**

Although there are no dates given in the Bible for the line of Nimrod, the dating from Noah to Peleg (brother of Joktan) is given in Genesis 11:10–17. Summarizing the data there we find that:

- The Flood is dated to about 2400 BC when Noah was 600 years old. Thus Noah was born about 3000 BC Noah lived after the Flood 350 years (or until **2050 BC**).
- Shem (age 100) begat Arphaxad two years after flood **or about 2398 BC** (Shem lived 500 years after he begat Arphaxad or until **1898 BC**).
- Arphaxad (age 35) begat Salah **about 2368 BC** (Arphaxad lived 403 years after he begat Salah or until **1965**.
- Salah (age 30) begat Eber **about 2338 BC** (Salah lived 403 years after he begat Eber or until **1935 BC**
- Eber (age 34) begat Peleg **about 2304** (Eber lived 430 years after he begat Peleg or until **1874.**
- Peleg lived 239 years or until about **2065**.

<u>Thus:</u>

- Noah outlived Peleg.
- Noah died (2050) when Eber was 288.
- Shem outlived Peleg.
- Arphaxad outlived Peleg.
- Salah outlived Peleg.
- Eber outlived Peleg (Noah died when Eber was 288).
- (Eber was the same generation as Nimrod).

So if Utnapishtim (Noah) had died as implied in the Epic of Gilgamesh, and if Gilgamesh can be equated with Nimrod (who was the same generation as Eber), then Gilgamesh would have probably been about 300 years old in the Epic. Because of their long lifespans, all of the Patriarchs listed above who followed Noah would have been living at the time of Nimrod and at the time of Peleg. Now Peleg was the brother of Joktan, and Joktan was the father of "Jered" and Ophir, so they had witnessed the "division" of the earth. It is also probable that "Jered" and his brother Ophir were contemporary with Nimrod.

36. SparkNotes: The Epic of Gilgamesh: Tablet X, http://www.sparknotes.com/lit/gilgamesh/section8.rhtml.

37. I will postulate the following: Urshanabi makes it possible for Gilgamesh to communicate with the immortal Utnapishtim (Noah—who has been given eternal life). Gilgamesh wants to ask Utnapishtim how to become immortal but rejects what Utnapishtim holds sacred. Gilgamesh rebels against the things of God and destroys the special stones and the serpent symbols that Urshanabi had used and cared for. These stones were considered sacred to Utnapishtim as they had helped him navigate his boat across the great waters and the Waters of Death (that is, they had helped Noah survive the Flood and gain eternal life). After Gilgamesh rejects the Godly things of Utnapishtim, he is commanded to depart. Gilgamesh returns to his city, which he makes a monument to man's power. In the epic story, for some unknown reason Urshanabi is sent away. As I established previously, if Nimrod (Gilgamesh) was contemporary with the patriarchs from Noah on down, it is possible for me to also equate Urshanabi with one of them (perhaps even Ophir, the brother of "Jered"), especially when Urshanabi was Noah's boatman and the caretaker of the "Stone Things."

Chapter 5

1. Thomas Crawford Johnston, *Did the Phoenicians Discover America?* reprinted by St. Thomas Press, Houston, 1965, pp. 33–34.

2. Johnston, *Did the Phoenicians Discover America?*, pp 17–18, 64–65

3. Historians Herodotus (as early as 445 BC), Pytheas (352–323 BC), and Polybius (ca. 160 BC) confirm that the tin mines of Cornwall were the source of the world's supply, exported by the Phoenicians (C. Dobson, *Did Our Lord Visit Britain as They Say in Cornwall and Somerset?*, London: Covenant Publishing Co., Ltd., 1986, p. 19.)

Source: Vaughn E. Hansen, "Israel's Lost Ten Tribes: Migrations to Britain and the United States, Springville, Utah: Cedar Fort, Inc., 2011, p. 75.

4. Johnston, *Did the Phoenicians Discover America?*, pp. 37, 76–77.

5. Ibid., p. 38.

6. Interestingly, Vaughn E. Hansen writes that after Jerusalem was destroyed by the Babylonian army (approx. 600 BC), the Bible implies that Jeremiah and his scribe Baruch went to Egypt with King Zedekiah's daughters (see Jeremiah 43). Hansen notes, "Jeremiah is reported (by several authors who quote from various ancient sources) to have taken [as guardian of their welfare] Tamar and Scota, daughters of the Jewish King Zedekiah, with him to Egypt." Hansen writes that, according to legend, these people were then taken by a Phoenician ship to Spain, "where one of the girls married into the reigning house of Spain" (Anthony W. Ivins, "Israel in History and Genealogy," *Utah Genealogical and Historial Magazine,* 23 [January 1932], pp. 6–8). From Spain, a ship continued on to the coast of Ireland with Jeremiah and Tamar, the eldest daughter. Once in Ireland, beautiful Tamar married Heremon, King of Ireland, who was a descendant of the tribes of the Northern Kingdom of Israel (Ernest L. Whitehead, *The House of Israel,* Independence, MO: Zion Printing and Publishing Co., 1947, p. 13).

Hansen notes that the concept of British Royalty being descended through the centuries from Hebrew and Israelite lines has been acknowledged by many genealogists and historians. W. M. H. Milner's *The Royal House of Britain, an Enduring Dynasty*

(Rochester, Kent: Stanhope Press, 1975) charts more than 800 names of royalty from early Judaic origins to Queen Elizabeth II.

Source: Vaughn E. Hansen, *Israel's Lost Ten Tribes: Migrations to Britain and the United States*, Springville, UT: Cedar Fort, Inc., 2011, pp. 71–73, 90–91.

7. Strabo (H.L. Jones transi. i.3.2), www.beforeus.com/email/article/art2-solfleet.html.

8. Johnston, *Did the Phoenicians Discover America?* pp. 42–43.

9. Ibid., pp. 45–46.

10. (Asiat. Res., vol. iii. p. 324). See also Johnston, *Did the Phoenicians Discover America?* reprinted by St. Thomas Press, Houston, Texas, 1965, pp. 59–60.

11. Johnston, *Did the Phoenicians Discover America?* p. 72.

12. Ibid., p. 82.

13. Ibid., pp. 73–74.

14. Ibid., p. 86. Although today all one needs to do is find the Big Dipper and follow its direction to Polaris, Amir Aczel notes that Polaris was not located at the pole during ancient times. "About 800 BC, Kochab (Beta Ursae Minoris), another star in the same constellation as Polaris, was located relatively close to the pole." That such differences in the pole star did not negate its use is brought out by the Greek mathematician Thales, who lived around 600 BC He wrote that the Phoenician mariners were capable of locating the pole star (Kochab) by using either the Big Dipper or the Little Dipper. Interestingly, Chinese navigators also oriented themselves to the Big and Little Dippers in ancient times by the use of a jade disk. "From the location of the star's positions on one such disk, called the Hsuan-Chi, scientists have been able to date it to 800 BC (Aczel, *The Riddle of the Compass*, pp. 22–23)

15. 1 Sanchoniathori, Rt. Rev. R. Cumberland, 1720.

16. See "Phoenician Theology" http://phoenicia.org/theomythology.html.

17. Philo of Byblius (Byblos) (AD 64–141) was a Phoenician scholar and Roman citizen, born in Byblos, and representative of the Roman Consul Herennius Severus. He wrote numerous works of grammatical, lexical, encyclopedic, and historical importance. His most important work is the translation of *Phoenician History* by Sanchuniathon. This work was thought to be made up, but since 1929, archaeological evidence of clay tablet texts dated to 1400–1200 BC from Ras Shamra, Ugarit, proved him true. He had a considerable reputation for honesty in his work, which archaeology confirmed. His Greek translation represents a valuable source for our knowledge of the Phoenician Canaanite religion.

18. 1 Sanchoniathori, Rt. Rev. R. Cumberland, 1720. Interestingly, in another translation in 1903 of *Extracts from Eusebius of Caesarae: Praeparatio Evangelica* (Preparation for the Gospel), E. H. Gifford interprets the phrase as follows:

> Philo . . . next begins his interpretation of Sanchuniathon by setting forth the theology of the Phoenicians.
>
> Chapter X
> Theology of the Phoenicians. . .
>
> 'Further, he says, the god Uranus devised the Baetylia, having contrived to put life into stones.' ("Phoenician Theology" http://phoenicia.org/theomythology.html)

19. Johnston, *Did the Phoenicians Discover America?*, pp. 90–91.

20. Ibid., pp. 92–93

21. Ibid., pp 96–97.

22. Herodotus, *The History*, trans. David Grene, IV:42.

23. Carl Peters, *The Eldorado of the Ancients*, pp. 317–19.

24. Johnston, *Did the Phoenicians Discover America?*, p. 93.

25. Jim Bailey, *Sailing to Paradise: The Discovery of the Americas by 7000 BC*, New York: Simon & Schuster, 1994, pp. 40–42.

26. Verneil W. Simmons, *Peoples, Places and Prophecies*, p. 99.

27. John L. Sorenson, "New Technology and Ancient Questions (part 2)," in FARMS, *Insights* (February 1997): p. 2.

28. McMenamin, M.A. 1997. The Phoenician World Map. *Mercator's World* 2(3):46–51; Scott, J.M. 2005. *Geography in Early Judaism and Christianity.* Cambridge University Press, pp. 182–83, as noted with other previous information on Phoenicia in an article titled "Phoenicia" on Wikipedia, the free encyclopedia. This claim is among many evidences that have been put forth regarding Phoenician contact with America. There are numerous websites containing such information.

29. Amir D. Aczel, *The Riddle of the Compass: the Invention That Changed the World.* New York: Harcourt, 2001, pp. 27–28. He notes, "bad weather posed a serious hindrance to navigation. When the skies were covered with clouds, it was impossible for mariners to find where they were going. Mostly for this reason, throughout ancient times, the seas were closed to navigation in winter."

Chapter 6

1. Interestingly, Jim Bailey notes the following on the Phoenicians and the Red Sea:

> Herodotus said that they came from the Red Sea to the Mediterranean . . . the name Red Sea can possibly apply to those places where "the Red Men," the Phoenicians, were concentrated. . . . Erythia in Greek means

red. (Jim Bailey, *Sailing to Paradise: The Discovery of the Americas by 7000 BC*, New York: Simon & Schuster, 1994, p. 49)

The above information is interesting when viewed against the detractors of the Book of Mormon who claim that the name "Red Sea" is a mistranslation in the Bible and thus an anachronism in the Book of Mormon.

2. George F. Hourani, *Arab Seafaring in the Indian Ocean in Ancient and Early Medieval Times*, revised and expanded by John Carswell. Princeton, New Jersey: Princeton University Press, 1995, pp. 7–8.

3. B. Keith Christensen, *The Unknown Witness*, pp. 60–61, unpublished manuscript.

4. W. Cleon Skousen, *The Fourth Thousand Years*, Salt Lake City: Bookcraft, 1991, pp. 248–51 in which he quotes from Werner Keller, *The Bible As History*, New York: William Morrow and Co., 1956, "pp.192–201 provides a rather complete summary of this expedition."

5. In an article titled "Austronesian Navigation and Migration," (http://www.geocities.com/Tokyo/Temple/9845/austro.htm) I found the following concerning the spice trade to the "East Indies" (Malay Archipelago):

> In ancient China it was required that people first chew cloves (gui) before speaking with the Emperor to ensure a pleasing breath. . . . cloves have [also] been found as early as 1,700–1,600 BCE in Terqa, Syria where a pot of cloves was found by archaeologist G. Buccelatoi. This date is very interesting because not too far away in Egypt during the reign of Queen Hatshepsut (1503 to 1482 BCE), there is mention in the hieroglyphic texts of *ti-sps* "cinnamon wood" being imported from the southern land of Punt. Now cinnamon also grew only in southeastern Asia before the modern period.
>
> Cinnamon is again mentioned in the 7th century BCE Hebrew biblical texts and by Theophrastus (372–288 BCE). The Hebrews claimed that cinnamon, cassia, and possibly also lemon-grass were used in the

> holy oil of the temple proscribed by Moses (Exodus 30). This correlates somewhat to the early dates for cloves in Syria and cinnamon in Egypt. The Hebrew word for cinnamon "quinamom" is believed to be derived from Malay *kayu manis* "sweet wood," and the English word is ultimately derived from the Hebrew. How did these spices arrive in Africa and the Middle East? Archaeologists have found that the medieval cinnamon trade followed a route across the vast expanse of the Indian Ocean from Indonesia to Madagascar. . . . in medieval time, cinnamon landing in Madagascar would then find its way to Rhapta in present-day Somalia. From there is reached the South Arabian traders in Muza, Yemen who carried on the trade along the coasts of the Red Sea. Now, this could be a medieval model explaining the ancient ships of Hatshepsut which sailed to the southern country of Punt to obtain cinnamon amongst other goods!

Continuing on, and in terms that to some might be reminiscent of the seagoing manner of the Jaredite barges (see the brackets), the author notes:

> Pliny the Elder (23/24–79 CE) wrote of how the Ethiopians bought cinnamon from their neighbors (probably to the south) who purchased it themselves from a seafaring people. These mariners:
>
> > Bring it over vast seas on rafts ["barges"?] which have no rudders to steer them or oars to push or pull them or sails or other aids to navigation; but instead only the spirit of man and human courage. What is more, they put out to sea in winter, around the time of the winter solstice when the east winds are blowing their hardest ["a furious wind bl[e]w upon the face of the waters, towards the promised land"? -Ether 6:5]. These winds drive them on a straight course, and from gulf to gulf.

The *Periplus of the Erythraean Sea*, written in the first century ACE, describes ships from Chryse in the Malay Archipelago known as *Kolan-diphonta* or "Kolan-ships." The "Kolan" here are probably the Kunlun of the Chinese annals. The ships are described as large vessels made of two whole logs roped together ["the length thereof was the length of a tree" (Ether 2:16)]. This sounds very much like the double canoes of Oceania ["they were light upon the water"

(Ether 2:16)]. Stone representations of such canoes have been found in Indonesia and northeastern India.

6. We find the following by J. A. Thompson under "Tarshish" in *The Illustrated Bible Dictionary*:

> W. F. Albright has suggested that the very word *Tarshish* suggests the idea of mining or smelting, and that in a sense any mineral-bearing land may be called Tarshish . . . An old Semitic root found in Akkad, *rasasu* means 'to melt', 'to be smelted'. A derived noun *tarsisu* may be used to define a smelting-plant or refinery (Arab. *rss*, 'to trickle', etc., of liquid). . . . The expression *'ni tarsis*, navy of Tarshish or Tarshish fleet, may refer more generally to ships which carried smelted metal either to distant lands from Ezion-geber or to Phoenicia from the W Mediterranean.
>
> [Some] view that Tarshish vessels were deep seagoing vessels. . . . These ships symbolized wealth and power. A vivid picture of the day of divine judgment was to portray the destruction of these large ships in that day (Ps. 48:7; Is. 2:16; 23:1, 14). The fact that Is. 2:16 compares the ships of Tarshish with 'the pleasant place" (RSV 'beautiful craft') suggests that whatever the original identification of Tarshish may have been, it became in literature and in the popular imagination a distant paradise from which all kinds of luxuries might be brought to such areas as Phoenicia and Israel. (*The Illustrated Bible Dictionary* vol. 3 [Wheaton, IL: Tyndale House Publishers: 1980], pp. 1517–19)

7. Ch. Rabin, *Studies in Religion*, III [1973/1974], p. 209; "Winds and Currents: A Look at Nephi's Ocean Crossing," *FARMS Update*, April 1986; cf. *National Geographic* (October 1967), p. 559, as quoted in Robert F. Smith, "Book of Mormon Event Structure: Ancient Near East," Provo, UT: FARMS, 1984, p. 23.

8. Additionally, iron might have come from the southern Arabia end of the Frankincense Trail. Responding to a FARMS request, in 1985 Eugene Clark, former geologist for ESSO in Oman, prepared a preliminary report of geological possibilities of mineral deposits in the Dhofar region, where the chief source of Frankincense for trade with other Near Eastern countries was located. (Eugene E. Clark, "A Preliminary Study of the Geology and Mineral Resources

of Dhofar, the Sultanate of Oman," Introduction). The report identifies a number of geological possibilities for accessible copper and iron ore. Most promising among the published studies are reports of specular hematite found in small, random deposits on the Mirbat plain east of Salalah. Specular hematite is the most readily available form of high-quality iron and would have been most attractive as a low-tech smelting source. The report also notes that Dhofar irons would usually occur in mixtures with manganese and carbon, yielding higher-quality steel that would be superior for tools.

On April 2, 2000, three BYU geology professors and a professional geologist reported on their work of evaluating the presence of iron ore in southern Oman, specifically the Dhofar region which has been proposed as the area of Nephi's Bountiful. According to Ronald Harris, although Oman has an abundance of ore deposits, most of these deposits are buried beneath a thick cover of sedimentary rock. However, the Dhofar region of Oman is an exception. In fact, it is one of the few places throughout the Arabian Peninsula where the ore deposits are exposed. Jeffrey Keith noted that the team found deposits of iron-rich carbonate, goethite, and hematite, which can be crushed, mixed together, and heated to make a very usable form of iron ore. In fact, the team extracted some of this ore material, brought it back to BYU, and made iron out of it. These deposits occur in two areas along the southern Omani coast in concentrations sufficient to make tools: Raykut and Mirbat (Ronald A. Harris, Eugene E. Clark, Jeffrey D. Keith, and W. Revell Phillips, "Nephi's Tools: An Overview of Iron Ore Occurrences in Oman," Brown Bag Lecture on 5 April, 2000. Reported in "FARMS Project Reports," in *Insights,* May 2000, p. 7).

Mirbat is located a few miles east of the Salalah coastal plain (the Hilton's proposed Bountiful site), and just west of Khor Rori (Potter's and Wellington's proposed site). It would have been easily reached by camel in Nephi's time. There is clear excavation evidence at a mountain site called Jebel Ali of a type of soft iron deposit called "goethite." Having gone through a natural process of breakdown by sulfuric acid, this soft deposit can easily be picked up and transported.

Raykut is located somewhat close to, and east of, Wadi Sayq

(the Aston's proposed Bountiful site); however, it is not reachable overland. One must approach it by boat from Wadi Sayq. Here the geologists found limited amounts of Iron carbonate, Hematite, and also Goethite.

Sur on the northeast of Oman (proposed by Hedengren as Bountiful) has the ore but not the water for a lush environment.

9. Bill Eyster, *Thataway: The Story of the Magnetic Compass*, South Brunswick and New York: A.S. Barnes and Co., 1970.

10. Eyster, *Thataway: The Story of the Magnetic Compass*, p. 27. On page 28 Eyster has a nice picture of a camel illustrating this point. The caption reads: "Nothing can express righteous indignation better than a camel with little stones sticking to his feet."

11. Eyster, p. 30.

12. In their book, *In Search of Lehi's Trail* (Salt Lake City: Deseret Book, 1976), the Hiltons write:

> (1) The Liahona pointed "the way whither [they] should go into the wilderness" (1 Nephi 16:10) as an indication to Lehi's party that they should keep going south-southeast rather than embarking on the sea at that point or going east into the mountains. This direction coincided with the relatively safe Frankincense trail. (2) However, the trail was as wide as the coastal plain-up to forty-eight miles at its widest point. Caravans seeking camel fodder would, of course, use its entire width. . . . [p. 73]
>
> We should note that the word *trail* is apt to be misleading. It does not refer to a well-defined, relatively narrow path or roadway, but to a more general route that flowed through this valley, that canyon, etc. The width of the route varied with the geography, ranging from a half mile to a dozen (even at one point up to fifty) miles wide. Travelers could thus camp great distances from one another and still be at the same point on the same trail. [p. 32]

13. George Potter and Richard Wellington, *Lehi in the Wilderness*, Springville, Utah: Cedar Fort, Inc., 2003.

14. Eyster, p. 29.

15. Aczel's full illustrated discussion is found on pages 39–52.

Chapter 7

1. Quoted in Ammon O'Brien, *Seeing Beyond Today with Ancient America*, England, 1995, p. 136.

2. Ibid., p. 149.

3. Ibid., p. 148.

4. Ibid., p. 151.

5. Clate Mask, "And They Called the Place Tulan," p. 4.

Chapter 8

1. Eyster, p. 29. Eyster's reasoning in this last statement leaves a lot of unanswered questions.

2. Tim Severin, *The Voyage of Sinbad*, New York: G. P. Putnam's Sons, 1983, pp. 91–95.

3. "Qin Dynasty," Wikipedia, the free encyclopedia. http://en.wikipedia.org/wiki/Qin_Dynasty.

4. Patrick Huyghe, *Columbus Was Last*, New York: Anomalist Books, 1992, p. 37.

5. Preston Chesser, "The Burning of the Library of Alexandria," posted June 1, 2002. Luciano Canfora, "The Vanished Library"; Edward Gibbons, "Decline and Fall of the Roman Empire"; and Wikipedia, "Library of Alexandria," which lists multiple sources.

6. Paul Fleury Mottelay, PhD, *Bibliographical History of Electricity & Magnetism: Chronologically Arranged*. London: Charles Griffin & Company Limited, 1922, p. 18.

7. Pliny, II.67.169. Pliny wrote about 250 years after the fall of Carthage.

8. "The Voyage of Hanno," www.metrum.org/mapping/hanno.htm.

9. Ibid., p.90.

10. Ibid., p. 81.

11. Paul Fleury Mottelay, Ph.D, *Bibliographical History of Electricity & Magnetism: Chronologically Arranged*. London: Charles Griffin & Company Limited, 1922, p. 22.

12. Frank Boott Goodrich, *Man upon the Sea or, A history of maritime adventure, exploration, and discovery, from the earliest ages to the present time*, Philadelphia: Lippincott, 1858, pp. 42–43.

13. Aczel, 111–13, 29. See also wikipedia.org/wii/Silk-Road.

14. T. A. Lyons, *A Treatise on Electromagnetic Phenomena and on the Compass and Its Deviations Aboard Ship*, Vol. II, John Wiley, 1903, 560–67. Quoted in "The Discovery of the Magnetic Compass and Its Use in Navigation" by H. H. Ricker III.

15. Ibid., pp. 88–89. I might comment here that with the devastating principle of "holy ignorance" came the rejection of additional truths—"A Bible, A Bible, We have a Bible, and there cannot be any more Bible." (2 Nephi 29:3–10). For me, a student for 20 years of ancient America and the writings on Indian origins, I found the parallels here between the destruction of Chinese "religious" writings and the destruction of Mesoamerican codices to be profoundly similar. The enlightened reasoning here is that if the evidence is destroyed, then there is no foundation for belief, and by

classifying what little remains as "legend" and "unscientific," it can be dismissed as the fables of an unenlightened people.

16. Lizana, *Historia de Yucatan*, part 2, 6:5; cited by Tozzer, *Landa's Relacion de las Cosas de Yucatan,* p. 78.

17. Joseph Lovell Allen and Blake Joseph Allen, *Exploring the Lands of the Book of Mormon,* second edition, Orem, UT: Book of Mormon Tours and Research Institute, LLC, 2008, pp.261.

18. Joseph Needham, *Explorations of an Ancient Tradition*, Cambridge, MA: MIT Press, 1973, pp. 3–19.

19. Cyrus H. Gordon, *Before Columbus: Links between the Old World and Ancient America*, New York: Crown Publishers, 1971, pp. 36–37.

20. Aczel, p. 78.

Chapter 9

1. There have been few published LDS works that have dealt in any great depth with early (1500–1830) perspectives on American Indian origins. For the past number of years I have been trying to read and collect as many pertinent writings as possible on Indian origins.

The first published LDS writings that dealt in depth with early perspectives on Indian origins were by B. H. Roberts (*New Witnesses for God*, vol. 2, Salt Lake City: Deseret News, 1909). Interestingly, he tended to bolster the idea that the Book of Mormon was about the Lost Tribes of Israel. In his *Chapter XXXII: External Evidences—The Hebrew Origin of the Native American Races*, Roberts presents a multitude of external evidences supporting the traditional Mormon thought on the origin of the Indians. Yet while Roberts's writings went out to the whole Church, they soon faded into the background.

In 1930, an LDS student at BYU named Alvah Fitzgerald wrote a 269-page master's thesis that represented (and would continue to represent for many decades) the most extensive LDS treatment of the "Progressive Opinion of the Origin and Antiquity of the American Indian." In this thesis, Fitzgerald defined, evaluated, and listed the books published about, the evidence cited in support of, and the credence given to the various different theories that were advocated in succeeding periods from the time of the discovery of America by Columbus. In addition to the above-mentioned theories, he also listed the "Indigenous Theory, Mixed Origin Theory, and PreAdamite Theory. He also divided his chronological approach to theories into five different periods: 1) Previous to 1800; 2) 1800 to 1830; 3) 1830 to 1860; 4) 1860 to 1900; 5) 1900 to 1929. Sadly, this work has been relatively unused, languishing on the bookshelves at the BYU library.

In 1984 an LDS review of early ideas on American Indian origins was given by Richard L. Bushman (*Joseph Smith and the Beginnings of Mormonism*, Urbana and Chicago: University of Illinois Press, 1984). In this book he has a section on some pre-1830 authors who wrote on American Indian origins (115–142), but there are no lengthy quotations, only commentary. He focuses more on the differences between their ideas and those in the Book of Mormon.

In 2005, a nice 600-page book, *Voices From the Dust: New Insights Into Ancient America: A Comparative Evaluation Of Early Spanish and Portuguese Chronicles with the Book of Mormon and with Archaeology and Art History* was finally published by David G. Calderwood.

In recent years, the focus of debate over American Indian origins has changed from the early historical accounts to the matter of DNA. According to critics, they have failed to find any support for the Book of Mormon story in DNA analysis of the various known American Indian tribes. For this apologetic debate, I will refer the reader to a multitude of sources that can be readily searched on the Internet. A good beginning site for LDS readers is FairMormon (http://en.fairmormon.org/DNA).

2. Neckam's book, *De Naturis Rerum*, contains the following description:

> The sailors, moreover, as they sail over the sea, when in cloudy weather they can no longer profit by the light of the sun, or when the world is wrapped up in the darkness of the shades of night, and they are ignorant to what point of the compass their ship's course is directed, they touch the magnet with a needle. This then whirls round in a circle until, when its motion ceases, its point looks direct to the north.
>
> Neckam's text gives no hint as to where or how he might have seen or heard about the magnetic compass. (Aczel, pp. 29–30).

3. "History of Magnetism and Electricity," History of Magnetism (http://www/rare-earth-magnets.com/t-history-of-magnets.aspx).

4. Amir Aczel tells of traveling to southern Italy to the coastal town of Amalfi to find out if this legend was true. In the center of town he found a plaque with the following inscription:

> All of Italy, and Amalfi, must give credit to the great invention of the magnetic compass, without which America and other unexplored places would not have been opened to civilization. Amalfi commemorates this pure Italian glory with special honors to its immortal son, Flavio Gioia, the fortunate inventor of the magnetic compass.—1302 (Amir D. Aczel, *The Riddle of the Compass: the Invention That Changed the World.* New York: Harcourt, 2001, pp. 4–5)

However, upon going to the Amalfi cultural center he was handed a pamphlet which quoted the following words from the Italian historian Padre Timoteo Bertelli:

> Flavio Gioia never existed. He represents only a kind of myth, created late after his presumed lifetime, and hence suspect. He is a fantasy produced by the fertile southern imagination of the people of Amalfi and elsewhere. (Ibid., p. 6–7)

Aczel continued to investigate. While he found that the inventor (variations on the name appeared in a variety of sources: Flavio Goia, Giovanni Gioia, Francesco Gioia or Goia or Giri, John Gioia or Goia or Goe) was most probably fictitious and the result of misinterpretation of documents, there is good evidence for the port of Amalfi being a power in the Mediterranean at one time. In the thirteenth century AD, Amalfi rose to great wealth through maritime trade under the Norman Kingdom of southern Italy. Amalfi's code of maritime law became universal throughout the whole Mediterranean from the thirteenth through the sixteenth centuries. This period was important because during this time, navigation became more efficient and scientific with new technology, and Amalfi became a primary source for those innovations. In respect to the compass, Aczel writes:

> Then, between the years 1295 and 1302, a true innovation took place in Amalfi. According to medieval and modern sources, the people of Amalfi attained a "perfection" of the magnetic compass, transforming it from a needle floating in water or supported in air into the compass we know today: a round box in which a compass card with a wind rose and a division into 360 degrees rotates, attached to a magnetic element. (Ibid.)

5. Peter Martyr of Angleria, *Decadas del Nuevo Mundo*, first published in partial form in 1511, first complete edition in Latin in 1530.

While the first Spanish edition was not published until 1892, Alexander von Humboldt gave consideration to Martyr's writings in the early years of the 1800s.

The quote is taken from Peter Martyr D'Anghera, *De Orbe Novo: The Eight Decades of Peter Martyr D'Anghera*. Translated from the Latin with Notes and Introduction by Francis Augustus MacNutt. Two Volumes. New York: G. P. Putnam Sons, 1912, vol. 1, p. 86.

6. In our modern Bible editions, the passages relating to Ophir are actually found in 1 Kings 9:26–28; 10:11; and 2 Chronicles 8:18; 9:10 RSV). This story is repeated almost verbatim in 2 Chronicles 8:18, 9:10—the only difference being that "almug wood" is "algum wood" in the Chronicles version. Most writers of the period included 2 Chronicles 9:21 ("For the king's ships went to Tarshish with the servants of Hirum; once every three years the ships of

Tarshish used to come bringing gold, silver, ivory, apes, and peacocks.") as part of the Ophir story, although they understood that the voyage lasted three years (Acosta, 1940, pp. 40–43).

7. Lee Eldridge Huddleston, *Origins of the American Indians: European Concepts, 1492–1729.* Latin American Monographs, no. 11. Institute of Latin American Studies, The University of Texas. Published by the University of Texas Press, Austin, 1967, pp. 40–42.

8. Bell, 1922, pp. 19–38; Rivet, 1960, p. 25.

9. Benito Arias Montano, "Phaleg, sive de gentium sedibus primis, oribisque terrae situ," in *Biblia Sacra* ("Polyglot Bible of Antwerp"). Antwerp, 1569–1572.

10. (1951:73–77).

11. Ibid., p. 141.

12. Chapter 19 of *Archaeology of Northern Mesoamerica* is an essay titled "The Peoples of Central Mexico and their Historical Traditions."

13. Quoted in Ammon O'Brien, *Seeing Beyond Today with Ancient America*, England, 1995, p. 142.

14. Ibid.

15. Joseph de Acosta, *Historia natural y moral de las Indias.* Sevilla: En Casa de Juan de Leon, 1590. See also *The Naturall and Morall Histories of the East and West Indies*, Translated by Edward Grimston, London, 1604. (Spanish edition-Madrid, 1590.) See also *The Natural and Moral History of the Indies*, Edward Grimston (English trans.), C. R. Markham (ed.), reprint ed., 2 vols. New York: Burt Franklin, 1963, pp. 47, 50, 53.

16. 2 Para., ix.; 3 Reg., x.

17. "Iman"—the load stone.

18. "Aguja de Marear"—Mariner's compass.

19. Plin., lib. iii, cap. 6; and lib. xxxiv, cap. 1, 14; and libi. vii, cap. 4.

20. Dios, lib. v, cap. 10. Lucret., lib. vi.

21. Aug. de Civit. Dei, cap. iv, 4, vbi mult de magnete.

22. Plin., lib. vii, c. 16.

23. Mozambique is located in southeast Africa opposite the shores of Madagascar and borders on the Indian Ocean.

24. A Moor is a designation given to any of the Northwest African Muslims, of mixed Arab and Berber origin. Emphasis might be given here to a connection with Arabia and to the seaports on the Indian Ocean.

25. Lib. i, de Ital. illust. reg. 13. Plin., lib. ii, cap. 72; and lib. vii, ca. vit.

26. Osorius de reb. gest. Eman., lib. i.

27. Gregorio Garcia, *Origen de los indios de el nuevo mundo, e Indias occidentales . . .* , Andres Gonzales de Barcia Carballido y Zuniga (ed.). Madrid: Francisco Martinez Abad, 1729. First published 1607 (Multivolume, Valencia).

28. Justin Winsor, *Narrative and Critical History of America*, vol. 1, New York: Houghton, Mifflin and Company, 1889, p. 369.

I will note here that Gregorio Garcia made an interesting observation regarding the tradition of the *Mexica* as recorded by Sahagun (see previous notation). He writes:

> In New Spain (Mexico) the word *Mesico* is found, which, as Stephen de Salacar remarks is Hebrew . . . and signifies "his anointed" . . . the

leader who conducted those who peopled Mexico was named Mesi, or as others write, Mexi; and the city and nation were afterwards called after him, in the same way as we see that many cities, provinces, and nations have been named after those who peopled or founded them, or to whom they owed their origin as we shall presently point out.

The word Mesi should be noted as being actually Hebrew, and it agrees surprisingly with the name of the chief, head, or captain of the Mexicans. (*Origen de los Indios del Nuevo Mundo*, 1607. Quoted in Ammon O'Brien, *Seeing Beyond Today with Ancient America*, England, 1995, p. 144)

29. *History of the Inca Empire . . . by Father Bernabe Cobo*, Translated and edited by Roland Hamilton. Austin, Texas: University of Texas Press, 1983. Roland Hamilton was the first to provide an English translation of any substantial part of the *Historia del Nuevo Mundo* by Jesuit scholar Bernabe Cobo.

30. *History of the Inca Empire . . . by Father Bernabe Cobo*, pp. 76–77.

31. In order to illustrate the problems with limited biased historical perspectives like that of Cobo, I will quote from a 2005 article in the *Journal of Book of Mormon Studies* titled, "Ancient Voyages Across the Ocean to America: From 'Impossible' to 'Certain'," by John L. Sorenson. On pages 6–7, he writes:

> Prevailing views by reputed experts . . . [on ancient transoceanic contact] assumed that "primitive sailors" would have found it impossible to cross the "forbidding" oceans.(n1) . . . Such views were not so much scientific conclusions as echoes of the prevailing isolationist political doctrine of the times that refused to grant value to "foreign" people or ideas. . . . Scholars who continued to claim that meaningful ancient voyages were made argued for the idea mainly on the basis of cultural parallels.(n6) [see note* below] . . . The [modern-day] skeptics maintained that any cultural similarities between the New World and the Old were simply coincidences, explainable because, they claimed, the human mind works the same everywhere in the world, so it should not be surprising that people independently come up with similar inventions or ideas. . . .

[**Note*** *As Sorenson notes, over the years skeptics have downplayed the many cultural similarities proposed to explain Old World–New World contact. Yet Cobo wondered where these similarities were. He writes:*

> *In conclusion, we see no difference from one region to another [in the New World], since they all lack any signs of the Hebrews. This is another strong argument in our favor, because without a doubt in some of the places where the ships came most frequently to trade, more signs and evidence of them would have remained than in other places, and in these places, from their communication and dealings with the Hebrews, the natives would have assimilated something, but that does not happen to be the case, since the natives are all the same.*

Interestingly, some of the very first lists of Old World–New World similarities involved similarities with the Hebrews. These authors also distinguished between the various types of Indians.]

In his article, Sorenson mentions that he and Martin H. Raish had published an exhaustive bibliography of "diffusionist" articles (n8), but it seemed to do no good. He then decided to change his approach. On pages 7–8 Sorenson writes:

> Over the last four years 98 species of plants have been identified that originated in either the Old World or the New yet were also grown in pre-Columbian times in the opposite hemisphere. That distribution cannot be explained the way cultural parallels have been. . . .
>
> [For example] In northern India archaeologists have recently found seeds of *Phaseolus vulgaris* (kidney bean), *Phaseolus lunatus* (lima bean), and *Macroptilium lathyroides* (phasey bean, a cousin of kidney and lima beans), in addition to *Argemone mexicana* (Mexican prickle poppy), all natives of America. The sites date from 1600 to 800 BC (n16)

Sorenson goes on to cite not just examples of actual plants, but realistic depiction of plants in art. He also notes that "references to imported American plants in Asian medical, botanical, and historical documents are a further source of evidence":

> A Chinese document written in the Jin dynasty (AD 290–307) by a minister of state who had served as a governor in southern China lists

some 80 plants that were known to him there. In the list was the sweet potato, *Ipomeoeca batatas*, another American species.(n24)

On pages 14–16, Sorenson makes an extensive categorized list of "plants for which there is decisive evidence of transoceanic carriage."

Sorenson's analysis does not stop with plants. He also writes about insects:

> Furthermore, two species of beetles that infested Egyptian mummies—*Alphitobius diaperinus* and *Stegobium paniceum*—have also been found in mummies in Peru. (n46) It is impossible to avoid the conclusion that intentional voyages across an ocean were involved in these transfers.

Sorenson notes: "Often several types of analysis, rather than a single method, combine to prove contact by sea. In our study we always demanded at least two lines of evidence before considering contact across the sea to be assured."

On page 17 Sorenson concludes by saying, "Research so far has not confirmed that ships did carry Jaredites, Lehites, or Mulek and his party from Eurasia to America. But now, for the first time, we have the clear backing of biological history that those voyages fit within a long-standing historical pattern."

Note 1: For a survey of thought on the topic, see Stephen C. Jett, "Before Columbus: The Question of Early Transoceanic interinfluences," *BYU Studies* 33/2 (1993): 245–71.

Note 6: *Man across the Sea: Problems of Pre-Columbian Contacts*, ed. Carroll L. Riley, J. Charles Kelley, Campbell W. Pennington, and Robert L. Rands (Austin & London: University of Texas Press, 1971)

Note 8: John L. Sorenson and Martin H. Raish, *Pre-Columbian Contact with the Americas across the Oceans: An Annotated Bibliography*, 2nd ed. rev., 2 vols. (Provo, UT: Research Press, 1996)

Note 16: A. K. Pokharia and K. S. Saraswat, "Plant economy during Kushana period (100–300 AD) at ancient Sanghol, Punjab," *Pragdhara* [Journal of the U(ttar) P(radesh) State Archaeology Department] 9 (1999): 99.

Note 24: E. Bretschneider, *Botanicon Sinicum: Notes on Chinese*

Botany from Native and Western Sources (London: Trubner, 1882), 38.

Note 46: J. M. Riddle and J. M. Vreeland, "Identification of insects associated with Peruvian mummy bundles by using scanning electron microscopy," *Paleopathology Newsletter* 39 (1982): 5–9.

Source: John L. Sorenson, "Ancient Voyages Across the Ocean to America: From 'Impossible' to 'Certain'," S. Kent Brown, ed., *Journal of Book of Mormon Studies* 14, no.1 (2005): pp. 1–7.

Chapter 10

1. Lee Eldridge Huddleston, *Origins of the American Indians: European Concepts, 1492–1729.* Latin American Monographs, no. 11. Institute of Latin American Studies, The University of Texas. Published by the University of Texas Press, Austin, 1967, pp. 111–12.

2. Quoted in Ammon O'Brien, *Seeing Beyond Today with Ancient America*, England, 1995, p. 152.

3. Pierre Francois Xavier de Charlevoix, *Journal of a Voyage to North-America.* 2 vols. London, 1761

4. Ibid, p. 53.

5. Ibid., pp. 52–63

6. Samuel Mather, *An Attempt to Shew, that America Must Be Known to the Ancients.* Boston, 1773, p. 18.

7. See the discussion on Flavio Gioia and Amalfi in a previous note (chapter 9, note 4).

8. Although the origin of the seafaring Phoenicians is obscure,

Herodotus (1.1; 7.89) wrote that they came by land from the Persian Gulf area by way of the Red Sea. Their ships are depicted on Egyptian monuments that date to around 2500 BC ("Phoenicia, Phoenicians," *in The Illustrated Bible Dictionary*, vol. 3, Wheaton, Ill: Tyndale House Publishers, 1980, p. 1223.)

According to the ancient *Extracts from Eupolemus*,

> Abraham excelled all in nobility and wisdom; he sought and obtained the knowledge of astology . . . and lpased God because he eagerly sought to be reverent. At God's command, he traveled to Phoenicia and dwelt there. He pleased the Phoenician king by teaching the Phoenicians the cycles of the sun and moon, and everything else as well. [compare Abraham Facsimile 3] (In T*raditions about the Early Life of Abraham*, compiled and edited by John A. Tvedtnes, Brian Hauglid, and John Gee, (Provo, UT: FARMS, 2001), p. 7.)

Abraham lived from about 1800 BC to 1600 BC Thus, the Phoenicians might have gained early knowledge from Abraham about the movements of planets and stars to such a degree that they obtained superiority in navigation over the seas.

9. James Adair, *The History of the American Indians*; *Particularly Those Nations adjoining to the Mississippi, East and West Florida, Georgia, South and North Carolina, and Virginia: Containing An Account of their Origin, Language, Manners, Religious and Civil Customs* . . . . London, 1775.

10. Jonathan Carver, *Three years Travels through the Interior Parts of North-America*, Philadelphia, 1784.

11. Jedidiah Morse, *Geography Made Easy: Being an Abridgment of the American Universal Geography*. Boston, 1802, p. 388.

12. Elias Boudinot, *A Star in the West; or, a Humble Attempt to Discover the Long Lost Ten Tribes of Israel*, Trenton, 1816. Boudinot was president of the Continental Congress at the time of the signing of the peace treaty with Great Britain at the close of the American Revolution. He subsequently served in the United States Congress and as Director of the United States Mint. In 1805, he

devoted himself to biblical studies and helping others. His book appeared 1816, the same year in which he became the first president of the newly formed American Bible Society.

13. Spaulding writes (original spelling):

Soon the whole crew became lost & bewildered—They knew not the direction to the rising Sun or polar Star—for the heavens were covered with clouds; & darkness had spread her sable mantle over the face of the raging deep. Their minds were filled with consternation & dispair—[*and unanimously agreed that*] What could we do? . . . [p. 4]

After being driven five days with incridable velocity before the furious wind, the storm abated in its violance—but still the wind blew strong in the same direction—Doubt whether the wind had not changed her point we gave the ship full sail & let her drive—On the sixth day after, the storm wholly subsided, the sun rose clear & the heavens once more appeard to smile—Inexpressible was the consternation of all the crew. they found themselves in the midst of a vast Ocean No prospect of returning—all was lost—The wind blowing westwardly & the presumption was that it had been blowing in that direction during the whole of the storm. No pen can paint the dolorious cries & lamentations of the poor mariners—for the loss of every thing they held most dear. At length a Mariner stept *forward* in the midst and proclaimed. Attend O friends & listen to my words—A voice from on high hath penetrated my soul & the inspiration of the Almighty hath bid me proclaim—Let your sails be wide spread and the gentle winds will soon waft you into a safe harbor—A country where you will find hospitality.—Quick as the lightnings flash joy sparkled in every countenance . . . On the fifth day after this we came in sight of Land—we entered a spacious River—& continued sailing up the *same* many leages until we came in view of a Town—. . . We anchored within a small distance from shore. . . . [p. 5]

As no alternative now remained, but either to make the desparate attempt to return across the wide boistrous ocean or to take up our residence in a country inhabited by savages & wild ferocious beasts we did not long hesitate. We held a solem treaty with the king & all the chiefs of his nation.—They agreed to cede to us a tract of excellent Land on the north part of the town . . . [p. 7]

[*The "Manuscript Found." Manuscript Story By Rev. Solomon Spaulding Deceased.* Printed from a Verbatim Copy, made expressly for this edition from the Original, now in the possession of President James H. Fairchild, of Oberlin College, Ohio. Printed and Published at the *Millennial Star* Office, Liverpool, England, 1910.]

14. I am taking my information from *View of the Hebrews* by Ethan Smith: a photomechanical reprint of the 1825 edition. Also *The Parallels between the Book of Mormon and the View of the Hebrews*, by the Mormon Historian B. H. Roberts, Salt Lake City, Utah: Modern Microfilm Co.

15. See B. H. Roberts, *Studies of the Book of Mormon*, edited and with an Introduction by Brigham D. Madsen. Salt Lake City: Signature Books, 1985 (1st ed.), 1992 (2nd ed.). Madsen writes the following in his section on "The Documents" (p. ix).

> "A Book of Mormon Study" is divided into two parts. Part I was originally 170 typed pages; Part II was 114 typed pages. The decision by Roberts not to present this additional material to the General Authorities of the Church is acknowledged in his October 24, 1927 letter to Richard R. Lyman; according to the Lloyd journal he later sent it to President Heber J. Grant. . . .
>
> The final document presented here is "A Parallel," which was originally eighteen typed pages. It presents similarities between the *View of the Hebrews* and the Book of Mormon and is arranged in parallel columns. It was presented to Richard R. Lyman as recorded in the Lyman letter of October 24, 1927.

16. Ibid., pp. 171–72

Chapter 11

1. This information is taken from the Adam Clarke Commentary on StudyLight.org, http://studylight.org. . .

2. This information is taken from the website "1828 edition of Webster's American Dictionary of the English Language," (http://1828.mshaffer.com/)

3. Elder George Reynolds, *A Complete Concordance to the Book of Mormon*. Salt Lake City, 1900, p. 147. Eldin Ricks, *Eldin Ricks's Thorough Concordance of the LDS Standard Works* (Provo, UT: Foundation for Ancient Research and Mormon Studies, 1995), p. 148.

4. The word topaz is also found in Exodus 28:17. According to Wikipedia:

> Many modern English translations of the Bible, including the King James Version mention *topaz* in Exodus 28:17 in reference to a stone in the Hoshen [the Israelite High Priest's sacred breastplate]: "And thou shalt set in it settings of stones, even four rows of stones: the first row shall be a sardius, a topaz, and a carbuncle: this shall be the first row." However . . . it should be borne in mind that [modern-day] topaz is likely not meant here. (n15)

Note 15: See the extensive discussion Oliver Farrington, Gems and Gem Minerals, Chicago, 1903 (http://www.farlang.com/gemstones/farrington-gems-and-gem-minerals/page_136). Farrington was curator of Natural History Museum in Chicago.

The King James Bible word *topaz* is derived from the Greek (*topazios* or *topazion*), the ancient name of St. John's Island in the Red Sea, which was difficult to find and from which a yellow stone (now believed to be chrysolite: yellowish olivine) was mined in ancient times. Pliny says that Topazos is a legendary island in the Red Sea and the mineral "topaz" was first mined there. The gem "chrysolite" (topaz) is also referred to as "olivine." The mineral olivine is a magnesium iron silicate with the formula (Mg,Fe)2SiO4 The ratio of magnesium and iron varies.

In the High Priest's breastplate, which had four rows of three gems representing the twelve sons of Israel, in addition to the "topaz" on the first row, the first gem on the fourth row is "chrysolite," which is another name for olivine or topaz. The Hebrew (masoretic) name for the stone was *tarshish* (although some have questioned the term). Interestingly, the word *tarshish* was a name given to ships (usually Phoenician ships) traveling to distant destinations. Again, although this word might be questionable, it is interesting that the

Greek word for topaz is *topazios*, which means "to seek."

Concerning the "topaz of Ethiopia," mentioned in Job 28:18, the ancient country of Ethiopia was located on the Egyptian side of the Red Sea, south of the Tropic of Cancer and south of St. John's Island. The mining of "topaz" was apparently associated with both areas. (Sources: Wikipedia: "Topaz," "olivine," "chrysolite," "hoshen," "ancient Ethiopia," and "St. John's Island Red Sea.")

Chapter 12

1. Reproduced in Richard Lloyd Anderson, *Joseph Smith's New England Heritage: Influences of Grandfathers Solomon Mack and Asael Smith*, Salt Lake City: Deseret Book Company, 1971, pp. 43–47.

2. Lucy Mack Smith, *History of Joseph Smith By His Mother, Lucy Mack Smith*, with Notes and Comments by Preston Nibley, Salt Lake City: Bookcraft, 1979, p. 37.

3. Ibid., p. 58.

4. Oliver Cowdery wrote two letters (August 4 and August 24) to his brother Warren Cowdery in Kirtland. Warren printed the letters in two issues of the *Messenger & Advocate* (September and October 1836).

Chapter 13

1. *Teachings of the Prophet Joseph Smith: Taken from his sermons and writings as they are found in the Documentary History and other publications of the Church and written or published in the days of the Prophet's ministry.* Selected and arranged by the Historian, Joseph Fielding Smith, and his Assistants in the Historian's Office of the

Church of Jesus Christ of Latter-day Saints. Salt Lake City, Utah: Deseret Book, 16th printing, 1967.

2. *An American Prophet's Record: The Diaries and Journals of Joseph Smith*, edited by Scott H. Faulring, Salt Lake City: Signature Books in association with Smith Research Associates, 1989.

3. Dean C. Jessee, *The Personal Writings of Joseph Smith*, Salt Lake City, Utah: Deseret Book, 1984.

4. According to the testimony of the Three Witnesses in the front of the Book of Mormon, they mention only that,

> "we have seen the engravings which are upon the plates; and they have been shown unto us by the power of God, and not of man. And we declare with words of soberness, that an angel of God came down from heaven, and he brought and laid before our eyes, that we beheld and saw the plates, and the engravings thereon."

Nothing is mentioned of the Liahona. However, David Whitmer, one of the witnesses, later confirmed that they had seen the "Directors." In a September 7, 1878 interview of David Whitmer by Joseph F. Smith and Orson Pratt, we find the following:

> Elder O. P. "Do you remember what time you saw the plates?"
>
> D. W. "It was in June, 1829—the latter part of the month, and the eight witnesses saw them, I think, the next day or the day after. (i.e. one or two days after). Joseph showed them the plates himself, but the angel showed us (the three witnesses) the plates, as I suppose to fulfil the words of the book itself. Martin Harris was not with us at this time; he obtained a view of them afterwards, (the same day). Joseph, Oliver, and myself were together when I saw them [the plates]. We not only saw the plates of the Book of Mormon, but also the Brass plates, the plates of the Book of Ether . . . and many other plates. The fact is, it was just as though Joseph, Oliver and I were sitting just here on a log, when we were overshadowed by a light. It was not like the light of the sun nor like that of a fire, but more glorious and beautiful. It extended away round us, I cannot tell how far, but in the midst of this light about as far off as he sits (pointing to John C. Whitmer, sitting a few feet from

> him), there appeared as it were, a table with many records, or plates, upon it, besides the plates of the Book of Mormon, also the sword of Laban, the directors—i.e., the ball which Lehi had, and the interpreters. I saw them just as plainly as I see this bed (striking the bed beside him with his hand), and I heard the voice of the Lord, as distinctly as I ever heard anything in my life declaring that the records of the plates of the Book of Mormon were translated by the gift and power of God."
>
> Elder O. P. "Did you see the Angel at this time?"
>
> D. W. "Yes, he stood before us. Our testimony as recorded in the Book of Mormon is strictly and absolutely true, just as it is there written." (The Testimony of David Whitmer, as related in an interview with Apostles Orson Pratt and Joseph F. Smith, at Richmond, Missouri, on September 7, 1878. *Millennial Star* 40: 771–74)

In a "Letter From Elder W. H. Kelley" printed in the *Saints' Herald* (1 March 1882) we find David Whitmer quoted as saying the following:

> I was plowing in the field one morning and Joseph and Oliver came along with a revelation stating that I was to be one of the witnesses to the Book of Mormon. I got over the fence and we went out into the woods, near by, and sat down on a log and talked awhile. We then kneeled down and prayed. Joseph prayed. We then got up and sat on the log and were talking, when all at once a light came down from above us and encircled us for quite a little distance around; and the angel stood before us. He was dressed in white, and spoke and called me by name and said, "Blessed is he that keepeth His commandments." This is all that I heard the angel say. A table was set before us and on it the records were placed. The Records of the Nephites, from which the Book of Mormon was translated, the brass plates, the Ball of Directors, the sword of Laban and other plates. While we were viewing them the voice of God spoke out of heaven saying that the Book was true and the translation correct.

Nevertheless, David Whitmer provided no further details on the appearance of the Liahona.

5. Joseph F. Smith, "Letter to Elder Edward Stevenson, December 5, 1889," in *President Joseph F. Smith, Personal Letterbooks*, pp.

396–97, LDS Church Archives, Ms f 271, Film Reel #4, Book #2. (Source: Dennis C. Davis, Ogden, Utah, typewritten copy, personal communication. See also Bruce E. Dana, *Glad Tidings Near Cumorah: Firsthand Accounts of Sacred Places, Angelic Visitations, and Ancient Relics*, Springville, UT: Cedar Fort, 2004, p. 126.)

Chapter 14

1. In my estimation, the logic necessary to accomplish proof of a partially magnetic Liahona is virtually impossible to provide, especially when compared to the evidence for a totally miraculous Liahona, which can be "miraculously" adapted to whatever the text says.

2. Joseph Needham, quoted in Amir D. Aczel, *The Riddle of the Compass: the Invention That Changed the World.* New York: Harcourt, 2001, pp. 77–78.

3. Terryl Givens, *"By the Hand of Mormon": The American Scripture that Launched a New World Religion*, New York: Oxford University Press, 2002, p. 246.

4. Richard Lyman Bushman, "Faithful History" in *Believing History: Latter-day Saint Essays by Richard L. Bushman*, Reid L. Neilson and Jed Woodworth eds., New York: Columbia University Press, 2004, pp. 3–4.

5. Ibid., p. 8.

6. For the last 22 years, I have been intensively studying the Book of Mormon, especially anything related to the geography and culture portrayed in the text. Having set the goal to collect, read, and organize on computer everything that was ever written on those subjects, I have been privileged over these many years to read and record hundreds of articles and books, and to see Book of

Mormon history portrayed from literally thousands of viewpoints by numerous authors (both LDS and non-LDS).

About the Author

Alan Miner grew up in Springville, Utah. He studied at BYU and served a mission in Guatemala and El Salvador. He took graduate studies at Washington University in St. Louis, Missouri. By profession he is a dentist. He resides in Springville with his wife, Barbara, where they have raised a family of six children who are all married to wonderful spouses. Alan and Barbara now look forward to their grandchildren's visits.

For the last twenty-two years, Alan has been intensively studying and researching the Book of Mormon and LDS Church history. He has been on the board of directors and lectured for the Ancient American Foundation.

For a partial listing of the thousands of pages of research and writing he has done for the Ancient America Foundation, visit their website at aaf.org.

0 26575 11374 7